L I V I N G
B U D D H A
ZEN

Early Comments on *Living Buddha Zen*:

"An invitation to enter directly into the awakening process itself—alive,
immediate, universal, leaping with broad warmth over discrimination of
gender and affiliation. I am deeply nourished."

—Susan Ji-on Postal, Zen priest,
Empty Hand Zendo,
Rye, New York

"The energies emanating from Lex Hixon's encounter with Zen Master Keizan
are those of celebration, rejoicing, and ecstasy. This serves to take us to the
heart of the matter."

—Nancy Baker, Professor of Philosophy,
Sarah Lawrence College

"Lex Hixon, in a warm and all-embracing way, offers an original and very
American interpretation of one of Zen's most important works, bringing it to
the attention of a wider western audience."

—Patricia Dai-En Bennage, Resident Senior Priest,
Mt. Equity Zendo, Pennsylvania

"Lex Hixon cuts through any notion of time or place to bring us the living
lineage of the Dharma Eye. His felicitous prose is like a sparkling brook; his
closing poems are remarkable expressions of intimacy and delight. With its
unimpeded warmth, its boundless generosity of spirit, **Living Buddha Zen** *goes*
directly to the reader's heart."

—Reverend Roko Sherry Chayat,
Dharma Teacher and Director,
Zen Center of Syracuse

By the same author:

Mother of the Universe: Visions of the Goddess and
 Tantric Hymns of Enlightenment

Great Swan: Meetings with Ramakrishna

Mother of the Buddhas: Meditation on the Prajnaparamita Sutra

Heart of the Koran

Coming Home: The Experience of Enlightenment in Sacred Traditions

Atom from the Sun of Knowledge

LIVING
BUDDHA
ZEN

LEX HIXON

Published for the Paul Brunton Philosophic Foundation by
LARSON PUBLICATIONS

International Standard Book Number (paper): 0-943914-75-2
Library of Congress Catalog Card Number: 95-78971

Published for the Paul Brunton Philosophic Foundation
by Larson Publications
4936 NYS Route 414
Burdett, NY 14818 USA

02 01 00 99 98 97 96 95
10 9 8 7 6 5 4 3 2 1

Calligraphy by Maezumi Roshi
    Cover: "A splendid branch issues from the old plum tree."
    Dedication: "The old plum tree."
Illustrations for book cover and interior by Eugene Gregan

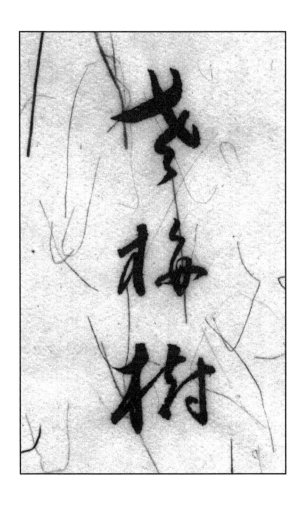

TABLE OF CONTENTS

APPRECIATION

In 1991, Center Publications published Zen Master Keizan's *Denkoroku: The Record of Transmitting the Light*, translated by Francis Cook, a retired professor of Religious Studies at the University of California, Riverside. Lex Hixon has written his commentary on this work, and I am honored to have the opportunity to write a few words about it.

I met Lex over ten years ago when my successor Bernard Tetsugen Glassman, Sensei, started the Zen Community of New York. Each time we met over the years, I was always surprised to learn that Lex was engaged in something new. At the time of our first meeting, he had his own radio show in New York City, interviewing spiritual teachers. I can't remember exactly the sequence of his involvements with various religious traditions, but I know that in the early years he practiced with a Native American Episcopal priest. After that, Lex studied in the Vedanta tradition with a disciple of Sarada Devi, wife of Ramakrishna. He visited Mount Athos in Greece to study in the Eastern Christian tradition and Istanbul and Mecca to study Islam. He later attended a Russian Orthodox seminary in New York. He is also a Sheikh in Islamic Sufism. In fact, during one of my semi-annual visits to Mexico City to lead *sesshin*, I learned that one of the *sangha* members was doing a Sufi retreat with Lex in the same city. In addition to all of this, Lex has also studied Tibetan Buddhism. I have sensed, from his practice and concerns, that his involvements with these various religions were not merely for satisfying his own curiosity, but rather something more than we can normally imagine.

Another astonishing fact is Lex's established scholarship. He completed his doctorate in world religions at Columbia University, translating and commenting on an ancient Sanskrit text as his thesis. *Living Buddha Zen* is the seventh book of his published so far. We expect others.

I enjoyed reading his present work, which is not a commentary in the usual sense, but rather a creative interpretation in which the main text appears partly as a translation. His unique style reads smoothly and gives rise to a sense of excitement, flowing with the vivid imagery Master Keizan himself created in his own writing. In contrast to Dogen Zenji, whose expression is the coolness of an immaculately clear vision of wisdom and the multi-dimensional dynamics of consciousness, Keizan Zenji, who appears in this book, is the warm sunlight of spring. Keizan Zenji's all-inclusive expression of bottomless compassion along with the clear insight of wisdom is often described as motherly, in contrast to Dogen Zenji as fatherly.

Lex's originality lies in the simple fact that no one, including many authors in Japan, has expressed these teachings of the *Denkoroku* with such distinctive style. Lex's seemingly ornate expression is firmly rooted in the ground of practice. Glassman Sensei and he spent three years together studying the *Denkoroku*, from beginning to end, case after case. The warmth and richness of Lex's expression is the natural outcome of his exuberant caring, devotion, and compassion. I hope the reader will enjoy Master Keizan's vision and warmth through Lex's high-spirited and irrepressible interpretation.

Now Lex Hixon is going to my father's temple in Otowara, Japan, for ordination and will be joining the White Plum Asanga, which consists of my spiritual successors in America.

Hakuyu Taizan Maezumi
Abbot, Busshinji
Zen Center of Los Angeles
Spring 1995

Less than two months after writing his Appreciation, my beloved Zen grandfather, Maezumi Roshi, died—suddenly, unexpectedly, peacefully. Comments an ancient master: "I came out by following the way of fragrant grasses, and returned home under the guidance of falling petals." It is always spring!

FOREWORD

I first met Lex Hixon more than twenty years ago in the antechamber of a house in the Flatbush section of Brooklyn. We sat waiting our turns to meet privately with His Holiness Dilgo Khyentse Rinpoche, a Tibetan lama renowned for his silent compassion and for his height. He was six foot seven. It was his first visit to the United States.

Over the following years, Lex and I would meet up again and again in circumstances which reflected the diverse channels through which the Buddha Dharma was flowing into the West. Together we have received teachings from Tibetan lamas, Vietnamese and Japanese masters, and American Zen teachers. We have encountered each other and the Dharma in hotel ballrooms, Bowery lofts, small apartments, elegant townhouses, a mansion in Riverdale, a waterfront warehouse in Yonkers. Each experience contained the quirky juxtapositions inevitable in the transmission of Dharma to the West.

Almost all these experiences evoked, at least for me, questions and more questions. For many years, I judged my own questioning harshly. I saw it as a sign of hopeless stupidity, of just not getting it. The fact that I had so many questions only seemed to indicate my attachment to a rational, faithless, logical way of understanding things. That my assessments were far from inaccurate made it all the more difficult for me to grasp that in Buddhist practice, ultimately, knowing nothing always eclipses knowing anything, and that questioning—or more specifically, the cultivation of a questioning mind—is integral to the practice itself.

Living Buddha Zen is a book of questions. In fact, it is a contemporary meditation on a Zen classic, *Transmission of the Light,* wherein the question—or *koan*—is used to transcend the parameters of rational thinking. Through complete absorption in the question itself, or, as it is said in Zen, by *becoming* the question, the practitioner uses a *koan* to dissolve the barriers that separate self and other, teacher and student. In this absence of any object or subject, "the transmission of light" occurs, and it is this illumination that Lex Hixon reflects, embodies, and communicates. But this is not a work of literal translation, for Hixon intertwines the traditional text with his personal investigation of the masters that make up the Zen line in which he himself is a lineage holder. Thus, *Living Buddha Zen*—as its title suggests—is a work of present history. By penetrating the all-encompassing wisdom minds of previous successors, *Living Buddha Zen* effects the collapse of time and space, making this journey, as Hixon says, both personal and planetary.

For Zen masters, Zen is life, this very universe in its entirety. And the transmission of light, upon which the authority and authenticity of the Zen tradition relies, transcends scripture, reason, words, and concepts. Nonetheless, Zen does have its own particular story, its distinct history and heroes, its location in time and place. Layered in its linguistic and cultural heritage, Zen arrived on Western shores in need of both literal and creative translators. This task of creating a new language for Zen in America provides an arena big enough to match Hixon's remarkable gifts.

Perhaps more than other modern contemplatives, Lex Hixon is the arch translator: from East to West, from old to new, from dead to living, from historical to contemporary, from the black and white calligraphic strokes of Zen to vibrant color and translucent imagery. And from the terse, often harsh and formidable language of the Zen patriarchs to a more universal and liquid language of love. In *Living Buddha Zen,* Hixon emerges as a conservative keeper of the Zen flame. At the same time, however, he pushes past the known boundaries of his own cultural alphabet as well as the verbal conventions of Zen, in order to retrieve from unknown territory a new way of retelling the classic teaching tales.

For all its idealization of silence—and perhaps because of it—Zen history has produced its fair share of written words. The Chinese masters of the Golden Era still inspire us, as they inspired Master Dogen, the thirteenth-century patriarch of Hixon's own lineage. But Zen words have played different roles at different times. In Asian

Zen—China, Japan, Korea—Zen classics and the Sutras of the Mahayana were studied almost exclusively in monasteries. These studies accompanied, inspired, and complemented a life devoted exclusively to attaining the very experiences indicated by the words. In traditional Asia, Zen words were not isolated from meditation, from working with a master, or from other aspects of daily life practice in a monastery. Words may have echoed in the Void but never in a vacuum.

In the West, by contrast, words came first and played the central early role in our Zen history. In the absence of monasteries and even masters, in social contexts where sitting still was anathema and godless Reality blasphemy, books alone spread the Zen word. One cannot underestimate the transformative force that writings on Zen have had in this country. Convincingly, Hixon continues this literary heritage.

The first Zen master to visit the United States was Shoyen Shaku, the esteemed abbot of Engakuji. He came from Japan to Chicago in 1893 to attend the World's Parliament of Religions. He spoke no English and his letter of acceptance to the Parliament was written by his young student, D.T. Suzuki. Within a few years, Suzuki himself would be in the United States, living in Chicago at the home of Paul Carus, and working on translations with Carus at the Open Court Press.

By the 1950s, D.T. Suzuki had become the voice of Zen in the West. The word-magician who used language to point out the way of no-language, he talked to audiences in New York and London about the futility of talk and explained the inadequacy of explanation. A prolific and singular writer, Suzuki's books influenced a generation of Western intellectuals and fertilized the soil for subsequent generations of Western Zen practitioners. Not wanting to burden his curious but unprepared Western audience with the Japanese cultural formalities that infuse Zen method, Suzuki did not emphasize practices such as sitting and bowing, but concentrated instead on philosophy. A Zen master at work, Suzuki evoked just the right teachings for the level of his students through his intimate perception of the West.

It is beyond my imagination to picture the American Zen landscape without the ubiquitous presence of D.T. Suzuki. But there were other writers as well who preceded the practice centers, the *zendos,* and who helped ignite the Zen boom of the 1950s: the iconoclastic writings of Alan Watts, which challenged the monastic ideals of Asia; the extraordinary appeal of Jack Kerouac, whose work today is impacting a whole new generation; and Paul Reps' widely circulated collected stories, *Zen Flesh, Zen Bones.* It was the latter specifically, originally published as five separate volumes from 1934 to 1955, that provided Americans with their first taste of the tough and unsentimental flavor of the Zen tradition.

Zen developed in China as a radical alternative to the prevailing Buddhist schools. From the first century C.E. to the sixth, Chinese Buddhism advocated memorization and recitation of the sacred texts. This conservative approach depended on what had been time-tested, esteeming the past over the present. Then came Bodhidharma, the blue-eyed monk who traveled East from India to China, only to manifest his perfect realization by facing a wall for nine years in silence. Today, Bodhidharma, revered as the first Zen patriarch, is still beloved, and still portrayed with the look of a pirate, rough and nasty, bearded, scowling, with a hoop in one ear. The enlarged look of his eyes is due to the absence of lids, for supposedly, the inclination of eyelids to close when sleepy interfered with Bodhidharma's resolute sitting meditation, and so he cut them off. Whether or not this story is factual, it remains an indication of the radical Zen school of awakened masters that emerged. Bodhidharma's successor, Hui-k'o in Chinese, Eka in Japanese, cut off his own arm as a testament to how serious he was about awakening. Eka succeeds Bodhidharma to become the second Zen patriarch.

After only two successions, between severed eyelids and an amputated arm, the uncompromising style of this Buddhist school could already be characterized by Barry Goldwater's memorable, *Extremism in the name of liberty is no vice.*

The liberty of which Senator Goldwater spoke referred to the American principles of democratic rule, while *extremism* argued in favor of the hapless effort to defend democracy by opposing

Communist forces in Vietnam. Bodhidharma's concerns with liberation were neither political nor dualistic, yet in both cases *extremism* is associated with shedding blood and fierce warriorship. This *extremism* is hard-edged, wounding, stoic, and sacrificial. In Zen history, as in war, the esthetic has been defined by men; and the intense muscularity of Zen remained very much part of the tradition inherited by both men and women in the West.

Eighty generations of lineage holders in the Soto Zen line have been patriarchs. Lex Hixon, as a Dharma heir of the American teacher, Tetsugen Glassman, is in the eighty-second generation. Beginning with Glassman Sensei's eighty-first generation, through the blessings of his teacher, Taizan Maezumi Roshi, women have been granted full teaching authority. The passing of the patriarchal era lies mercifully in sight. For those concerned with this issue, *Living Buddha Zen* proves to be an unexpected ally.

Living Buddha Zen excels at the difficult task of speaking of silence in a language that expresses the authentic Zen terrain while releasing the imagery from its masculine stronghold. Here, the whip-cracking exchanges of bare-boned Zen discourse convert into generous, aromatic prose; tough love is replaced with unabashed devotion; the confidence of the disciple softens the hierarchical authority of the master. Here, love for the teacher, love for the Buddha Dharma, and love for life itself is emotionally charged, passionate, sensual. Tales of Zen life on the razor's edge are retold in language that is pliable and poetic. Pick a paragraph at random, and you may hear Rumi, Milarepa, or the Song of Solomon, but not Zen—at least not the Zen to which we have grown accustomed. You may even hear the voice of a woman.

Translation for Hixon is a process of transformation, translating from the inside out, from the heart and from his own understanding. If he has circumvented certain rules of the game, his choices have not been arbitrary. With a Ph.D. in religion from Columbia and seven books in print, he has spent thirty years investigating the initiatory lineages of various sacred traditions. The modern, secular, skeptical, scientific view has not been casually jettisoned by Hixon, but shed slowly, through trial and error, personal inquiry, reliable spiritual guidance, and fearless commitment to a naked vision.

Living Buddha Zen is not just a contemporary rendering of an old text, nor a lyrical account of one man's Zen story. Rather, like the great Zen classics, it embodies Zen in the manner of Master Dogen as "the full moon way, complete from the very beginning." *Living Buddha Zen* is not a manual for enlightenment, yet it contains the essentialized teachings of Zen.

With Zen practice centers flourishing all over North America and the modern world, Hixon's audience is vastly different from D.T. Suzuki's. So he offers not just an introduction, but an invitation to receive initiation and to pursue face-to-face study with a master, as he himself has done. As well, this book is a compendium of warnings against subtle forms of avoidance and inflation which masquerade as spiritual practice and realization.

As a genuine lineage holder, Hixon writes with the full empowerment of successive generations of adepts. But his special genius is to become the flexible vehicle through which this prodigious spiritual energy flows, while steadying himself in its midst long enough for his heart to find its voice for our benefit. This is the vow of the *bodhisattva*, and it affirms *Living Buddha Zen* as an authentic continuation of the transmission of light.

HELEN TWORKOV
AUTHOR OF *Zen in America*
EDITOR, *Tricycle: The Buddhist Review*
NEW YORK CITY, SPRING 1995

Author's Introduction

What is This Book?

This book is a union of personal and planetary history. To begin within the personal dimension, in 1991, when the October full moon, the orange harvest moon, was setting at dawn, on the day the Dalai Lama offered the ancient Tantric Kalachakra initiation at Madison Square Garden, I drove to meet my Zen master, Bernard Tetsugen Glassman Sensei. He is a Brooklyn kid who migrated West to the aerospace industry in southern California, becoming spiritual successor in 1976 to Taizan Maezumi Roshi, a Japanese Zen master living in Los Angeles. In 1979, Sensei Glassman returned to New York City to take his Zen seat here. I encountered him immediately.

So it was as old friends that Sensei and I sat together in radiant silence that early autumn morning in 1991, and then engaged in easy conversation, exploring the enlightenment experience of Shakyamuni Buddha. The essence of this meeting, and our subsequent fifty-two meetings over three years, tracing the transmission of Shakyamuni's enlightenment down fifty-two generations, is now recorded by *Living Buddha Zen*.

The present pages were born from Sensei Glassman's intuition that I should write a book about our mutual study of these *koan,* these dramas of spiritual transmission between living Buddhas and their destined successors—twenty-eight generations in India, twenty-two generations in China, two generations in Japan. Sensei's understanding of my need to write—a need which, as essentially a non-writing person, he does not share—reminds me of anthropologist Carlos Castaneda and his Yaqui Indian guide, Don Juan. The Native American sage realized that his modern apprentice could not get the rational mind out of the way unless he wrote voluminous field-notes.

The timeless sage in the present case, Bernard Glassman, emerged from modern culture with a Ph.D. in mathematics and an instinctive sense of business organization as a vehicle for social and spiritual action. Glassman is a Jewish Zen master who has vowed to end homelessness in Yonkers, the depressed community where he lives just north of New York City. He began from the entrepreneurial base of a gourmet bakery, staffed at first by his Zen students and now by inner city persons who have come through the Greystone Bakery job training program. The Sensei presently receives state grants to fund his programs for housing single mothers, infant day care, and now a residential AIDs facility for the homeless. Glassman has also founded the House of One People, an inner city community center where members of all religions can come to worship, meditate, and celebrate, both together and separately, in an atmosphere of social renewal and spiritual harmony.

These and many other projects are all undertaken in the unitive spirit of Shakyamuni Buddha's enlightenment. Glassman's own resolution of some one thousand Zen *koan* prepared him to develop a social vision rooted in the Buddhist principle of nonduality. Even his Zen teaching program, *How to Raise an Ox,* integrates the practical wisdom of the twelve-step movement, originally inspired by Alcoholics Anonymous, into the traditional Buddhist understanding of the path to enlightenment. Twice a year, Sensei leads a seven-day Street Retreat, when he and a few Zen students wholeheartedly join the homeless population of New York City, living in shelters and eating at soup kitchens, to which they later give anonymous financial contributions.

Bernard Glassman is hardly the romantic figure from another world, or worlds, that we encounter in the sorcerer Don Juan. Yet when seated face to face with Sensei in silence, an ancient wisdom-being is clearly manifest—mysterious, belonging to all worlds and to no world, a great being inseparable from the fifty-three Awakened Ones we approach through the pages of *Living Buddha Zen.*

The original work at the base of *Living Buddha Zen* is the fourteenth-century Japanese masterpiece by Keizan Zenji, *Denkoroku: The Record of Transmitting the Light*. This text purports to trace the transmission from master to successor of the enlightenment of Shakyamuni Buddha through one thousand seven hundred years to the world-teacher, Dogen Zenji, in thirteenth-century Japan. Master Dogen is considered the father of the Soto Zen Order, which has twenty-five thousand temples and ten million practitioners in contemporary Japan. His seminal work, *Shobogenzo: The Treasure House of the Eye of True Dharma,* has profoundly inspired both Eastern and Western philosophers and spiritual practitioners during this century, after remaining in obscurity, even in its native land, for some seven hundred years. Master Keizan is considered the mother of Soto Zen, his *Denkoroku* being the reservoir or womb of the lineage.

The *Denkoroku* is a fifty-three stroke ink and brush drawing of essential Buddhist history. Seen more broadly, this text presents in the direct Zen manner the essential nature of awareness, the single Light celebrated by all ancient wisdom traditions. The *Denkoroku* is a work of art whose subject is sacred history. It is not historiography.

Even more than a work of art, this text is a vehicle for mutual study between Zen masters and their successors, honing the insight of each and insuring the actual continuation, without diminution, of Dogen Zenji's radical spiritual teaching, perpetual plenitude—the perfect awakeness, here and now, of all beings and worlds. This transmission of Light remains continuous throughout the unpredictable developments of planetary history, such as the transplanting of Zen from Japan to America and, from America, to the strange global landscape called the *postmodern world.*

These are some reasons why Sensei Glassman chose the *Denkoroku* as the text for our mutual study, preparing me for the Dharma transmission in which I will be invested with responsibility for pouring Light into the next generation. The formal ceremonies are scheduled to be celebrated in Japan and New York during 1995.

The model of Dharma transmission presented by the *Denkoroku*, one living Buddha for each generation, is symbolic. In actual fact, all fully awakened men and women in each generation constitute the living Buddha of that generation. According to the reckoning of his

Soto lineage, Maezumi Roshi in Los Angeles represented the eightieth Buddha generation to descend from the Shakyamuni Buddha of ancient India, enlightened two thousand five hundred years ago. Glassman Sensei and other Western successors represent the eighty-first generation. Along with the next wave of successors, I represent the eighty-second Buddha generation. Members of these three contemporary Buddha generations—spiritual grandparents, spiritual parents, spiritual grandchildren—are scattered across the earth, some recognized by formal ceremony, others remaining hidden. Some are teaching, some are writing, others are simply waiting.

Also to be understood symbolically is the *Denkoroku's* single-pointed focus on the Soto lineage of Dogen Zenji, which seems to ignore the rich complexity of Buddhist history. This focus is the simplification of nature by the Zen artist, a simplification which permits the participant-observer to enter a much fuller, more profound experience of the landscape. Soto Zen here represents all realized Buddhist lineages and all wisdom traditions on the planet whose initiatory transmission of Light remains unbroken, providing a direct spiritual experience at the highest level of authenticity, not just a cultural inheritance or a romantic aspiration.

Glassman Sensei encouraged me at the beginning of our work together to experience direct encounter with Keizan Zenji, author of the *Denkoroku.* That is precisely what occurred. The six hundred ninety-one years that appeared to distance me from Master Keizan's Zen talks melted away. I encountered his text as living and breathing. His presence shone vividly as the brown-robed presence of my contemporary Zen master. I encountered with similar directness each of the fifty-two living Buddhas in the *Denkoroku* and the fountainhead of their lineage, Shakyamuni, whose enlightenment flows through and as them all. This enlightenment, or Light, suffers no diminution, and actually increases the breadth and profundity of its expression as Buddha generations pass.

To resolve any particular *koan,* to pass through any of the gateless gates along the pathless path of Zen, is simply to become this *koan.* Through the motherly encouragement and guidance of my ancient Japanese guide, Keizan Zenji, and my contemporary American guide, Tetsugen Glassman, I was somehow pushed, pulled, and inspired to become in turn each of these fifty-three living Buddhas. Without a qualified Zen master—in my case, two masters, one ancient, one contemporary—such a process would be impossible, even unimaginable.

Living Buddha Zen is my personal presentation of each *koan,* each drama of Dharma succession, as well as my personal commentary on each. These presentations and commentaries represent a fusion of my own perspectives as a practitioner of several sacred traditions, including the Tantric Buddhism of Tibet, with the perspectives of Keizan Zenji from fourteenth-century Japan and Glassman Sensei from our century. This fusion of insights cannot be analyzed into its component streams. As with any dish, some of the seasonings can be discerned, but we taste and enjoy it as a new experience, beyond any of its original ingredients. The ancient, the contemporary, and the timeless interact alchemically in these pages, which I would never claim as my own separate creation.

The same basic format followed by Keizan Zenji is followed here. First there is a condensed presentation of the ineluctable moment of transmitting Light, called *koan,* a presentation which I originally made orally to Tetsugen Glassman, opening our face-to-face meeting, or *daisan.* Then follows a free-flowing reflection on the transmission, called *comment,* composed from notes taken directly after my early morning Zen interviews—generous, loving conversations, not the staccato dialogues often associated with Zen. These records were later expanded, as I continued to reread the Zen talks of Master Keizan. Finally, I conclude each chapter as our ancient Japanese guide does by expressing *koan* and *comment* in a single poetic flash, called *closing poem.* These poems took shape inwardly, during or immediately following the Zen sitting, the Zen interview, and the Buddhist morning service—chanting, bowing, and offering incense, accompanied by deep bell, high bell, and wooden drum. *Living Buddha Zen* is not a book about Zen history, Zen philosophy, or Zen method. Nor is it autobiography. This book is simply a reservoir of Zen, envisioned by Dogen Zenji and others as the full moon way: Total Awakeness, complete from the very beginning.

What is this book? It is an invitation to the full moon way, the spontaneous awakeness which is total in every moment. It is an invitation to receive initiation and to pursue profound face-to-face study within any of the living wisdom traditions on the globe.

My gratitude flows primarily to my Zen master, Bernard Tetsugen Glassman, and to my spiritual grandfather, Hakuyu Taizan Maezumi who, along with his contemporary, Suzuki Roshi, and others, has helped to open the full moon way of Soto for America.

I joyfully acknowledge deep connection with another contemporary Soto full moon, Shundo Aoyama Roshi. Among the most prominent women Zen teachers in Japan, she is abbess of Aichi Women's Monastery in Nagoya. On the eve of the formal ceremony in New York City, 1983, when I became a senior student of Tetsugen Glassman, she gave me the Dharma name, Jikai, *oceanic compassion*.

I am also deeply grateful to Francis H. Cook, the scholar-practitioner whose accurate and sympathetic English translation, *Denkoroku: The Record of Transmitting the Light*, helped to make this entire experience possible. There are two other English translations of the *Denkoroku* by Western scholar-practitioners, indicating the immense importance and attraction of this text. The *Denkoroku: The Record of the Transmission of the Light* by Reverend Herbert Nearman O.B.C., was edited and contains an introduction by the prominent Western woman Zen teacher in America, British-born Jiyu-Kennett Roshi. The other translation is *Transmission of Light* by Thomas Cleary. These translations will provide inspiration to the interested reader. My version is not a translation but an assimilation. Yet *Living Buddha Zen* always aspires to remain loyal to the basic meaning of the *Denkoroku* and to the living spirit of its author, Keizan Zenji, fourth Buddha Ancestor of Japanese Soto, disciple of his own mother, profound devotee of the female Buddha, Kuan Yin, and initiate in the Japanese Tantric tradition.

Someone might ask, "How can your personal assimilation of this text have real value for someone else? Why not simply allow the accurate translations of the classical Japanese to stand alone?" This argument has the merit of simplicity, but somehow Buddha Dharma will not remain silent about itself. It continues to speak out, orally and in writing, through Buddha generation after Buddha generation. Sometimes the Dharma speech is completely authentic; other times, it remains veiled to various degrees by layers of personality and society. But the primordial urge to express truth continues to spring up spontaneously.

Living Buddha Zen is a manifestation of this urgency—boiling, fermenting, fructifying. At the very least, my study of Soto Zen teaching can inspire others to recognize that personal assimilation is possible—without knowing Japanese, without leaving aside social, family, and religious responsibility, without becoming someone who meditates for days or weeks on end, and without becoming so inflated as to deny personal limitations, to claim full enlightenment, or to claim any enlightenment whatsoever.

Living Buddha Zen is conceptually transparent. It will not further clutter the complex ideological, intellectual and religious landscape of modern times. It may even serve as antidote for this disease of complexity, as well as for the disease of over-simplification, two prominent modern maladies. Whether my book serves or does not serve, however, I had no choice but to write it.

WHO ARE THESE LIVING BUDDHAS?

Many of these living Buddhas, before awakening, were personal attendants of the previous living Buddhas, cherishing the selfless, responsive, transparent presence that the attendant's role entails. One successor served as attendant for forty years under two living Buddhas before awakening into Buddhahood. Another continued to serve as attendant after his awakening, after his beloved master finally passed away, and even after his own biological death, declaring that his own unmarked tomb should be placed near the tomb of his beloved guide in the position of attendant.

These characteristics of the attendant, invisibility and pure attention, reflect throughout the lives of living Buddhas. At least two Awakened Ones regularly cleaned latrines after the unveiling of their inconceivably sublime nature—one remaining within the monastery, the other taking care of public latrines in the town, living there and speaking only the rough language of the common folk.

These two concealed their recognition as living Buddhas, as many other destined successors did. One living Buddha hid among hill tribes for ten years, constantly moving and changing his personal appearance to conceal his identity. Another waited sixty-seven years before revealing his revolutionizing wisdom. Ten years of concealment after being unveiled as living Buddhas was quite natural for these Awakened Ones. Some transmitted Light to hundreds or thousands, but most transmitted only to a few. Some taught the families of princes and emperors, but most refused invitations from places of temporal power, eating and dressing exactly like their monastic disciples or like the humble common people with whom they enjoyed associating. One gave his eye to a blind beggar.

Many of these destined inheritors of Buddhahood began the intensive process of unveiling during childhood or youth. One boy reached up and touched his own face while the *Heart Sutra* was being chanted—*no eye, no ear, no tongue*—astonishing his Sutra teacher with the confident Zen affirmation, "But I have eyes, ears, tongue!" Another destined successor, while his mother was washing a wound on the young boy's hand, stated in a straightforward manner, "My hand is a Buddha's hand."

Mothers are immensely important to these successors, and are mentioned more prominently than fathers. Many mothers of these living Buddhas had dreams of the diamond beings destined to come forth from the wisdom womb of Mother Prajnaparamita, mystically unified with their own wombs. One mother dreamed she drank a liquid jewel on the night of conception. Another, already pregnant, dreamed of her future child standing on the summit of Mount Sumeru at the center of the visible and invisible cosmos, holding a golden ring and calmly reporting, "I am here." Several bedchambers were filled with golden light at the moment of conception or birth.

Wherever one successor walked, the earth turned a beautiful golden color.

In several instances, spiritual instructions from their mothers were the main source of inspiration for these destined successors to Buddhahood. Several renounced royal palaces or courtly careers particularly associated with their fathers, escaping by night into the wilderness of nondual Mother Wisdom, the realm of Goddess Prajnaparamita.

Some fathers and mothers voluntarily gave up their gifted children to the way of living Buddhahood upon hearing songs and affirmations of wisdom spring forth unexpectedly from the lips of these beloved young persons. One astonished father observed his mute, paralyzed son, fifty years old, become a successor to Buddhahood by taking his first steps toward the living Buddha and uttering his first words as a wisdom poem. Another destined successor was considered insane by his entire village as he wandered about moaning, night and day, carrying a gourd of wine. Yet another successor cut off his own arm to demonstrate radical commitment, an act that could not be considered sane by the standards of any culture.

Two among these successors to living Buddhahood were young homeless persons. One called himself *nameless* and the other immediately recognized his destined master from a previous eon. Two among these living Buddhas were executed by corrupt political authorities, and a third, by nonviolently extending his neck to the sword, touched the conscience of the emperor and received the royal reprieve. From the headless trunk of one precious Buddha body, milk gushed forth.

Many of these successors never studied Buddhism or practiced formal meditation, while others were profound scholars and intense monastic practitioners of Buddha Dharma from their youth. One successor insisted upon leaving home for a monastery at age six. Some began their relentless push to unveil intrinsic enlightenment later in life. One successor started practicing by becoming a monk at age sixty, remaining sleepless for three years until his awakening.

Some destined successors were already deeply realized when they approached their destined masters, others had more experiences to go through. One was a famous philosophical debater of the Buddhist Sutras of Liberation, another had delivered charismatic lectures on the *Lotus Sutra* since age seventeen. Some were profound meditators, realizers of emptiness, immersed in silence. One was a holy mendicant. Another was a shaman with thousands of followers. Other successors to living Buddhahood were adepts of various sacred traditions and yogic practices. One had read extensively in Taoist and Confucian philosophy. At least two lived in caves.

One successor studied the Sutras delivered by Buddhas from previous eons, scriptures preserved only on the subtle plane of the Naga kings. Another successor was born with left fist clenched, this disability only being healed by meeting the living Buddha and releasing to him a tiny miraculous gem from the Naga plane—a crystallized manifestation of Prajnaparamita, Perfect Nondual Wisdom.

Some who became living Buddhas continued to remain focused on the richness of Buddhist tradition, often resounding with Tantric overtones, while others polished all the colors of Buddhism from the rice of essential nature, leaving it brilliantly white. One living Buddha invited sincere non-Buddhists to practice in his monastery. In one instance recorded here, Shakyamuni Buddha opened the highest realization to a non-Buddhist practitioner.

Some who became living Buddhas were simple village persons, who received their destined masters in mud-walled huts. Others were princes or members of important families, who met with living Buddhas in palaces or beautiful old gardens. One cleansed the local temple of degenerate practices before he even reached the age of ten. One was constantly followed by a flock of cranes. Another was followed by a brilliant round mirror, visible only to those with spiritual sight.

One successor suffered from leprosy and was healed by his unveiling as living Buddha. Several successors were so transparent as to provide no details whatsoever about their existence prior to becoming living Buddhas. Several died in meditation, eyes open. One did not lie down to sleep for sixty years after his unveiling as a living Buddha. The body of at least one of these diamond beings remained incorrupt. When his tomb was opened by an earthquake, one year after death, the body was still sitting at ease in the position of meditation, only hair and nails had grown long.

At least one of these Awakened Ones was married and had a child—Shakyamuni Buddha, fountainhead of the lineage. Monastic sensibility may have prevented frank reporting of this dimension in the lives of other living Buddhas. Another dimension, even more obviously suppressed, is the existence of female living Buddhas. Even though the mothers of these fifty-three Awakened Ones are always near the center of their spiritual unfolding, the absence in the *Denkoroku* of living Buddhas who experience a woman's body and a woman's sensibility raises questions.

The fact that the living Buddha of each generation is constituted by all the fully awakened men and women of that generation permits the enlightened women of Buddhist history, and human history in general, to take their proper place. To one degree or another, however, awakened women are always concealed by male-oriented culture. But this pervasive pattern of male-orientation is changing. The continuous yet hidden stream of women's spirituality is emerging. When future lineage trees are drawn, women's awakening will be openly recorded, their teaching gestures will be widely cherished, and their spiritual successors, both men and women, will be more numerous and more visible.

As we celebrate female practitioners and female living Buddhas from the past, as well as those from present and future who will be recognized and strongly supported by their surrounding cultures and religions, there is another perspective which must be considered. The living Buddhas are androgynous beings. Awakened Ones enjoy immediate conscious access to fatherly and motherly qualities, to sisterly and brotherly qualities, to the qualities of passionate female lover and passionate male lover. Female living Buddhas are therefore no more exclusively female than male living Buddhas are exclusively male. Whatever our cultural sense of maleness and femaleness may be, we will find in these fifty-three fluid and elusive sages of the *Denkoroku* a wonderfully broad spectrum of human response and expression.

Nor are living Buddhas purely transcendent beings—some mere essence of light without humanity, without personal integrity, without history. Total Awakeness does not erase the experience of being human or being Indian, Chinese, Japanese, American. Living Buddhas are fully human. Being the most complete flowering of humanity, they are more passionately and compassionately human than we can imagine, for we are still lost in abstractions and patterns of avoidance that separate us from our true humanity.

The living Buddha can appreciate a cup of plain tea more profoundly than a museum curator can appreciate an ancient masterpiece. Why? The Awakened One is not curating, not defending or controlling, not separating past from present, not isolating museum, temple, or self from the miraculous flow of ordinary events.

This full humanity of the living Buddhas is precisely what demands that there be equal numbers of male and female Awakened Ones, whether they remain hidden or revealed. Gender experience and its nuances are a vivid dimension of full human experience.

The existence of female Buddhas, both celestial and earthly, was discovered and clearly proclaimed by Buddhist Tantra, beginning in India some fifteen centuries ago, but was strongly hinted at before that by the feminine nature of Prajnaparamita, Perfect Nondual Wisdom. In the Upanishads, the wisdom literature of ancient, pre-Buddhist India, the existence of fully awakened female sages is clearly documented.

However, the mainstream cultures of Buddhist lands, with the partial exception of Tantric India and Tibet, retained their fundamental male-orientation. For instance, none of the exalted female Buddhas of Tantra, such as the Vajradakini, ever entered Japan with the great wave of Tantric Buddhism called Shingon.

The spiritual principle of the equality of feminine and masculine has been irrefutably established by Tantric Buddhism and by other great sacred traditions, but· the social and religious implications of this principle have yet to be worked out with genuine completeness anywhere on the globe.

Let us consider once more the fifty-three living Buddhas presented by the *Denkoroku.* They are lepers, princes, nonviolent revolutionaries who face execution, shamans, yogis, deep meditators, scholars, debaters, cleaners of latrines, homeless children, the mute, the paralyzed, those who are apparently insane, mendicants, members of wealthy families, woodcutters, rice-huskers, persons spiritually awake from birth, anonymous persons who keep their backgrounds unknown, persons advanced in age as well as those who are surprisingly young, those with thousands of followers, those who conceal themselves among the common people, those in touch with subtle and divine beings on other planes of being, cave dwellers, village dwellers, city dwellers, adepts with miraculous powers, selfless attendants who regard themselves as utterly insignificant, devout Buddhists, members of other sacred traditions, practitioners without any religious identification.

Who are these living Buddhas? We are these living Buddhas! Whoever we are, however we are, whatever we are, wherever we are—in our naked awareness, unveiled, here and now! Welcome to the wonderful and auspicious realm where living Buddhas recognize and serve living Buddhas! Welcome to Living Buddha Zen!

JIKAI
LEX HIXON
NEW YORK CITY
1995

LIVING
BUDDHA
ZEN

WONDERFUL OLD PLUM TREE STANDS DEEP IN THE GARDEN

SHAKYAMUNI BUDDHA

koan

From beneath the Bodhi Tree before dawn, Shakyamuni perceives the morning star directly and awakens beyond all awakening, exclaiming: "I, the broad earth, and all conscious beings are enlightened and effortlessly manifest the Great Way together."

comment

The amber autumn full moon sets before dawn, balancing on the black rock palisade, reflecting across the wide river. As beloved Master Keizan proclaims in his talk this morning, our own true nature stands like an eighty-thousand-foot precipice within each movement, within each perception.

Seeing directly. This alone is the morning star of enlightenment, unveiling Total Awakeness, here and now. The Bodhi Tree is our precious human body. Awakening, we cry spontaneously: "I am the living universe. I am the six realms of transmigration—elemental, animal, etheric, human, subtle, divine. All this, functioning harmoniously, is already enlightenment." There are no separate sentient beings, yet the enlightened way naturally and tenderly serves sentient beings. How? By unveiling them as limitless awareness.

Leaving the palace of convention at nineteen, practicing adamantine sitting, manifesting enlightenment at thirty, for the remaining forty-nine years of his life, Shakyamuni Buddha is never alone. He is continuously giving nonduality to all beings, both through his words of Light, abundantly diverse, and through the silent evidence of his actions—walking, standing, sitting, lying down—free from the slightest sense of separation or division.

Never alone. This means oneness. There is nothing separate to be known, no one separate to perform the act of knowing. Great Compassion is simply the absence of separateness. This unique compassion without subject or object springs forth instantly from the realization of nonduality. Utter inclusiveness. A moon so full it engulfs the sun. There is no way to approach nonduality, to cultivate or even be aware of nonduality. It is all-consuming.

The living Buddha possesses only robe and alms-bowl. When there is no more sense of being a separate individual, what needs can there be that are not spontaneously fulfilled? This is the secret meaning of every monastic discipline, every form of external or internal renunciation. The separate individual disappears, leaving only robe and bowl and Light.

The living Buddha can resemble any mendicant, dusty from the road. Who can perceive that his human form contains all the mountains and rivers of the universe? He is our eye of wisdom, we his wisdom eye. This discerning eye is not two, not one. It is our entire being, now fully awake. Where is Shakyamuni? Where are we? Where is multiplicity? Where is unity?

The lion's roar—*I am Buddha! I am awake! All beings are completely awake!*—is not a statement by Shakyamuni, not a perception belonging to Shakyamuni. Rather, Shakyamuni Buddha and countless Awakened Ones come forth from this primordial *I am*. The entire cosmos comes forth moment by moment, without subject or object, from this one fundamental innate Mind of Clear Light. With great kindness, Roshi Keizan, who is known as the mother of Japanese Soto Zen, now presents us the record of the unveiling of this limitless clarity through fifty-two generations. This is the drama of Dharma succession, the transmission of Light from one living Buddha to the next, from one Buddha generation to the next.

When Shakyamuni pulls up the boundless net, all openings in the net, all phenomena, are instantly liberated. Did this happen twenty-five hundred years ago? If so, it is not the timeless principle of enlightenment. There is no cosmos apart from the living Buddha, no living Buddha apart from this burgeoning cosmos, this pupil of his wisdom eye.

Our very skin, nerves, and senses are the morning star of enlightenment, yet Total Awakeness has absolutely nothing to do with skin, nerves, senses. Although both sides are true, leave both sides behind! There is only limitless awareness in this hermitage!

A wonderful old plum tree stands deep in the garden. It is more ancient than the memory of our ancestors. It appears more giant boulder than tree. Is it alive? Yes! A single green branch springs from the gnarled trunk. This branch manifests thorns. Thorns on a plum tree? Impossible! Suffering beings on the tree of enlightenment? Impossible! Yet they continue to appear, right before our eyes.

Now the plum branch is bearing fragrant blossoms, the first to bloom in the spring. Miraculously, fruit of every kind comes forth. Not only the delicious plums of living Buddhas but awakened guides and holy prophets, women and men from all sacred traditions—pear, mango, cherry, tamarind, flourishing on a single branch. Comments Master Dogen, who is known as the father of Japanese Soto Zen, "This old plum tree is boundless. Its whirling, miraculous transformation has no limit. All blossoms of the inexhaustible lands that lie in the ten directions are one family of plum blossoms."

closing poem

What magnificence! What splendor!
Morning star everywhere!
At this very moment
Shakyamuni sees,
and we celebrate
the inconceivable harmony
of the Great Way.

TRANSMISSIONS

Two Clear Mirrors Facing Each Other outside Time

Transmission One
Shakyamuni to Mahakashyapa

koan

When Shakyamuni raises a wildflower, his destined successor smiles. The living Buddha responds to his intimate companion with the great intensity of transmission: "I am Wonderful Mind. I am Nirvana. I am the inexhaustible treasure house, the Eye of Nonduality. Now this Light is manifest as you, as Mahakashyapa."

comment

Mahakashyapa plays the role of mirror to the living Buddha within the luminous circles of all past Awakened Ones. During this present lifetime, Shakyamuni always shares his diamond teaching seat with the magnificent Mahakashyapa, most profound among practitioners of the Great Way. Total Awakeness must now manifest outwardly as transmission, unveiling the Three Jewels of unfailing refuge.

In Shakyamuni's awakening beneath the Bodhi Tree, the Three Jewels—teacher, teaching, community—remain fused. On Vulture Peak, the jewels Buddha, Dharma, and Sangha are clearly displayed. On the sacred mountain outside linear time, Shakyamuni has already revealed all-embracing Prajnaparamita, the Sutra of Transcendent Wisdom. However, the playful transmission of this wisdom from generation to generation is yet to manifest. On the elusive mount of revelation, Shakyamuni now raises a flower, the living, blossoming Prajnaparamita—wisdom beyond words and letters, wisdom beyond wisdom.

The flower is the Treasure House of the Eye of True Dharma, the *shobogenzo* raised by Dogen Zenji fifty-one generations later on the mountainous islands of Japan. The Unveiling of Boundless Clarity, the *denkoroku,* is Master Keizan's responsive smile. Dogen is *koso,* transmitter or father. Keizan is *taiso*, receiver or mother. This very flower, ever new, has been raised by Awakened Ones everywhere, always bringing forth the smile of transmission.

The living Buddha chooses to manifest this transmission of Light on Vulture Peak right before the eyes of his entire community— eighty thousand practitioners, mindstreams of the principal male and female transmitters of Dharma that will descend from Shakyamuni during our long planetary history.

Without verifiable transmission, there can be no fully manifest jewel of Sangha, *enlightened community.* Without this outward demonstration of transmission, there cannot be the authentic leadership that makes the Sangha an accessible place and principle of refuge. Now these eighty thousand practitioners and their concentric circles of disciples down through history can open the Eye of Nonduality under the illumined guidance of Mahakashyapa and his destined successors. We are no longer satisfied to remain merely good meditators and loyal followers, but desire passionately to awaken as living Buddhas.

Shakyamuni raises his eyebrows slightly as he raises the flower, his deep eyes sparkling with love for his old friend, Mahakashyapa, inseparable companion in this theater of transmission that extends throughout beginningless time, this theater of the repeated manifestation and recognition of Wonderful Mind.

Shakyamuni is the metaphorical masculine principle: active compassion, skillful method, diamond thunderbolt, blissful *vajra.* Mahakashyapa is the metaphorical feminine principle: wisdom that discerns emptiness, bell of boundless space ringing miraculously, inexhaustible receptivity.

This flower and this smile are the father-mother union of diamond thunderbolt and diamond bell so cherished by Tantric tradition. They are timelessly united, neither two nor one. What appears as the transmission of Light has therefore already and always taken place. This explains the humorous gleam in Shakyamuni's eyes, the subtle raising of his eyebrows: "It has been accomplished beginninglessly, you see!" Only by becoming Mahakashyapa can we know this.

Our smile is Mahakashyapa, our gleaming eyes Shakyamuni. Forget the flower. Forget the universe. Between Shakyamuni and Mahakashyapa, two clear mirrors facing each other outside time, there is nothing to reflect. Yet nothing is lost. No beloved being or structure of value is negated.

Shakyamuni and Mahakashyapa are passionate human beings, not merely principles. There is great tenderness in the eyes of Shakyamuni at this moment, great delight on the lips of Mahakashyapa. There is wonderful intimacy between the living Buddha and his destined successor. It bathes the vast assembly of practitioners—monks and nuns, laymen and laywomen—in radiant waves of love. Love, tenderness, and delight are now revealed as the basic functioning of the Sangha Jewel, the world-enlightening community.

This is simply raising a flower and smiling. No analysis of experience, no transcendent insight, no silent meditative equipoise, no separate action and response. This is the touch of the living Buddha, the tender love without subject or object shared equally by Shakyamuni and Mahakashyapa. The precious human forms of both these Zen masters and the community surrounding them are golden with the Light of transmission. This is the perpetually rising sun—Buddha, Dharma, Sangha.

When Mahakashyapa was born, golden light filled the mother's room and entered the child's blessed mouth. The sublime body of the destined successor was always filled with this luminosity of Dharma, the completely pure teaching of nonduality, free from sign or configuration, free from lack or fragmentation. This is our real body, our essential humanity.

Shakyamuni the principle manifests as enlightened master and Mahakashyapa the principle as humble disciple, whenever and wherever this beginningless drama of transmission manifests throughout the universe, generating countless living Buddhas. Now, in the blissful company of Awakened Ones, we await Maitreya, the next Lord Buddha of our present inconceivable Thousand Buddha Eon.

Mahakashyapa is so receptive! At their first meeting, when

Shakyamuni cries joyfully, "Welcome, O mendicant yogi!" the long hair of Mahakashyapa falls away, rather than needing to be cut and shaved with a blade. Shakyamuni's word alone is the razor. How much more powerful is the living Buddha's silence as he raises the flower? Receiving this silent transmission, Mahakashyapa and all destined successors smile the smile of Total Awakeness.

closing poem

Ancient pine tree roots deep
on the mount of transmission
not found in India, China, Japan, America.
Here is the glade of sudden realization,
sometimes remote, other times near,
sometimes lost in clouds,
other times clear.

KNOCK DOWN THE FLAGPOLE BEFORE THE GATE!

TRANSMISSION TWO
MAHAKASHYAPA TO ANANDA

koan

Ananda inquires of his spiritual brother, the fully awakened Maha-kashyapa: "Did the limitless awareness manifest as Shakyamuni give you anything other than the gold brocade robe?" The present Bud-dha whispers intensely: "Ananda!" Younger brother gazes with com-plete attention. Whereupon the first successor of Shakyamuni pow-erfully proclaims: "Knock down the flagpole before the gate!" Pre-cisely as Shakyamuni manifests as Buddha when he sees the morn-ing star, and Mahakashyapa when he sees the flower, so Ananda now unveils the borderless, divisionless expanse of Wonderful Mind.

comment

Born into a warrior family on the very morning that Shakyamuni awakened beneath the Bodhi Tree, Ananda has been inseparable from the living Buddha for eons, as are all those who receive the transmission of Light. Attentive throughout twenty years of intimate discipleship as personal attendant to Shakyamuni, Ananda not only assimilated his master's verbal teachings but also learned his body language. After the passing away of the Great Sage, when Maha-kashyapa requests Ananda to take the diamond teaching seat and present Lord Buddha's scriptural outpourings in their entirety, this recitation is not just verbally perfect, but the spiritual mood and even the physical movements of Shakyamuni are clearly displayed. As the other senior disciples confirm, it is as though Shakyamuni Buddha has returned from *mahanirvana* to offer them the fullness of his formal discourses.

Yet even such miraculous knowledge of the teachings of his origi-nal master does not bring about Ananda's complete awakening. For twenty more years, Ananda serves Buddha Mahakashyapa, calmly awaiting the moment of transmission. This highlights the fourth Jewel of Refuge, which is traditionally mentioned first—Master, Buddha, Dharma, Sangha. When Ananda is finally unveiled as living Buddha, this enlightenment is called forth and confirmed by his master, Mahakashyapa, not by a transcendental vision of Shakyamuni Buddha. When Ananda prostrates in gratitude after this experience, the deep bow is offered not to an icon of Shakyamuni but directly to Mahakashyapa, to the living Buddha, the fusion of the Three Jewels, just as they were originally fused beneath the Bodhi Tree.

Subliminally, Ananda received the Wonderful Mind of Luminosity when Mahakashyapa received it, along with eighty thousand practitioners on Vulture Peak. But complete, personal clarification of this original transmission is alone what constitutes full awakening. Patiently and humbly, Ananda prepares for his unveiling through forty years of discipleship.

Without any sense of expectation, the moment comes. Ananda inquires of Mahakashyapa if there was some secret transmission that his master received from Shakyamuni in addition to the gold brocade robe, that is to say, in addition to the royal way of Total Awakeness from the very beginning.

Perceiving the preparedness of his beloved brother, who does not ask this question naïvely, Mahakashyapa firmly yet intimately whispers, "Ananda!" The Dharma brother gazes attentively and directly, with the clear, selfless awareness developed during long years of study, contemplation, and devoted discipleship. Ananda's awakened response, his full attention, is an instant echo, inseparable from the original sound. It is the spark that comes forth when two flints are struck. There is no hierarchy here, no master-disciple relationship, no Buddhist doctrine, no expectation, no separation. Timeless transmission alone. Only flint can strike sparks from flint.

Like raising the flower and smiling, this event appears very natural. Yet look again! There is not one person whispering and another one responding with clear attention. There is no twoness. At this pregnant moment, Ananda is already unveiled as Total Awakeness.

From his vast reservoir of compassion, Mahakashyapa now utters a Zen phrase of even deeper clarification.

Knock down the flagpole before the gate! Do not take the position of Buddhism. Do not play the role of discipleship. Knock down the notion of *me* and *you* which has been set up as a conventional sign, as an arbitrary form of debate. As we actually pass through the gate of awakeness, the transparent banner of boundless clarity flies by itself, without any flagpole. This gate has no pillars, no dimensions. The victory banners of Buddhism and all sacred traditions fly from one axis. Plum, mango, cherry, pear, tamarind, all growing from a single branch.

There is nothing more than or other than pure attention, limitless awareness. There is no secret transmission outside sacred scriptures. There is no hidden Buddha nature outside the subject-object patterns of awareness called *skandhas*. But neither do Sutras or *skandhas* constitute Buddha nature. "Mind simply transmits to Mind, yet no one understands," remarks our ancient Japanese guide, Keizan Zenji. There is no one separate from Wonderful Mind, and therefore no one to understand. This realization is the gold brocade robe of transmission, which now manifests as the golden body of the fully awakened Ananda. This is the robe of Light which instantly puts out the fires of universal suffering. This is the very robe to be worn by the coming Buddha Maitreya.

There is only the robe, with no one wearing it. But do not get stuck in pristine emptiness. The historical Ananda actually wears this robe. In fact, the boundless clarity at the core of awareness is wearing this magnificent robe right now. Do not feel nostalgia for the companionship of Mahakashyapa and Ananda. There is no pole before the gate.

The flagpole of reliance upon scriptural teaching has been brought down, yet the victory banners of Sutra and Tantra shine in the wind. The conventional flagpole of teacher and student has been eliminated, yet each living Buddha serves as guide for the next. Scriptural mountains crumble and vines of study wither, yet we still investigate and venerate the *Prajnaparamita Sutra in 8,000 Lines*. Separate body and mind fall away completely, yet the living water of transmission continues to gush forth in the valley of our precious humanity. Sparks of transmission still spring from living stones, both masters and disciples.

closing poem

> Fire unites with fire!
> Ananda knows the meaning of his name,
> Great Bliss of Awakening.
> One spark ignites the universe!

BUDDHA IS ALIVE! BUDDHA IS ALIVE!

TRANSMISSION THREE
ANANDA TO SHANAVASA

koan

Successor inquires of living Buddha: "What is the original, uncreated, unborn nature of all phenomena?" The sage responds by pointing to one corner of the aspirant's monastic robe. Destined successor asks illumined master: "What is the original nature of Buddha's awakening?" The playful sage grasps the corner of the disciple's robe and pulls down sharply. Suddenly and totally, the new living Buddha is awake.

comment

Shanavasa, powerful adept who practiced contemplation for years in the Himalayas, has worn consciously since birth the natural, formless, colorless clothing of Unborn Nature—warm in winter, cool in summer. When he embraced the monastic way as a youth, this transparent clothing spontaneously manifested as the traditional upper and lower robes. Predicted one hundred years before his birth by Shakyamuni Buddha, Shanavasa now asks Ananda questions that no one ever thinks to ask. Why are these questions so rare? Because no one is fundamentally confused or even uncertain about Unborn Nature. Nothing ever substantially comes into being and therefore nothing ever substantially goes out of being. This fact, veiled only by its own transparency, stands naked at the core of daily awareness.

What is Unborn Nature? In the same way that Mahakashyapa whispered to him at the culminating moment, Ananda now points to a corner of Shanavasa's robe. At this moment of transmission, in which Shanavasa is completely receptive, Ananda could point anywhere in the universe. Yet the sage chooses to point at the sacred *kesa,* the robe of the Buddhist monk. This beautifully clear expression of Unborn Nature, this robe of nonduality, is what is most intimate to Shanavasa. This vow-body is closer to him than physical body or mental body.

The Buddhist monk is much more radical than homeless. He or she is birthless. Shanavasa understands this enlightened gesture of Ananda instantly, because he has been wearing the natural cloth of birthlessness for many eons, since his prediction to full enlightenment by previous Buddhas, to whom he humbly offered the whole cloth of his body, speech, and mind—his very life, breath, and being.

As Ananda once asked "Is there some secret that Buddha transmitted other than his robe?" Shanavasa now inquires, "What is this Unborn Nature which we call Buddha's awakening?" The question implies, "What is there other than birthlessness, which I already wear as my natural clothing, even in the *bardo* state between incarnations?" Ananda reaches out suddenly and tugs at the *kesa.* In no way flamboyant yet streaming with warm friendship, this intimate touch awakens Shanavasa. Previously he contemplated Unborn Nature, while now he actually feels its living touch. The Unborn is concrete, not abstract. Active, not passive. It is more obvious than the obvious, not esoteric. There is nothing to renounce or to acquire. Without this Buddha touch, our very eyes will obstruct their own vision. And the Buddha touch is a sharp tug, an energetic movement. The Unborn is tangibly manifesting. Even playing.

With this Zen gesture, Ananda expresses wordlessly: "Your *kesa,* your life of homelessness, is the very nature of awakeness. Your breath, your spiritual practice, your consecration, your natural awareness, the natural cloth of spontaneity you have worn for lifetimes, is awakeness in its original, unborn, uncreated nature. Feel it directly! Total Awakeness is tugging at you right now!"

Manifest as a body born from blessed mother and father, every precious human being perfectly expresses the Unborn. This present seeing and hearing are essentially no different from the awakeness of the ancient sages. This present life is not fundamentally different from the life of Mahakashyapa and Ananda, nor separate from the lives of ants and mosquitoes. Why would the true nature of existence be different for different beings? How could limitless awareness constitute some beings and not others? Can there be more than one Eye of Nonduality, more than one Mind of Luminosity?

We are here this morning face to face with our Zen teacher. How wonderful to meet such a person at last. Now our efforts will be fruitful. We are no longer the hungry ghosts of metaphysical speculation. We are no longer the lower heavenly beings of egocentric religious aspiration. We must have been predicted to Buddhahood, just as Shanavasa was predicted, for we are now knee to knee with the glorious Ananda. Smiling broadly, he is tugging at the *kesa* of our natural awareness. The transmission is ours. It is like reaching up to touch our own face. We do not need mirror or method. We are Great Mother Prajnaparamita, the brilliant dark womb where living Buddhas manifest.

closing poem

>Continuous stream plunges
>over ten thousand foot palisade.
>No dust mote comes to rest
>on this pure silk
>that forms our seamless robe,
>this awakeness always dancing
>and singing, "Buddha is alive!
>Buddha is alive!"

SPACE IS CONSUMED BY FLAMING SPACE

TRANSMISSION FOUR
SHANAVASA TO UPAGUPTA

koan

Living Buddha asks destined successor: "Did you renounce home in an external or an internal sense?" Wide open at this moment, the young monk replies: "My renunciation was not just internal but also external." With great intensity, the old sage now transmits the Light of Shakyamuni's realization: "How can the astonishing teaching of all Awakened Ones have anything to do with external or internal, with body or mind?" The new living Buddha is instantly awake.

comment

At age fifteen, through profound karmic propensity, the successor meets his illumined master and follows him. At seventeen, this un-educated, low-caste boy shaves his head and leaves home in the deepest sense by entering the Buddhist Sangha in a spirit of great clarity. Perceiving the vastly increased receptivity of this young man, now merely twenty-two, Shanavasa asks: "Was your home-leaving based on the level of external renunciation or on the level of inward renunciation?" Upagupta replies: "My renunciation was physical, not just mental." Now the living Buddha speaks like a sudden clap of thunder from the clear sky: "How can the boundless teaching of nonduality that radiates through all Awakened Ones have anything to do with physical or mental, with monastic or lay, with categories or limits of any kind?"

Ananda directly indicated Unborn Nature to his successor Shana-vasa by pointing at his monastic robe. Shanavasa, now the conscious embodiment of Unborn Nature, opens his successor Upagupta by penetrating through the young man's powerful sense of monastic re-nunciation to the open space beyond vows, beyond religion.

Later, as living Buddha, inheritor of the gold brocade robe, bearer of the lineage of Light, Upagupta inspires so many aspirants to enter monastic life that his community equals in numbers the visible Sangha of Shakyamuni. Evidently, open space also contains monastic vows. Reports Keizan Roshi, the charismatic power of this new living Buddha causes the dark palaces of demons to tremble. In fact, Upagupta manifests Buddha power by transforming many demonic energies into protectors of the Dharma.

Although freed by enlightenment from the slightest adherence to body or mind, to being monk or lay person, Upagupta carefully keeps count of his monastic disciples who attain the fullness of the Great Way by using thousands of small sticks. Following his request, these wooden counters are cremated with his body after Mahanirvana. This gesture indicates to everyone the merely provisional reality of any form of renunciation, pointing directly to the pure flames of Unborn Nature as source and goal of renunciation, as source and goal of every subtle principle from the eighty-four thousand teachings.

Consciously established as the Unborn, one can value even more highly the most transparent expressions of Unborn Nature, such as monastic renunciation or *bodhisattva* commitment to awakening all beings, without regarding such vows as some substantial, independent reality that actually comes into being. Consciously established as the Unborn, never coming into being or going out of being, one has no difficulty becoming sincerely engaged with various sacred traditions, participating fully in their sacraments and ceremonies. Consciously established as the Unborn, as the open space beyond religion, one immediately finds the core of every religion one encounters, surprising the most profound practitioners with genuine devotion to their practice and intuitive understanding of the teachings, symbols, and living presence of their sacred way. Consciously established as the Unborn, one does not have to enter any particular religion or person through the clothing or even through the skin, but can enter directly into the heart and circulate throughout the body as life-giving blood.

That Upagupta attains Great Awakening after a mere seven years of discipleship, while Ananda waits forty years, indicates that awakening as the Unborn is not related to time. In his Zen talk this morning, Master Keizan remarks most simply: "Awakening is unobtainable." Therefore, mature practitioners do not seek Wonderful Mind nor feel the slightest nostalgia for some Original Awakeness which is imagined to have been lost. They do not cultivate holiness any more than they would cultivate obsessive negativity. They realize that any attempt to exterminate personhood is a spiritual sickness, like anorexia, and that the drive to contemplate and become lost in some formless Absolute is a dangerous ploy of the subtle ego. These are the enlightened persons who have truly left home, truly renounced. As our ancient Japanese guide says: "Their minds are pure as the autumn moon, their eyes clear as a bright mirror."

Buddha Shanavasa proclaims uncompromisingly that the Unborn has nothing to do with home-leaving, whether it becomes visible or remains internal, nothing to do with any vow or religious structure. When one truly hears this, routine and convention break apart like sugar crystals metabolized in the fire of the body. All roots are cut. Trees and plants now blossom in the sky. Unborn Nature is never born into the conventional world and therefore never renounces or serves the world, no matter how noble such renunciation or service may be. Unborn Nature does not advance toward Buddhahood. Without this clear realization, the eighty-four thousand beautiful teachings of Lord Buddha remain mere provisional knowledge. This realization of Unborn Nature is, in fact, not a teaching of the Buddha, but the source of all teaching, the Mother of all Awakened Ones.

Do not imagine that affirmations such as *I am Buddha* or *I am the Original Face before my parents were born* actually constitute Unborn Nature. They may or may not be authentic expressions of it, but they are not it. The Unborn is neither mind nor no-mind, neither birth nor no-birth. These are but teachings. It is the source of all teaching.

Neither master nor disciple can be found within the Unborn, which is the elusive sound of a stream, a sound with no border or identity. This is the only meaning of transmission: the absence of boundary between one living Buddha and the next. This is why Upagupta, functioning in his turn as living Buddha, attracts so many persons to plunge into the Great Way, because he is the fire of Unborn

Nature in which not only dry sticks but even green trunks of banana trees are easily consumed. This is made evident at Upagupta's cremation ceremony, where not only his precious body and the wooden counters of his monastic disciples are burned but where space is consumed by flaming space, leaving no trace.

This borderless conflagration of Unborn Nature appears as the attractive form of Buddha Upagupta. He never presents the detailed teachings of Dharma, but concentrates solely on the Unborn, which contains them all. Buddha Ancestors, Buddha teachings, and noble renunciates are transformed by this fire of the Unborn to pure ash, black as fine lacquer. Compassionately, Master Keizan writes on this dark sky, on this midnight ocean without surface or depth. When we look for his words, they are gone!

closing poem

> Every cloud
> dissolves.
> Only blue fire
> of clear sky,
> unborn.
> Here is true body, true mind!
> Where can they hide?

NOT ONE CONVENTIONAL COIN
IN THIS TREASURY

TRANSMISSION FIVE
UPAGUPTA TO DHRITAKA

koan

Destined successor boldly proclaims: "One who leaves home may gradually become *me-less* and *my-less,* but Original Mind never ceases to be just itself. Therefore the Great Way is timeless, without any trace of development. Original Mind never becomes *this* or *that.*" Living Buddha responds with the thunderbolt of transmission: "Now you must simply be Original Mind! Embrace it as your daily awareness! Absorb it into your body completely!" The new vessel of Light is instantly full to the brim.

comment

The Awakened One is listening to the dream of a father at the birth of his unusual son, Dhritaka, whose name means *intimate with reality.* The father dreamed about a golden sun emerging from his ancestral home, illuminating both heaven and earth. A vast mountain also arises, adorned with seven jewels. A spring gushes forth from its summit, overflowing in the cardinal directions.

Buddha Upagupta now interprets. "The rising sun is the home-leaving, the perfect renunciation, destined for your son, who will bless your noble family for seven generations in each direction. The mountain is the present living Buddha. The overflowing spring is your son's abundant *prajna,* his transcendent insight. Dhritaka will present the inexhaustible teaching of nonduality to the entire universe. The seven jewels are seven *chakras,* inner energy spirals fully activated. The wisdom spring bursts forth from the crown *chakra.*

The living Buddha is the thousand-petaled lotus at the crown of the subtle body. The destined successor is the transcendent insight flowing abundantly from this crown. Master and successor are not two. They are like milk and its whiteness, fire and its power to burn."

Seated with quiet dignity beside his father, young Dhritaka now responds to the dream interpretation in a surprising manner. He sings about the clear spring of Prajnaparamita, timelessly gushing forth, transmitting not merely the teaching of nonduality but the very taste, refreshment, and freedom of indivisible awareness. Buddha Upagupta replies in kind with a spontaneous poem, indicating his intention to transmit Light to his young friend. The right key immediately opens the lock. Master serves as key for disciple and disciple as key for master. Without this miraculous mutuality, there is no transmission. The transmission of Light is effortless and inevitable. Sings young Dhritaka, deep in ecstasy: "The spring of transcendent insight is always overflowing."

The timeless disciple now makes three prostrations before his timeless master, humbly requesting the ceremony of home-leaving. Without flawless renunciation, flawless nonduality, no deep awakening is possible. Buddha Upagupta chooses to enlighten the youth immediately, not even waiting the minimal seven years that his own master waited with him. The probing question is the same one originally used to break through Upagupta's own presuppositions.

Living Buddha asks destined successor: "Is it your intention to leave home with body or with mind?" Manifesting profound insight, the young sage replies: "It is not for the sake of either body or mind." The Awakened One further probes the innate wisdom of this youth: "If not body or mind, who or what is it that leaves home, that renounces selfish habits and dead conventions?" Unhesitatingly, this amazing disciple responds: "The *no-self self,* neither arising nor ceasing, constitutes the timeless way of the timeless Buddhas. This is essential mind, free from form or focus."

Dhritaka's response is not intellectual, not the fruit of Buddhist study, but flows spontaneously from the summit of the mountain. The old sage now insists that this overflowing insight must belong directly to Dhritaka, not only to the mountain. "You must greatly awaken by realizing this as your ordinary mind!" Dhritaka awakens beyond all awakening.

The primal principle of the Great Way, transcendent insight, exists timelessly, but without a timely awakening, it is not truly transmitted. It remains the dead *Prajnaparamita Sutra,* mere words and concepts, not the living Wisdom Goddess. The Great Way must be born anew, generation after generation. This birthless birth from the womb of Prajnaparamita can occur only through the master's motherly concern, compassion, care.

The wisdom spring of the successor can gush forth only from the lineage holder. The living Buddha must actually transmit Light. Awakening is not some independent project of the successor. Radical renunciation of self must be intended by the receptive disciple. Otherwise, apparent sages may arise who cannot truly transmit Dharma, whose expression of the principle of nonduality is tinged by arrogance, by formalism, by the nihilistic rejection of lineage, by subtle denigration of discipleship, by absence of compassion.

At the moment of authentic transmission, successor merges consciously with master, becoming the royal seal for the new generation that guarantees this teaching as Buddha teaching. Remarks our beloved Roshi Keizan: "When you see the royal seal, you know the product is not poison." Sutras and Tantras can be propagated by someone without this seal of awakening, but they will remain dead scriptures. They may even contain poison. This royal seal cannot be found inside any of the eighty-four thousand teachings of the Buddha, nor can it be developed by means of any supernatural powers. We must discover our own boundless treasury, the Eye of Nonduality, the *Prajnaparamita Sutra* of our own natural mind and body. This is the only seal of authenticity.

There is not one conventional coin in this treasury. There is nothing here merely repeated from the past. It is all new, never before encountered in the history of Buddhism, in the history of consciousness. This seal is not the teaching *all is empty* or *mind only* or *the whole being is Buddha nature.* This seal is not religious convention, nor even genuine Buddhist understanding. It is the Great Seal, *mahamudra*, the awakening beyond all awakening.

Reveals Keizan, tender mother of Japanese Soto Zen, each awakening is a gem which radiates its own unique aura. Each sage is a gourd, entwined with its own unique pattern of vines. The uniqueness of each mind is not effaced by realization. By awakening, we do not become impersonal principle, but the ever unique *no-self self*. Now we can enter the inner sanctuary of all Buddhas and wander through our own homeland. The essential energy of such awakening brings all eighty-four thousand teachings alive and clear. But each illumined sage, like the Taoist wheelwright Lun-pien, unveils a unique subtlety that was never manifested before and will never be repeated again.

closing poem

> Remove the mask of Buddha
> from your own face!
> Weeping and laughing,
> transmit the treasure!
> Mind
> is enlightened
> just as it is!

HAZY MOON OF SPRING

TRANSMISSION SIX
DHRITAKA TO MICHAKA

koan

Living Buddha transmits indivisible Light to destined successor through these passionate words: "Shakyamuni taught: *To exercise any occult power or to immerse the mind in any finite doctrine is to be bound and dragged by a rope.* But you can be completely certain that the moment you abandon the small stream and come directly to the great ocean, you will realize Unborn Nature." The new living Buddha stands suddenly unveiled.

comment

Successor Michaka is brought before Buddha Dhritaka through intriguing karmic conditions, established six eons earlier in the heavenly dimension of Lord Brahma. In that distant time, Michaka had already begun to acquire magical powers in order to control other beings, while his companion, Dhritaka, had chosen to practice selfless meditation, seeking the transcendent power of enlightenment in order to liberate all beings.

At their first meeting on the earthly plane, Michaka, with his marvelously developed psychic powers, perceives and comprehends this ironic karmic situation. He acknowledges his ancient friend Dhritaka to be his destined master, and requests liberation from the endless cycles of self-involvement. The Awakened One graciously confers upon Michaka the monastic precepts. This potent initiation is instantly effective, clarifying and preparing the successor for the transmission of Light.

The thousands of shamans who travel with Michaka as their guide and who are intensely proud of their ability to manipulate subtle energy are transformed as well by witnessing Buddha power, which manifests in all universes simultaneously, without any effort and without needing to establish a base in any substantial energy whatsoever. These adepts are so genuinely moved that they also decide to become Mahayana monks, in order to attain complete awakening for themselves and for all sentient beings. This revolution at the core of consciousness occurs simply when they hear the Awakened One repeat the original teaching of Shakyamuni Buddha: "Manipulating limited energies and inquiring into the nature of Reality from limited perspectives is like being bound and dragged."

With powerful gaze, the present embodiment of enlightenment turns to Michaka and proclaims: "You should confirm for yourself, here and now, that the moment you leave the limited stream and enter the limitless ocean, you will realize Unborn Nature." Through the authenticity behind these words, Michaka, former magician, awakens as the ocean of the Unborn.

In the narrow stream of psychic science, which investigates and manipulates the subtle characteristics of energy, one can perceive eighty thousand eons in both directions. But fundamental questions are left unanswered. Even advanced spiritual science, formless contemplation, is a narrow stream leading to rebirth in a formless dimension, faced with inevitable and involuntary remanifestation in the realm of form. Raptly contemplating formlessness is to be bound and dragged by the rope of most subtle karma. Struggling to overcome delusion and attain enlightenment is still to remain stuck for eons in the small stream. Even wiping away absolutely all imperfections on all levels is not yet to reach the great ocean. Such cleansing, too, is a conditional effort, which can produce only conditional results.

What is the nature of this ocean of the Unborn? If we imagine it to be empty of phenomena, we are being bound and dragged. Do not regard anything as false, illusory, or separate from essential mind. The Unborn is right here. No one is ignorant of it, although she may claim ignorance. No one has knowledge of it, although he may claim knowledge. It manifests as skin, nerves, and spontaneous poems—waves rising and falling, leaving no marks.

The ocean of the Unborn is always at play. This faceless consciousness is forever on the move, forever creating faces. It weaves clothes and grows food, but is never limited by any of these fluent manifestations. Awakening as this ocean of awakeness, we lack nothing and possess nothing. We simply *are* the golden peach, the delicate green bamboo. Every other meditation is trivial compared to this meditation beyond meditation.

The Unborn is free from bondage and liberation, from *samsara* and *nirvana,* yet it manifests compassionately as the path to enlightenment. There are actually no small streams at all. There is nothing but the great ocean, the Great Way. Every dust mote and every star is a dream image of the Unborn. Unborn Nature is the only possible subject of inquiry. If we laboriously travel to some ocean from some small stream, it is certainly not the great ocean. The great ocean already contains every spring, every waterfall, every dewdrop. There is nowhere to leave, nowhere to arrive.

In a single moment, six eons of calculation and manipulation drop away from the mindstream of Michaka. Simultaneously, he becomes humble monk and living Buddha. What wonderful destiny! It belongs to each of us equally! We are meeting and acknowledging our ancient friend, now a living Buddha, who is closer to us than we are to ourselves. The currents of student and teacher flow together within the great ocean. Even this cannot be stated. Is there any difference between water and water?

Master Keizan's closing poem this morning warns us not to misperceive the landscape of the Unborn. It is not a clear autumn moon. It is not the beginning of winter hibernation. Leaves are not drying up and falling away to expose black limbs against cold sky. Unborn Nature is the hazy moon of spring. Life is burgeoning. There is a cloud of tender new growth floating about the trees. Mist veils the moon, concealing its form while revealing its most subtle light. Air is humid. Soil is damp, dark, and fragrant.

closing poem

> Sitting before dawn,
> blackness becomes light.
> Can this broom
> sweep the earth away?
> Can this cup
> empty the vast sea?

THERE IS NO NEED FOR AN EMPTY CUP

TRANSMISSION SEVEN
MICHAKA TO VASUMITRA

koan

Successor places large gourd of wine before living Buddha, bows, and waits. The Awakened One asks: "Is this mine or yours?" The next vessel of Light ponders silently. The master's words flash like a lightning bolt opening a raincloud: "If you think this wine gourd is mine, you have liberated your own being. If you think it is yours, you have received my complete transmission." Now there is no master, no successor, only Total Awakeness.

comment

While demonstrating Buddha activity by roaming freely through the mysterious landscape of India, the Awakened One approaches a mud-walled village. With Buddha perception, he notes a strangely shaped golden cloud rising from within it. He informs his companions that they are about to encounter the diamond being who is destined to receive the transmission of Light.

Vasumitra has always appeared mad to the undiscerning eyes of the villagers, spending his days and nights wandering about with a gourd of wine, never letting it go, sighing and moaning with profound longing. But unlike any mad person, he always keeps his body and clothes immaculate.

Recognizing the visitor instantly as the living Buddha, this ecstatic raises his mystic vessel of wine and inquires: "Do you know what this is?" The surprising answer comes: "It is still an impure vessel." Vasumitra places the gourd on the ground before his destined guide, for the first time letting it out of his grasp. He bows profoundly and waits. The Awakened One picks up the wine gourd and places it back in front of Vasumitra, indicating the open door to enlightenment with the question: "Is this mine or yours?"

The hidden sage is again surprised and plunges into contemplation. Buddha Michaka now pushes the unconventional yogi through the open door with the force of these words: "If you think this is mine, you have become free from relative existence. If you think it is yours, you have become a living Buddha, beyond such notions as absolute and relative." The Arhat is liberated by completely giving away his own being. The Buddha liberates all beings by completely affirming his own beingless being. Vasumitra, remaining silent, awakens to the indivisibility of Unborn Nature—neither *here* nor *there*, neither Arhat nor Buddha. At the very moment of awakening, the vessel of wine miraculously disappears, along with the entire network of conventional thought and perception.

Destined successor Vasumitra has never revealed to anyone his personal and family name, so committed was he to forgetting himself and finding his destined master. Now the master asks his name and Vasumitra replies with a poem, revealing the name that he has always borne, lifetime after lifetime, eon after eon. Buddha Michaka, in turn, responds with a prophecy. Shakyamuni predicted that three hundred years after his *mahanirvana* a holy being by this very name, Vasumitra Bharadvaja, would receive responsibility to embody the Great Way. Empowered by these prophetic words, the new living Buddha now remembers hearing the prediction of an ancient Buddha from a previous eon that he, Vasumitra, would eventually become a successor in the lineage of Shakyamuni during a distant future to be called the Fortunate Thousand Buddha Eon.

Whatever the master knows must be reconfirmed by the direct experience of the successor—not at a lower level, or even at the same level, but at a significantly deeper or higher level. Thus the Light of transmission becomes more rich and intense through the course of generations, rather than diminishing in power or remaining on the same plateau.

First the disciple must present the vessel of his or her entire being before the master, who alone truly embodies the Unborn, who alone can drink the radiant wine of Unborn Nature. The offered vessel is always impure, no matter how clean and clear the disciple is, no matter how spiritually advanced. There always remains the subtle impurity of falsely perceived duality— between master and disciple, between enlightenment and something else. Then the master returns the vessel, completely purified of duality, and the disciple realizes that the vessel contains the intimacy of his or her own unique awareness, essentially no different from the master's awareness. Now where is *mine* or *yours?*

This is the penultimate step. If the process stops here, a tinge of realization-ego may remain, and future transmission will be impossible. The vessel must utterly disappear for the lineage of indivisible Light to continue. Even the slightest conceptuality about realizing our essential nature or becoming a living Buddha must merge into Total Awakeness. As soon as the vessel disappears, however, it subtly reappears. In the present case, it manifests as Vasumitra's secret Buddha name, prophetically confirmed by Shakyamuni and by the Awakened One from a previous eon. Only because it has truly disappeared can the vessel now function transparently as lineage-holder, as liberator and awakener.

Any sense of personal realization and personal functioning must disappear. Even the amazing experience of this body as Buddha must disappear. Asks our ancient Japanese guide very pointedly: "Is there anyone ready to accept this elusiveness, this inconceivability, among you contemporary persons who always want clear answers and demonstrable knowledge?"

Teacher and student are like the bell and its resonance. Student and teacher are like intersecting cords in a fishing net—nodes, not separate strands. When the teacher is ready, the student will appear. Successor Vasumitra longed and moaned for Master Michaka, but Michaka was searching even more avidly for Vasumitra. Reveals our compassionate Keizan Roshi: "The disciple rises up to the master's head, and the master comes down to the disciple's feet." Master and disciple need not engage in any long drama of transmission. They are already pure transmission, pure plenitude. As the poem delivered spontaneously by Keizan Zenji this morning suggests: "From the very first, there is no need for an empty cup."

closing poem

> During profound penetration,
> the vessel disappears—
> no contact, nothing to contact.
> At bell sound,
> the vessel arises, walks, talks.
> Simply condensed sky!

DO NOT IMAGINE YOU ARE GOING TO BECOME A STILL POND

TRANSMISSION EIGHT
VASUMITRA TO BUDDHANANDI

koan

The complete embodiment of enlightenment immediately recognizes his spiritual inheritor, who enters the master's presence proclaiming: "I have come to debate truth." The Awakened One
responds, smiling: "Dear friend, if we debate, it will not be truth."
The indivisible Light of transmission suddenly shines.

comment

Buddha Vasumitra is wandering freely through India, releasing persons from limited religious, social, and metaphysical views by opening their minds to the unutterable principle of Unborn Nature. A
certain Buddhanandi, deeply committed to philosophical investigation, invincible in dialectic, is the karmically destined successor
whom Vasumitra is patiently seeking. The crown-protuberance, one
sign of Buddhahood, already manifests on Buddhanandi's head. The
exalted term *buddha,* meaning *awake,* already appears in his name.
Entering the presence of the Awakened One with intense confidence, even before sitting down he announces: "I have come to debate with you about the nature of truth." Buddhanandi presumes
that he can confront this wandering sage eyebrow to eyebrow, as he
has done in so many other instances during his distinguished debating career. He is surprised and fully enlightened by the delightful
response of the living Buddha, who speaks gently and harmoniously,
without a trace of the usual intellectual or religious rivalry. "Beloved
friend, truth does not have two sides and therefore has never been
debated and can never be debated. Whatever one may debate, no
matter how profoundly, is therefore simply not truth." Buddhanandi
is dedicated to following deep philosophy wherever it may lead, and

therefore cannot avoid being awakened to unformulatability and in-divisibility by these simple words, which bear the transforming power of realization. The successor has been skillfully debating for many years about various expressions of truth without experiencing truth directly. He now effortlessly mirrors the Light of transmission.

Buddha Vasumitra kindly addresses the newly unveiled living Buddha. "Whatever can be asserted about reality, however coher-ently and correctly, must remain on the level of discussion. There is always some other perspective from which any assertion can and must be debated. Even the slightest intention to assert or discuss already veils what is real. No verbal claim, such as the correct asser-tion that mind and its objects are not fundamentally separate, can be truth. The verbal claim that truth is beyond words and thought is also not truth. To assert that subject and object are forgotten in the blessed experience of enlightenment, or to express the higher view that subject and object are not forgotten in enlightenment—neither is truth.

"Bodhisattva Manjushri's enlightened affirmation that reality is ut-terly beyond speech is an excellent expression of truth but not living truth. Even the radical response of the sage Vimalakirti, who sits in *thunderous silence,* is but an expression of what is real. So long as any sense of defining or even expressing truth intervenes, the principle of Unborn Nature cannot be clarified, and we will remain confused, even if we are disciples of an Awakened One.

"To extinguish body and mind in unbroken concentration is a se-vere obstruction. Even the much higher way of rejecting the separate categories, *delusion* and *enlightenment,* avoiding the notions *impurity* and *purity,* is an opaque veil. Both *form* and *formless* misrepresent truth, like the mirage misrepresents the desert. We should neither seek truth through the golden forms of Buddhas nor through their brilliant formlessness. If you claim cyclical existence to be a dream, there remains someone dreaming and someone claiming. How funny! Even the distinction between *false* and *true* remains on the level of perennial discussion, and is therefore not truth. Simply be truth! But do not imagine you are going to become a still pond or a stainless sky!"

The first full moon of Soto Zen, Tung-shan, thirty-eighth successor of Shakyamuni, was consciously unified with all phenomena and could clearly hear all phenomena preaching the Dharma of nonduality. Yet this great sage sensed that he remained subtly involved with expressions of truth. His master simply advised: "You must experience this situation very carefully and completely." *Carefulness* means distinguishing indirect expressions of truth from direct truth. *Completeness* means embodying the direct truth. Tung-shan awakened only after leaving the monastery of his teacher, leaving the context of systematic inquiry into truth and dedication to the expression of truth. While wandering freely through the wilderness, he crosses a stream, glimpses the reflection of his own face, and is awakened beyond all expression.

Ananda simply hears his own name and is enlightened. The transmission of Light always comes from itself to itself, dissolving the duality of master and disciple as well as the duality of disciple and himself or herself. Yet the delightful, transparent play of twoness always remains in play. Fully awakened, Tung-shan can now sing about the principle of the living Buddha: "Avoid seeking him in someone else or in yourself, but meet him everywhere. Certainly he is me, but this dusty, foolish traveler that I am is not him." This is the secret of Living Buddha Zen—its great power, its great humility. Be Buddha! Be Total Awakeness!

Master always sits on a cushion higher than disciple, yet the master secretly merges with the disciple and thus accomplishes the transmission. The disciple never elevates himself or herself to the position of master. In realization, the disciple simply disappears. Only the full moon remains, transmitting truth day and night, along with the ancient temple pillars and the dancing votive lanterns.

Leave aside worldly opinions and religious opinions as well, no matter how strongly bastioned they may be by cultural expectation, by study of the scriptures, by meditation experience. Leave aside marketplace and monastery. Every thought, no matter how sublime—such as the naturally manifesting enlightenment of all phenomena—remains in the ambiguous realm of opinion and discussion. Both sublime and mundane thoughts are equally laughable, as is the stupid state of no-thought. We must experience this situation very carefully and completely.

It is irresponsible and incomplete to dwell in the purity and clarity of emptiness. It is never a solution to remain in silence or to dispense with meditation, study, and rigorous debate. A certain Chinese Zen master reported that after thirty years of relentless spiritual investigation, he finally understood how foolish it was "to conceal body and mind in transcendent purity."

Master Keizan's core question this morning illuminates the situation—not over a period of thirty years but instantly: "When is seasoning not appropriate?" The delicious, subtle seasoning is the play of phenomena, the dance of body and mind, the inexhaustible expressions of truth. It is not hospitable to offer bland food to the honored guest in this hermitage without gates or walls. Who would pine for an empty winter sky, when the full moon is rising over a fragrant countryside, seasoned by spring?

Our beloved guide Keizan recommends only that rare carefulness which always remains immersed in the fact of spiritual fullness. With great tenderness, he whispers to us: "Work carefully and do not be hasty." We must come outside the realm of discussion and debate. Yet if we rush toward truth past all the wonderful expressions of truth, we may miss the most delicately seasoned dish. "O taste and see that the Lord is good," proclaims the singer of the Psalms. Too much seasoning, however, is unpalatable, and seasoning alone, without food, inedible.

closing poem

> Mother bird hears
> insistent pecking from within.
> With mature beak,
> she breaks the shell.
> Only a thin surface
> separates mind
> from flight.

How Sweet These Seven Steps!

Transmission Nine
Buddhanandi to Buddhamitra

koan

The living Buddha proclaims to the inheritor of Total Awakeness: "Your speechless speech is one with essential mind. Not even intimacy with mother and father can compare to intimacy with essential mind. Your actionless actions spontaneously express the Great Way. This is what constitutes the Wonderful Mind of all Buddhas. If you create any Buddha image, it will never completely correspond to your own reality. If you desire to know essential mind directly, you must realize that you are neither one with Mind nor separate from Mind." Deeply receiving these words of transmission, the destined successor awakens beyond every level of awakening.

comment

The Awakened One, traveling and teaching spontaneously, now arrives before the house of a certain merchant and, with Buddha perception, discerns white radiance emanating from its inner chambers. He remarks to his companions: "A great being resides here. No word comes from his lips, as he is a vessel of transcendent wisdom and the destined inheritor of the wordless teaching. His feet never touch the earth, because he is an adept of transparency, perceiving not an atom of substance anywhere."

At this moment, the head of the household appears and salutes his visitors. The radiant Buddhanandi says: "I am seeking a qualified person to accompany me." The white-haired householder replies humbly: "Revered sir, I have only one son. He is fifty years old and has never walked or spoken." Buddhanandi responds: "He will be my Dharma successor!" Hearing this potent prophetic utterance from his bed within the house, Buddhamitra arises and walks for the very first time. Coming forth into the presence of his destined master, the hidden sage speaks his first words in the form of a poem.

> Even mother and father are not close enough.
> Where is true intimacy?
> Even Buddhas are not close enough.
> Where is the Great Way?

To this uniquely prepared person, the living Buddha now speaks. "Your speech has not manifested during this lifetime because you have been in a state of spontaneous union with essential mind. Although your love for your parents is so intense that you hesitate to walk, lest you renounce your home and walk away from them, intimacy with essential mind is infinitely more intense. It is the intimacy of nonduality. You have not manifested external action during this lifetime because your activity has already been merged in the Great Way, which cannot be expressed by any external or internal form, even by the auspicious golden forms of the Buddhas, toward whom you feel such deep devotion. You must now awaken to the full appreciation of essential mind by realizing that you need not remain silently merged in it. Whatever you think or do, you are never separate from it." Instantly manifesting enlightenment at these words of Light, Buddhamitra takes seven sacred steps, exactly as Shakyamuni did at his miraculous birth, clearly confirming the transmission.

Living Buddhas wander freely, effortlessly searching for destined successors who are karmically prepared to reincarnate their masters while these Awakened Ones are still visible to earthly eyes. Thus Light transmits to itself, playing as two unique sages. This approach differs from methods which seek the departed master's reincarnation as a small child or attempt to select a successor, after the master's passing, by dreams or by consultation among advanced practitioners. For Living Buddha Zen, the master and the full incarnation of his or her awakened mind are equals and best friends, face to face here on earth, sometimes sharing years of rich companionship, each enhancing the subtlety and profundity of the other. This deep mutual affection permits the awakened successor to refine the enlightened art of compassion, the capacity to transmit the Light of nonduality. This wonderful friendship becomes easy and natural, even though it usually begins in the mood of mystery and intensity.

How can one distinguish between an autistic child and a hidden sage such as Buddhamitra? Each case is karmically different. Our Roshi Keizan warns: "Do not assume that either speech or silence has anything to do with the freedom of Unborn Nature to manifest as all phenomena or to remain immersed in radiant darkness." One Dharma successor may be an eloquent speaker who becomes rather silent after the earthquake of transmission. Another may be unspeaking and unmoving, immersed in longing or in sheer transparency, and then become extremely active and discourse extensively after awakening. Each successor must take over his or her own responsibility to transmit the single Light uniquely, whether in Asia or America. Only the illumined sage can recognize the new vessel of Light. Spiritual succession cannot be confirmed with the eyes of socially or religiously conditioned perception. The destined successor is always surprising and often unacceptable, even to close disciples of the master.

What is the difference in the consciousness of these highly prepared persons, these Dharma successors, before and after transmission? Nothing new is placed into them during the process, since their karmic receptivity is already complete and their enlightenment can manifest only from within. What happens? Each case is distinct. The state of Buddhamitra before transmission was relentless immersion in the Unborn. This state is called *ri* in Japanese, meaning to be separate or aloof from words, actions, phenomena. His master skillfully opens him into the mirror-image of this state, called *bi* in Japanese, the secret freedom of Unborn Nature to manifest transparently as words, actions, phenomena. *Inside* is not close, *outside* not far. This transition from *ri* to *bi* is often part of the mystery of Dharma transmission, although no conventional pattern can ever be established.

Whatever exists in seed form before the transmission of Light now appears to bloom into plenitude at the touch of the living Buddha, as lotus bud becomes full blossom beneath the rays of the sun. Yet this lotus of Wonderful Mind actually blossoms night and day, under all conditions.

O sisters and brothers, this is true for all of us. We are the successor Buddhamitra, whose name means *friend of awakeness*. The living Buddha is our best friend, our most intimate beloved, our own core reality manifesting as innumerable awakened sages and evolving conscious beings throughout space and time.

closing poem

> After spinning our cocoon
> of Buddha form,
> we burst it open.
> Deep in the ocean of emptiness,
> we take giant breaths of air.
> Free from speech and silence,
> unconfined by action or stillness,
> how sweet these seven steps!

CURLING WHITE LIKE PERPETUALLY BREAKING WAVES

TRANSMISSION TEN
BUDDHAMITRA TO PARSHVA

koan

Without even once entering the state of sleep, destined successor focuses full attention on living Buddha. After three years of this unimaginable intensity, this ceaseless gaze, disciple hears master chanting the Sutra of Birthlessness and is suddenly awake.

comment

Parshva is tremendously gifted from birth, as first revealed by the dream of his father: the newborn infant appears as a brilliant pearl, resting on the back of a white elephant, sending forth wisdom rays into countless hearts. Yet Parshva's period of spiritual gestation is sixty years. When he enters monastic life at age sixty, he is ridiculed by conventionally minded monks and nuns, laymen and laywomen. But the hidden sage is not even slightly distracted by these taunts. He is profoundly prepared. When he receives monastic initiation, a wonderful brilliance shines from his meditation seat. Buddha relics materialize before him and then disappear again. Parshva immediately vows sleeplessness, continuous practice of study and meditation, and continuous companionship with the living Buddha.

The destined successor is not awakened by anything in particular—no unexpected sound or flash, no dramatic question and answer exchanged with his master. There is no particular phrase that finally opens the disciple, either from the Sutra of Birthlessness or from the living Buddha's inspiring oral commentary. There is not even a key word or wordless gesture. Parshva does not receive or proclaim anything. He just awakens. How?

The new living Buddha is unveiled simply by perceiving the totality of his master, the totality of Buddhamitra's life, the totality of his awakeness. During three years, no detail of the master's existence has been ignored by this careful attendant, who is attending to infinite life, not just to a particular life-form. During the day, the successor contemplates with intense commitment the entire range of Sutra teaching. At night, in his master's transparent presence, he practices the profoundly peaceful meditation of nonduality—*mahamudra*, the Great Gesture, that does not obsessively wipe away motes of dust nor attempt to exterminate erroneous thoughts but that waits tenderly with all beings in the mystic womb of the Wisdom Mother.

Diligence in nondual insight, both day and night, is Parshva's goalless path, his pathless goal. Every day is a good day for nonduality! Every moment is as auspicious for realization as the birthday celebration of the Buddha. Parshva pays full attention to relative and absolute, never making the slightest division between them. Only in this way can we become direct disciples of the living Buddha— wherever we are, whoever we are. Parshva does not flip through Sutras, presumably understanding them, but penetrates them skillfully, line by line, never remaining on the surface of meaning but plunging to the depth. Neither does he turn the Sutra scroll of his life in some casual or complacent manner. He does not waste precious body and mind. Though weakened by age, he ignores mental and physical fatigue, heat, cold, illness. He perseveres to the end of the race, sprinting continuously for three years, and becomes one with the Great Way. He demonstrates that whatever adverse conditions may prevail, this can be done.

Parshva awakens by encountering not scriptural phrases or principles of doctrine but the living truth at the root of every teaching, the indivisible Sutra of Birthlessness, which embraces all Sutras and Tantras, all masters, all breaths and heartbeats, all phrases, verses, words, letters, all dreams, visions, and events. After awakening into this ever deepening way of wholeness, egocentricity, no matter how subtle, becomes impossible. Why? Because egocentricity is partial, and this is whole. There is nothing that is not included, elucidated, and sustained by this wholeness, this Great Mother Sutra, this scroll always turning, always unrolling and rolling back up. No place to come from, no place to abide, no place to go. Simply the play of simultaneous evolution and involution, breath by breath. Veda is time, Sutra is space, Torah is life, Gospel is love, Quran is cosmos.

The diamond verses of the *Prajnaparamita Sutra,* the master's beautiful Buddha voice, Parshva's intense hearing and illumined understanding of the text, our own consideration of the present transmission—all these are living words and letters in the sole scripture of Unborn Nature, the Mother Book. Nothing is separable, isolatable, identifiable. There is no special way. Nothing is obscure. Nothing is ordinary.

The Sutra of Birthlessness is the completeness of life. Anyone can say these words. They must become our life-breath. We must speak as we breathe, not out of distraction but to live. For all beings to live.

This morning our ancient Japanese guide provides an open door to this unlocked, unguarded treasure. Softly, he sings: "Turning, turning—so many Sutra scrolls." Conscious beings are Sutra scrolls, curling white like perpetually breaking waves. Ever-unfolding abundance, without end or beginning. This is the blissful Sutra of Birthlessness. We need not meditate on deathlessness, for birthlessness is more profound. "Born here, dying there," continues Keizan Roshi's poem, "are chapters and phrases." This universally fruitful meeting of Buddhamitra and Parshva, this transmission of boundless clarity, is simply one chapter. The present words of appreciation and participation are simply one phrase.

closing poem

> Breath scroll turns
> night and day—
> teaching, teaching.
> Taste of bitter herbs,
> taste of honey.
> There is no key.
> The scroll simply turns.

PATIENCE! SMALL BIRDS ARE SPEAKING!

TRANSMISSION ELEVEN
PARSHVA TO PUNYAYASHAS

koan

Destined successor, palms joined in reverence, now stands silently before living Buddha. The Awakened One asks: "Where do you come from? Where are you residing?" Immersed in formlessness, the aspirant replies: "My mind does not come or go. My mind does not dwell anywhere." Playfully, the master probes: "You seem somewhat disoriented." The contemplative is not shaken, responding confidently: "All Buddhas are in this state." Like a diamond thunderbolt, the sage strikes: "This notion, *all Buddhas,* is falsification." Ignited by the enlightened power of the reply, Punyayashas enters continuous inward inquiry for twenty-one days. Finally, he dissolves the obstacle of formlessness and experiences transcendent patience, joyfully accepting the constant arising of universal manifestation—free from birth, root, origin. Returning to his master, Punyayashas remarks: "The notion, *all Buddhas,* is indeed falsification. And so are the notions *holiness, sacredness, specialness.*" The living Buddha recognizes the proper level of preparedness and transmits Light in silence. Wordlessly, free from every notion.

comment

When the Awakened One arrives in the kingdom where Punyayashas dwells, he informs his traveling companions that a hidden sage will soon approach and that the earth will turn the color of gold in his presence. This golden omen indicates the precious realization of formlessness, in which the mind neither comes, stays, nor goes. But this spiritual state is definitely not full awakening. The ground does not turn golden in the presence of the living Buddha but remains pure earth color. For Awakened Ones, all phenomena manifest transparently, just as they are. This natural nonduality, humorous, free from any special sanctity, is not just golden color but authentic gold—inexhaustible spiritual wealth to distribute among all conscious beings.

The destined successor now tastes transcendent patience. Oak grows slowly, redwood more swiftly. Patience enjoys each growing at its own rate, by its own principle. Patience delights in transparent manifestation, not in formlessness. Each wisdom tradition actually comes from somewhere—from a particular lineage and fragrance of realization. It abides somewhere—in a world of organic ceremony, abounding with disciplines, sacraments, responsibilities. And it goes somewhere—to a life of ever greater universality and compassionate maturity. Remaining immersed in formlessness, as young sage Punyayashas does, is a profound spiritual level indeed, but fails to appreciate oak, redwood, cypress, mahogany, gingko—Hindu, Buddhist, Jewish, Christian, Muslim, and many others—each with its own unique principle of manifesting, each inseparable from the rich soil of Unborn Nature.

As our ancient Japanese guide subtly indicates: "My mind is not composed of such abstractions as *formlessness* or *all Buddhas*. It actually comes from somewhere, abides somewhere, and goes somewhere." The living Buddha is fully living human life! To claim that all religions are one is another abstraction which falsifies. As Keizan Roshi warns: "My mind is not your mind." Do not succumb to the abstraction of oneness or sameness. Do not place meditation cushions of many colors in the *zendo*. Zen is a black cushion. Do not fill the *zendo* with rose perfume. Zen is the fragrance of aloeswood.

After ceaselessly releasing his attachment to brilliant formlessness for twenty-one days, disciple is recognized by master as fully receptive. Punyayashas now attains selfless patience toward persons, religions, and entire worlds, each arising uniquely and transparently from the groundless ground of the Unborn. Since there is nothing special or separate about realization, the transmission of Light occurs spontaneously. There is no flash. There is no separate subject or object for awareness to flash between. There is no strange opacity called *formlessness,* nor any leap beyond it. There are no high walls of spiritual states which can impede the natural flow of awareness. Do not try to analyze Total Awakeness, either with native intelligence or with traditional Dharma categories. It fills up master and successor equally. There is simply no more separate sage.

closing poem

> Patience! Dawn is breaking!
> Patience! Small birds are speaking!
> Patience! Wooden drum is sounding!
> Where are all Buddhas now?

THE UNCOMMON RED
OF THE PEACH BLOSSOMS

TRANSMISSION TWELVE
PUNYAYASHAS TO ASHVAGHOSA

koan

Advanced aspirant asks living Buddha: "What is Buddha?" The Awakened One replies: "The person who truly does not know Buddha is Buddha." Still involved in knowing, the disciple enquires: "How can one definitively know that the state of not-knowing is Buddha?" The master responds powerfully: "How can one know that the state of not-knowing is not Buddha?"

Disciple comments with deepening insight: "This conversation is like a sharp saw." Master nods and adds: "It is also like fine wood." Master now asks disciple what he means by *sharp saw*. "Beloved teacher, you and I are exactly matched, like the teeth on a saw. And what do you mean, revered sir, by the term *fine wood*?" Commenting softly, "Time has come," the living Buddha transmits Light with a sudden downward gesture of his right hand, crying out: "Now you are cut through!" There is only boundless clarity.

comment

Ashvaghosa, predicted as a world-liberator six hundred years earlier by Shakyamuni, now comes directly to Buddha reality. Nothing else concerns him, only *What is Buddha?* Ashvaghosa is superior to all the aspirants of his generation in the transcendent virtues of patience, generosity, goodness, commitment, meditation, and insight. His practice of ordinary moral virtue is also impeccable. This supremely worthy person has now reached the point of utter focus. He is manifest as a great vessel. His inquiry is about nothing other than Buddha. He does not even inquire about the thirty-two major marks and the eighty minor marks of the Buddha. Only Buddha. Anything else would not be definitive.

Yet now this intense focus needs to melt into not-knowing. True not-knowing is infinite. It is not comparable to any ordinary condition of not knowing some information or not perceiving some object. True not-knowing, though faceless, can manifest any face. It has no particular way to be, no mark by which it can be recognized. It is always simply us. Our own most intimate awareness.

In conditional not-knowing, there is a subject who remains in a frustrated state of separation from some object of knowledge that is being sought. True or unconditional not-knowing is pure being and pure doing, wisdom and compassion, without subject or object. There is not a single thread of frustration, only blissful release.

True not-knowing never excludes careful knowing on every level. We simply must not remain confined within knowing, even within the transcendent knowing at which Ashvaghosa is already adept when he approaches the living Buddha. Master Keizan calls this awakening from the dream of transcendent knowing, "coming forth from the confining cave of brilliant clarity." One then enters true not-knowing, which is neither light nor dark, neither absolute nor relative. There is no more dialectic. There are no more teeth on this saw, no more master and disciple. The wood has been cut through. With a shout, the carpenter makes the last precise stroke with his saw. Both sides, knowing and conditional not-knowing, instantly fall away.

Keizan Roshi's closing poem this morning is most helpful. It alludes to the Chinese Zen teacher, Ling-yun, who was inspired by some rare red peach blossoms to allow all knowing and conditional not-knowing to drop away. Sings our ancient Japanese guide: "The red of the rustic village houses is unknown to the peach blossoms." A certain common red clay pigment is used by traditional artisans as an artifice, a knowing, whereas the uncommon red of the peach blossoms is an effortless red. It does not know the artifice of red. It is true not-knowing. Consider the tender expression in the eyes and the subtle smile on the lips of Ling-yun when he simply becomes these startling red blossoms, far beyond any concept or experience of red, untouched by any tradition of red, any method of producing red, any expectation of achieving red.

closing poem

> Master and disciple,
> intimate as saw and wood,
> inquiring, responding,
> knowing, not quite knowing.
> Be! Be! Be!
> Now it is cut through!

PALE BLUE MIRROR OCEAN

TRANSMISSION THIRTEEN
ASHVAGHOSA TO KAPIMALA

koan

With profound inspiration, the Awakened One speaks to his destined successor about the Ocean of Reality. "Mountains, rivers, and the broad earth appear simply as waves on this Ocean. The superknowledge and superaction of fully realized human beings appear simply as waves on this Ocean." Hearing and absorbing these potent words flowing from the present Buddha, the next Buddha springs forth spontaneously.

comment

Kapimala is an advanced student of various religious and esoteric traditions, as well as an adept in the shamanistic art of transformation. He has some three thousand fervent followers. Coming into the transparent presence of the living Buddha, this great adept is so amazed that he enters *samadhi*, profound absorption, and collapses on the earth before Ashvaghosa's Dharma throne, where the Awakened One is offering diamond teachings of nonduality to his radiant assembly. Buddha Ashvaghosa remarks simply: "This is no ordinary person." Now Kapimala returns to relative awareness and, through his control of subtle forces, begins a series of magical transformations, metamorphosing from a feminine being of great beauty, to an insect beneath the Buddha's throne, to a golden dragon rising high into the sky. With his infinitely superior Buddha power, Ashvaghosa simply cancels these manifestations as they arise, asking his destined successor: "Could you also transform the vast ocean with these apparent powers of yours?" "Certainly," comes the confident reply.

"What about the Ocean of Reality?" the master asks softly. The adept has never even heard of such an ocean. He is stunned. Now Ashvaghosa transmits Light through a few precise words, and

Kapimala suddenly and directly awakens as this primordial Ocean, in which all manifestations of all worlds are just waves. Kapimala suddenly realizes the humorous fact that his great mastery has been merely over waves, with no sense at all of the whole ocean.

Reality ocean is an expression introduced by the oceanic sage Dogen, father of Japanese Soto Zen. For him, there is no word or concept *buddha,* only pebbles, hedges, giant mountains, nerves and senses—only waves of *reality ocean.* Every moment or event is the boundless realization of *reality ocean.* Whatever we see and our way of seeing are already the Ocean of Reality. Not a single drop of existence falls outside this oceanic expanse. Nothing is useless or meaningless. Nothing is unenlightened.

Our Roshi Keizan, with wonderful kindness to his Zen students, points to the word of the Chinese Master Hsueh-feng, who once fearlessly proclaimed: "There is an ancient mirror within me. When a Mongolian appears before it, a Mongolian is reflected. When a Chinese appears before it, a Chinese is reflected."

The Ocean of Reality is a borderless mirror. The ceaseless waves on *reality ocean* are reflections in a mirror. If a Buddhist appears before me, I reflect Buddhism. If a Muslim appears before me, I reflect Islam. But if I remain only an adept in transformation, merely playing multiple roles as Buddhist, Muslim, Hindu, Christian, Jew, my adept's ego will leap into the sky and expand, perhaps taking the form of an impressive golden dragon. When Buddha Ashvaghosa manifests simply as *reality ocean,* the huge dragon of Kapimala's spiritual ego immediately ceases its proud display.

Only when fully awake as the mirror-like Ocean of Reality, can I participate in all sacred traditions without becoming a mere trickster, as Kapimala had become before meeting face to face with *reality ocean* in the form of his destined master. The Ocean of Reality must be recognized as the conscious heart of the human being. Then its waves will function skillfully as waves of wisdom and compassion—guiding, protecting, and maturing precious human persons by means of all sacred traditions, by means of all events, rather than confusing or manipulating them through dualistic claims of rivalry or exclusivity.

Like Kapimala, we have not yet imagined or even heard about this oceanic heart, even though we have studied so many systems, even though we play expertly with words and methods. Only face to face with the living Buddha can we truly meet *reality ocean*. Now waves are no longer experienced as separate from ocean. Nor is *reality ocean* ever without its stormy waves of living beings and its great tidal waves of enlightened sages, mysterious waves which are neither moving nor still. Yet, as Master Keizan sings this morning: "Even when great waves rise high as heaven, flooding the realms of Paradise, essential water remains the same."

closing poem

> Pale blue mirror ocean
> contains tree-tops and roof-tops
> but no golden dragon.

IT SIMPLY SHINES, SHINES, SHINES!

TRANSMISSION FOURTEEN
KAPIMALA TO NAGARJUNA

koan

The present Buddha receives a wish-fulfilling gem from the Nagas, serpent-beings who guard the treasure of transcendent wisdom at the bottom of the ocean of nondual awareness. The intimate attendant and destined successor asks his master: "Is this gem essentially formless or does it have an actual form?" The Awakened One transmits suddenly, opening and clearing the entire being of the chosen vessel with these uncompromising words of Light: "You are still obsessed with parallel logical structures, *having form* and *not having form*. Why not perceive this gem directly? It neither has form nor is it formless. Beyond that, the gem is not even a gem." The new living Buddha stands unveiled as the diamond of open space.

comment

Even before meeting Buddha Kapimala, Nagarjuna is thoroughly adept within various wisdom traditions, especially Buddhism. He has even examined various Sutras transmitted by Buddhas previous to Shakyamuni, scriptures which are in the possession of Nagas on subtle planes. The wondrous Nagarjuna has genuinely assimilated these rich teachings, but is still holding on to his identity as a sage.

When the living Buddha comes humbly to visit him, Nagarjuna reflects: "Why is this venerable person approaching me? Is he really awakened or is he just seeking my knowledge?" Kapimala clearly perceives these thoughts and calls out, still at some distance: "I am not venerable, nor have I any agenda. I am simply coming to greet someone of great spiritual knowledge. Why concern yourself about whether I am awakened? Why not consider instead the full implication of homelessness?" These words stream with the flavor of true homelessness—identitylessness. Nagarjuna, shocked at his own limited attitude, longs for liberation, and immediately requests the ceremony of home-leaving. Kapimala joyfully complies, and the sacrament of renunciation is immediately effective, immensely clarifying this well-ripened mind. Yet Total Awakeness still remains elusive.

Nagarjuna now functions as close attendant to the living Buddha, traveling with him everywhere for four years. The Awakened One is presented one day with a wish-fulfilling gem from another dimension of being. Nagarjuna comments to his guide that this gem is the most precious one on the earthly plane, because it comes from the Naga realm and is composed of powerfully condensed devotion to nondual wisdom.

To express his own advanced understanding, Nagarjuna asks his master: "Is this brilliant, healing, wish-fulfilling gem with form or is it formless?" These words indicate the basic realization expressed in the *Heart Sutra:* "Form is none other than emptiness, emptiness none other than form."

Kapimala responds by taking Nagarjuna beyond the correlative equivalence of form and formless, beyond Sutra teachings, and all the way to enlightenment. The triple negative of his reply, "This gem has no form, nor is it formless, nor is it even a gem," is the ultimate realization expressed in the *Heart Sutra:* "No path, no wisdom, and no goal." The successor does not receive mere letters and words from the dead *Heart Sutra,* but receives instead the breath of the living Buddha.

This triple cry from the heart of Mother Prajnaparamita rises like a springtime stream, right now, flooding the intuitive mind and freeing it from the wisdom position, *form is emptiness, emptiness form.* There is no more form or path. No more formlessness or wisdom. No claim to enlightenment. No jewel or goal. Now we awaken as Nagarjuna. Now the whole universe appears coherently as the insubstantial brightness of Wonderful Mind. Not one detail is blurred, not one responsibility deferred.

Keizan Roshi stresses in his remarks this morning that practitioners should not succumb to pride or romanticism by retreating into the wilderness. Or by practicing Zen on our own. We should remain instead in or near the monastery, the ceremonial context, close to our teacher, whether lay or monastic, struggling in community and in communion to awaken to the source of all wisdom teaching. There is no isolated self-realization. This way of sweet, selfless intimacy our ancient Japanese guide calls "the true secret teaching of Buddha." Only nonduality is true home-leaving. The adept who stays in a wilderness retreat or in any self-defined context, including self-realization, is establishing a substitute home—some separate place apart from the confusion and noise of other practitioners or simply other suffering beings. Some separate citadel. This person has therefore not truly left home. Even if the adept does not dwell somewhere obviously removed, he or she may subtly solidify the wisdom teaching to make it a separate home, a place to live elevated above less evolved beings, a high personal distinction. The stronger the wisdom position, the more intractable becomes the reliance on this subtle home, which remains invisibly in place even after the powerful home-leaving ceremony. This is why inconceivability, unencounterability, and unformulatability are the *true secret teaching of Buddha*. When truth ceases to be a secret and becomes a doctrine, it inevitably takes the form of a home, a personal and communal identification and agenda.

The great Nagarjuna takes four years as attendant to the living Buddha to become truly homeless, to free himself from subtle identification with the wisdom position. Actually, Nagarjuna does not free himself. The compassionate and diamond-sharp word of his master, who is the *Heart Sutra* come completely alive, is what frees Nagarjuna from Nagarjuna. This was the master's first suggestion to the destined successor: "Why not consider the full implication of homelessness?"

Awakening is like removing our focus from the fingers and placing our attention fully in the palm. The fingers are the various wisdom traditions, including Buddhism. The fingers are personal and communal identity. These fingers still remain harmoniously functional, but the new orientation in the palm is unique. It can only be felt, never described. Consider the traditional metaphor for enlightenment: a ripe fruit placed in the palm of the hand. When the Awakened One opens his palm, hand held high in *abhaya mudra*, the fearlessness of perfect nonduality is experienced by those who witness his gesture. Dwell in the palm!

In his poem this morning, Keizan Roshi describes Total Awakeness as "the orphan light—marvelously vast, never darkened." This orphan light has neither mother nor father, neither source nor direction. This is the secret of its marvelous vastness and indicates why it cannot be darkened or eclipsed in any way.

closing poem

> Orphan light
> has no home, no analogy,
> casts no shadow, pervades no space,
> conceals nothing, cancels nothing.
> It simply shines, shines, shines!

White Crane Standing Still in Bright Moonlight

Transmission Fifteen
Nagarjuna to Aryadeva

koan

Hoping to be accepted as disciple, the destined successor seeks audience with the Awakened One, the embodiment of Shakyamuni's enlightenment. The living Buddha immediately recognizes this aspirant as someone of exceedingly profound wisdom. He requests his attendant to fill a bowl with water and place it before the visitor. The successor, in turn, drops a needle into the bowl and offers it back to the playful sage. The two laugh together, joyously manifesting One Mind.

comment

Om mani padme hum. Jewel embraced within lotus. Aryadeva's bright needle is the jewel of skillful means, compassionate method, liberative art. Nagarjuna's bowl of water—deep, clear, pure to the very bottom—is the lotus of emptiness. Needle is *vajra:* diamond thunderbolt that opens the black rainclouds of compassion. Bowl is bell: open space, ringing spontaneously with the wisdom of emptiness, nonduality. This blissful union of metaphorically male compassion and metaphorically female wisdom graciously awakens all sentient beings from their terrible dream of separation.

Aryadeva is enlightened, right before our eyes. Without Zen words, without Sutra phrases, without red peach blossoms, without pebble striking hollow bamboo, without tugging on robe. It already happened! Needle and bowl, *vajra* and bell, masculine and feminine are already in harmonious embrace. As our beloved Keizan remarks: "From the very first, Aryadeva was one with the Great Way."

Nagarjuna treats Aryadeva just as intimately as Shakyamuni Bud-

dha treated Mahakashyapa when he requested his destined successor to sit with him on the Dharma throne. Nagarjuna and Aryadeva
are more like host and honored guest than master and disciple. The
host, who is the wisdom of emptiness, is not in a higher station than
the guest, who is active compassion. In traditional hospitality, in
fact, guest is exalted above host. As the *Jewel Mirror Samadhi Sutra*
suggests, compassion and wisdom are like snow in a silver bowl, like
a white crane standing still in bright moonlight. Brightness within
brightness.

Buddha Nagarjuna now manifests an astounding spiritual transformation, his body appearing to the gathered practitioners as a full
moon of boundless radiance. The next living Buddha, the diamond
of activity inside this moon disk of emptiness, calmly elucidates the
master's transformation to the assembly: "Buddha nature is precisely
this clarity and brightness, this fullness, roundness, completeness."
Nagarjuna's full moon manifestation is the water bowl, the full circle,
Total Awakeness. Aryadeva's words of elucidation are the sharp
needle, the skillful functioning of this awakeness. Bowl and needle
must remain unified to generate and release the compassionate wisdom of Mahayana. Where are master and disciple now? Where are
self and other? There is only transparency, functioning helpfully,
blissfully, playfully. Aryadeva gave away one of his eyes to a blind
beggar. Like a needle, he has only one eye, the Eye of Nonduality.

Deep absorption in the essence of awareness, or *samadhi*, is the
water bowl. Greeting reality in all its forms with reverence and gratitude, palms together, fingertips pointing, or *gassho*, is the needle.
Inbreath is bowl, outbreath needle. To meditate with eyes partially
closed is the bowl. To open the eyes with a sharp, penetrating glance
is the needle placed by Aryadeva in the bowl. Without leaving any
trace, the water in the bowl pervades, embraces, and sweeps away all
phenomena. The needle, more indestructible than diamond, manifests its single sharp point everywhere, piercing through both gross
and subtle with its compassionate eye.

Bowl is the comprehension of emptiness. *There are no separate
sentient beings.* Needle is *bodhicitta,* the mind of enlightenment, the
adamantine aspiration that all sentient beings be awakened into con-

scious Buddhahood. Without the needle, which is an instrument designed to be used, without what Mahayana calls *method,* the water bowl of wisdom could never become the Great Way. Thus the needle is primary. Compassion takes precedence to wisdom in their inseparable correlation. This is why Keizan Roshi proclaims this morning in his closing poem: "A needle can lift up all the water of the ocean."

However, as our ancient Japanese guide warns, if we succumb to the error of swallowing the needle along with the water, it will stick in our throat. That is to say, if we become focused on particular cases instead of drinking the pure water of emptiness, we may become helpers of humanity and other creatures, but we will never awaken all beings into Buddhahood. Realizing Buddha nature is not a finite giving or receiving of help or blessings.

Keizan Zenji suggests this solution: *swallow completely and vomit completely.* Swallowing is the bowl. Vomiting is the needle. Bowl and needle are not two objects but part of the same organic process, like peristalsis and emesis, like the flower blossom and the stamen within the blossom. By placing the needle in the water bowl, Aryadeva does not join two entities but unveils and activates again for his generation the timeless union of wisdom and compassion.

The needle is superactive, penetrating all dimensions more swiftly than eye can see or thought can think, continuously sewing phenomena into conscious interdependence and mutual support. Yet in its own right the clear water, the wisdom of emptiness, is by no means passive. As our beloved guide reveals: "This water bores through mountains and floods the heavens." But the compassionate activity of the needle takes precedence. "It pierces the bottom of the water as well as the top; so there is no more absolute or relative." This needle ever remains the indestructible *vajra* of simple, pristine awareness, even during the eons empty of all phenomena which intervene between eons of manifestation. Can water, fire, or wind touch this adamantine awareness, even if the whole universe is flooded, consumed, or blown away?

Those who awaken fully, as diamond needle plunges into water bowl of transparency, are like fierce dragons. What adversary or adversity can possibly overcome them? These dragons, such as

Nagarjuna and Aryadeva, recognize each other immediately. Sings our Zen master Keizan this morning in his closing poem: "Wherever fierce dragons go, it is hard for them to conceal themselves."

closing poem

> Bell is large brass
> bowl that waits
> during meditation,
> empty, patient, deep.
> Needle of lightning
> now plunges and strikes.
> Ah, rolling thunder!
> Great Compassion!

THIS DELICIOUS FUNGUS GROWS EVERYWHERE

TRANSMISSION SIXTEEN
ARYADEVA TO RAHULATA

koan

The destined successor is attentively serving refreshments to the living Buddha at their first encounter. Simply by hearing the Awakened One reveal clear karmic causes from previous lifetimes, signs invisible to ordinary eyes, the young boy awakens beyond all levels of awakening.

comment

Shakyamuni awakened suddenly beneath the Bodhi Tree by discovering the principle of dependent origination. All possible manifestation was revealed to his gnostic eye as an indivisible expanse of interdependence and inter-illumination, without final frontiers or fixed descriptions. Free decisions of countless conscious beings, past and present, are constantly producing the rainbow of phenomenal structures. These intertwined moral threads, alive with the immense energy of intention, extend continuously throughout beginningless and endless time.

Rahulata was predicted by Shakyamuni Buddha to appear in the second five-hundred-year period of his Dharma in order to receive the transmission of Light and to assure its further transmission. The mind stream of Rahulata was once perhaps the son of Shakyamuni, named Rahula. Rahulata is tasting the ultimate karmic fruits of his earlier lifetime as companion of a living Buddha.

This boy now quietly and humbly serves refreshments to the present embodiment of Shakyamuni's enlightenment, Buddha Aryadeva, who has unexpectedly come to visit his father. The highly intelligent child overhears his father discussing with the sage a certain mysterious, ear-shaped fungus that grows on an ancient tree in the garden of the family mansion. As the Awakened One reveals, this is not really an organic fungus but the karmic manifestation of a certain Buddhist monk. Generations ago, this wandering *bikshu* received alms from the family ancestors in this very garden. The monk had not yet attained awakening, and so received the alms as if they actually belonged to him. Neither a drop of water nor a blade of wheat nor a grain of rice belongs to anyone, but only to Mother Wisdom, the infinite womb of brilliant blackness.

After becoming a genuine *bodhisattva,* inseparably joining wisdom and compassion and inviting all beings to awaken into nonduality, the wandering monk, as a gesture of gratitude to his early benefactors, mentally manifested this peculiar fungus. Its distinct ear-shape is karmically designed, Aryadeva now reveals, as a message to the boy Rahulata: "Listen! Listen carefully to the words of the living Buddha who is destined to visit you here!"

Farfetched as it appears to conventional thinking, our world is entirely composed of such subtle karmic signs, karmic events and links, karmic attractions and confirmations—clearly recognizable by awakened persons, almost unnoticed by others. The sound of a car starting up in the early morning when the engine is cold. A dog barking in the predawn darkness. A cat walking unexpectedly into the *zendo* during quiet meditation and leaping to a high windowsill. A local convent, gradually emptied of sisters after seventy years of ceaseless vigil, becomes available as a sanctuary for all religions and for persons dying of incurable illness.

The mysterious fungus in Rahulata's family garden happens to be delicious. The boy somehow discovered this, and has been amazed to observe the portions that he eats grow back again. We are inexorably attracted to taste our karma, whether bitter or sweet, but it can never be consumed without playing out its drama, without delivering its message. This fungus, points out Master Keizan, remains invisible to the other members of the extended family, except for the boy's father. Not everyone can see the karma that plainly unfolds before our eyes.

Father and son happen to be alone together in the garden when Buddha Aryadeva arrives unexpectedly. The numerous family members and servants each have someplace else to be. Something draws them away from this most auspicious encounter, more astonishing than meeting a wild tiger roaming through Delhi, Beijing, Tokyo, New York. The living Buddha explains this situation: "You and your son alone can give pure offerings, free from egocentric involvement." Egocentricity, the automatic central-point perspective of consciousness, is what conceals the beautiful karmic display of infinite waves and infinite dimensions, this symphony without a single false note. As Keizan Roshi proclaims, speaking from the Mind of Luminosity: "Can you not see? Do you not realize that from the prehistoric past to the present, no one has ever been fundamentally separate or separated? If you do not awaken to this fact today, when will you?"

In the peaceful garden of his ancestral home, Rahulata now effortlessly comprehends this unerring moral interdependence, inter-illumination, and vast harmony. There is no renunciation, no quest, no questioning. The living Buddha comes precisely to where the boy is waiting, here at the confluence of countless karmic streams. Through these words addressed to his father, Rahulata thoroughly awakens and becomes the overflowing vessel of Light for his generation. Aryadeva now receives the father's permission and shaves the boy's head. But the home-leaving has already occurred. There is simply no separate, independent place to call home in this intricate, borderless, transparent karmic play.

Karma is evolutionary consciousness. Yet insentient phenomena, like the fungus or the tree, which are not mindstreams evolving lifetime after lifetime in karmic continuity, can still manifest as clear karmic signs, springing into being as karmic results. The old monk's mindstream can manifest the fungus only because of the ancient tree, and the fungus can inspire Rahulata's awakening only through the words of the living Buddha.

Pen, ink, and paper are now flowing with the karma of writer and reader, and in this sense they are alive. In this sense, even the mineral kingdom is morally alive, inseparable from the intentions of the conscious beings who are swimming in this boundless karmic ocean, pursuing and fleeing, helping and educating. Awakened Ones are the entire ocean, experienced in essential tranquillity as brilliant diversity without division.

When we hear about karma from a living Buddha, it is not

depressing or binding but liberating. Without the realization of the Great Way as karma, karma, karma, we will continue to take food and breath for ourselves, as belonging independently to us. Let us become instead an edible, inexhaustible fungus for the pure-hearted. Let us silently attract them to their destined encounter with the Awakened One. Let us cease to be superficial monks, nuns, and laypersons.

As Master Keizan gently hints in his Zen talk this morning: "You cannot make all your own clothing." We exist in interdependence, in mutual supportiveness. The open space of Mother Reality is perpetually pregnant with life—arising in relativity, awakening as relationality. Karma is her mother's milk, karma her cleansing, curing, comforting, consoling, and correcting hands. Buddha Mind is the formless, placeless Mother Prajnaparamita who protects, guides, chastens, educates, liberates, enlightens. Body and personal consciousness are her servants. Karma is her mystic womb, her palace of wisdom. This perception is what Keizan Roshi calls the Eye of the Way. The one who is known as the mother of Japanese Soto Zen kindly elucidates: "Once your Dharma Eye is clear, even if the sky becomes a bowl and sacred Mount Sumeru becomes rice, you will eat night and day without taking a single grain for yourself." The sky bowl is wisdom, the mountain of rice compassion. Together inseparably, they nourish all beings.

Successor Rahulata's Dharma Eye becomes clear simply by listening to the living Buddha speak about karmic causes and conditions, invisible to most observers. Is our present listening any less worthy? Any less fruitful? Look around! This delicious fungus grows everywhere!

closing poem

> Cat enters Zen hall,
> every careful step karma,
> karma, karma.
> Countless moral threads
> fuse in my fingertips.
> Universal Eye opens.

COME OUT OF THE CAVE TO TASTE THE SWEETNESS

TRANSMISSION SEVENTEEN
RAHULATA TO SANGHANANDI

koan

The present Buddha proclaims to his unique inheritor: "Through me, who am without limited self, you can clearly see limitless self. If you intimately attune with me, you will realize that limited self can never merge into limitless self during the deep absorption of *samadhi*. Why? Because for the one who sees limitless self clearly, limited self simply does not exist. Nor has it ever existed." Upon receiving this transmission of Light, the new living Buddha compassionately proclaims the liberation of all consciousness from the illusion of limited self.

comment

Even as an infant, Sanghanandi could speak, and he always praised Lord Buddha. At seven, he lost all taste for conventional existence and begged his royal parents for permission to leave the palace and become a monk. They refused, and he refused to eat. To placate the boy, the king imported an unawakened Buddhist monk into the palace to teach Sutra to the prince. At nineteen, Sanghanandi saw through the sham of this superficial study. One full moon night, he left his pleasure garden, walked many miles through unfamiliar landscape, and discovered a cave on the face of a huge precipice. With great intensity of intention, he entered the cave and plunged into *samadhi*, deep absorption in tranquillity.

After twelve years of Sutra study in the palace and ten further years of *samadhi* practice in the wilderness, Sanghanandi is profoundly prepared, in one sense, and yet remains thoroughly bound up in his dualistic understanding and practice. This adept in meditation can now remain in *samadhi* for twenty-one days, indicating the *nirvikalpa* level of contemplative absorption, in which breath and heart-beat become so subtle as to be indiscernible. There are no *vikalpas* in this state, no modifications of mind or nervous system. This *samadhi* has a great purifying effect but is far from full enlightenment. It can become the most subtle obstacle to enlightenment.

As a young man of twenty, Vivekananda told his master, the Tantric sage Ramakrishna, that he longed to enter this unwavering *samadhi* for two or three days at a time, coming down into relative awareness only to take enough sustenance to keep body together. Ramakrishna replied: "O foolish boy, I will show you a realization much more advanced than *nirvikalpa samadhi*. Sing that beautiful Sufi hymn by Jaffar!" While pouring forth with his whole heart the mystic hymn, "O Lord, whatever exists is You, for You alone truly exist," Vivekananda awakened to pure spontaneity, not correlated with any process of concentration or absorption. This natural, nondual *samadhi* does not exist in relation to any special state of the nervous system. Nor does this *samadhi* exist in relation to any particular focus of thought or to the suspension of thinking.

Because Sanghanandi is confined within his dualistic *samadhi,* as well as within the narrow view of the Sutras which he received from a teacher without full awakening, the young man argues at length with the living Buddha who comes to visit the remote cave which the palace guard, searching for months, was never able to find.

Sanghanandi vigorously defends his assumption that one can enter ultimate *samadhi* and come forth from it again. He basically argues that *samadhi* is located and locatable, while Buddha Rahulata, with great patience and compassion, demonstrates dialectically to this precocious twenty-nine year old that true *samadhi,* Total Awakeness, is never located anywhere, either inside or outside body or mind. How could Total Awakeness come and go, start and stop? Being without limited self, every phenomenon is already in spontaneous *samadhi*. Awareness cannot enter into *samadhi* or come out of *samadhi,* because by its very nature, awareness is awake in the *samadhi* of limitless self.

The living Buddha opens the door for this young sage, whom he clearly recognizes as destined successor, by asking: "Is your *samadhi* a physical state or a mental state?" Sanghanandi replies: "Both body and mind enter into *samadhi* and disappear there." The Awakened One laughs and responds: "Then how do body and mind come out of *samadhi* again?"

A technical debate now ensues, during which the Awakened One repeatedly distinguishes the effortless awakeness that neither comes nor goes from the effortful *samadhi,* into which this young adept enters and from which he comes forth again after twenty-one days. Many layers of stubborn fixation are removed from the mind of Sanghanandi by the words of the living Buddha, which are simply selfless awareness—incisive, tender, intimate.

At last, the young sage gets a taste of this natural selflessness, sweeter and more refreshing than the pure mountain stream that flows below his cave. Astonished, he asks the name of Buddha Rahulata's teacher. The response comes like a life-giving peal of thunder: "Under Buddha Aryadeva selflessness was demonstrated." Simply by hearing the name of this Great Master spoken with selfless power, the profound Buddhist predilection in the mindstream of Sanghanandi is activated. The young man humbly requests: "Please ordain me as truly homeless, since you are truly selfless."

Radical home-leaving is now transmitted to Sanghanandi through the words of the *koan.* All sense of dualistic *samadhi,* the presumed merging of limited awareness into limitless awareness, is instantaneously removed from this disciplined and aspiring mind. This is the ordination beyond ordination, the homelessness beyond monastic vows. Immediately upon awakening, Sanghanandi leaves his spiritual isolation, his home-abstraction, and begins fervently to proclaim the liberation of all conscious beings from the illusion of limited self. This is instant Buddha activity, more powerful even than the long-term Bodhisattva vow to save all sentient beings. Rather than aspiring to future universal enlightenment, this is liberating activity based upon universal enlightenment as the present fact. This is the rejection of any fundamental distinction between ordinary mind and awakened mind.

At this final point, Buddha Rahulata remarks to the newly unveiled Buddha Sanghanandi: "Your mind is free and unique, not bound by my mind. Your Buddhahood is not defined or confined by my Buddhahood." It is suddenly revealed that Sanghanandi is the emanation of an Awakened One from some ancient aeon. The two living Buddhas now eat heavenly sweet rice together that manifests miraculously, enjoying the wonderful taste that the monastic disciples around them, although deeply realized, cannot yet enjoy. The disciples of Rahulata complain: "How can it be? This stubborn young man was a previous Buddha?" But did not Shakyamuni Buddha, eight centuries earlier, also abandon his palace and engage in six years of *samadhi* practice, attempting to extinguish relative awareness, before he awakened beyond relative and absolute? This drive for total absorption is just a thin veil which covers living Buddhas until their full awakening. But there is a very significant difference here. Shakyamuni, the Lord Buddha, removed this veil by himself, whereas his successors must rely on the present lineage holder to create the luminous environment in which this most subtle veil dissolves. The destined successors do not project their own independent realization, but humbly receive and transmit Shakyamuni's Light. Their true nature is not something that belongs to them.

Sanghanandi would have sat without enlightenment for a lifetime, even a thousand years, here in this remote canyon, beside this wild, rushing stream, if the Awakened One, engaged in the wandering which is characteristic of Buddha activity, had not sought him out and patiently debated with him. Yet this veiling and unveiling is just play, the cathartic theater of the transmission of Light that cures practitioners from their dualistic sense of struggling to reach some goal. We need such theatrical display—eon after eon, wisdom tradition after wisdom tradition—until we can simply enjoy the taste of sweet rice. Throughout this beginningless and endless drama, Total Awakeness always remains totally awake!

closing poem

> Limitless! Self-manifesting!
> Come out of the cave
> to taste the sweetness!

BOTH BELL AND WIND ARE THE SILENCE OF GREAT MIND

TRANSMISSION EIGHTEEN
SANGHANANDI TO GAYASHATA

koan

The destined successor is observing the wind blow the large bronze temple bell, causing it to ring slightly. Intuiting the ripeness of his young attendant, the living Buddha asks: "Is bell ringing or wind ringing?" The reply is instantaneous and unpremeditated: "Neither bell nor wind but Great Mind is ringing." Probing to the uttermost depth, the Awakened One inquires further: "To whom is Great Mind now appearing?" This inquiry itself is the complete transmission of the Light that always shines. The new living Buddha demonstrates enlightenment by responding obliquely: "Both bell and wind are the silence of Great Mind."

comment

This astonishing person of knowledge, destined successor Gaya-shata, was born with transcendent knowing, which manifested to those with spiritual sight as a round, bright mirror that followed the retiring boy wherever he went. Whenever Gayashata gazed into it, all teachings of the Buddhas were reflected on its brilliant surface, free from any distortion. This clear moon disc even floated like a canopy over the boy's head while he was sleeping.

Buddha Sanghanandi travels in spontaneous, joyous search of his successor. Arriving in the land of Magadha, the entire party feels a fresh wind that delights both body and mind. It is the presence of young Gayashata. The Awakened One remarks to his companions: "This is the life-giving wind, the power of the Great Way."

When master and successor meet face to face, the boy claims to be one hundred years old, playfully indicating the depth of his knowing. When he is enlightened, not even claiming to be one hundred eons old will be sufficient to indicate the depth of Total Awakeness. The master immediately perceives the miraculous mirror hovering behind the boy, and inquires about it. The successor responds effortlessly in verse: "The round mirror of all Buddhas has no distortion, for it possesses neither interior nor exterior. All conscious beings have the potential to see this mirror, for the mental eye of all beings is essentially the same."

When the boy's parents hear this amazing wisdom streaming from their son, they permit him to receive monastic ordination from Sanghanandi. Since this home-leaving ceremony is not just surface renunciation but the complete renunciation of duality, the miraculous mirror now disappears. Truth is no longer subtly externalized or internalized, and successor Gayashata lives peacefully, traveling as the personal attendant of the living Buddha.

No matter how great the knowledge of any advanced aspirant— even if it is pure Buddhist knowledge in the form of direct vision, not mere intellection—this knowledge remains a bright mirror. A mirror implies reflection and original. A mirror invites someone to gaze into it. Subtle duality remains. Only radical renunciation, perfect home-leaving, can open the way to omniconscious nonduality. This round mirror of all Buddhas must dissolve, along with mental eye, heavenly eye, and even wisdom eye. There is no longer any separate organ of vision or object of vision.

Bell is body. Wind is mind. Are these bodies around us moving and speaking or is it minds that move and speak? Neither. Great Mind wholly constitutes both body and mind. Actually, there is nothing separate which constitutes or is constituted. There is only Great Mind, and Great Mind is silence. Its unique silence is not the absence of sound. This silence is inconceivability, unencounterability, unformulatability. The intrinsic formlessness of all form even as it forms, the intrinsic stillness of all movement even as it moves, the intrinsic silence of all sound even as it resounds—this is the ringing of Great Mind. "Soaring mountains and deep ocean," sings our beloved Roshi Keizan. What a wonderfully profound tone! What a soaring koan! What luxuriant green growing and knowing! The whole universe is Great Mind—ringing, dreaming! There is no burden from the very beginning!

closing poem

> Zen master smiling,
> mirrorless.
> Breath bell,
> mind wind,
> silent ringing
> without boundary.

BRIGHT BLUE RIVER RUSHING IN A CIRCLE

TRANSMISSION NINETEEN
GAYASHATA TO KUMARATA

koan

The present Buddha proclaims with great power to his destined successor: "Shakyamuni, the sage spontaneously adored by all mindstreams, predicted that one thousand years after his Mahanirvana a great being would be born in this small village, a diamond being who would receive and transmit the Sudden Teaching. You have actualized this inconceivable good fortune simply by meeting me." The moment the master speaks these words of transmission, the successor awakens into all previous lifetimes and shines as boundless clarity alone.

comment

Master and successor are the two thumbs in the *mudra* of meditation. When they touch, ever so lightly, the circle is complete. The life-blood of the lineage of awakeness circulates. After successor in turn becomes master, another destined heart-disciple must appear to receive transmission, for this Mind of Luminosity can never remain fixed or static. This is why living Buddhas wander through the multidimensional realms of India, China, Japan, America—actively seeking or quietly awaiting their successors.

Simply by meeting me. These words of Light mark the precise moment of transmission. This is not the indirect encounter of two persons but the direct meeting of identity. Both thumbs belong to the same body. This is clearly known, not a mystery. As our two thumbs touch, completing the circuit, the sensation is subtle, yet natural and ordinary.

Buddha awakening is always to limitless knowing—not to knowledge of any conventional object, such as particular doctrine, particular previous incarnation, particular Dharma teacher. The successor awakens to the limitless knowing which has radiated throughout all past lives and will radiate throughout all future lives—equally through awakened sages and through all conscious beings. This radiant knowing never increases or decreases. This sublime knowing is Prajnaparamita, Mother of all the Buddhas. There is no separate knower or known. In his closing poem this morning, Keizan Roshi refers to Mother Wisdom most intimately. "Numberless past lives, one body after another, yet now I directly encounter our Old Friend —very intelligent, very bright, utterly unconcealed."

Successor Kumarata remembers glimpsing this Original Friend during a previous existence, when he heard divine Indra preaching Prajnaparamita in one of the lower celestial realms. Later, he attained deeper acquaintance with this wonderful Friend by himself offering the teaching of birthlessness in higher celestial dimensions. But not until hearing the intense words of the living Buddha, when the wandering sage approaches his mud-walled village home, does Kumarata meet this faceless Friend even closer than face to face.

When destined successor first hears the powerful name, *Shakyamuni,* from his destined master standing outside, he falls back in awe and cries instinctively from within the house: "No one is here!" The sage calls back: "Who is it that utters the words *no one*?" Kumarata is taken instantly to the source of *I hear* and *I speak,* to the source of personal identity and personal agency. Opening the door curtain wide to gaze upon this brilliant Mind Source standing there in human form, the new living Buddha receives the transmission of Light simply by direct encounter. Buddha Kumarata instantly ceases to be a particular being in a particular lifetime, ceases to be a mindstream by becoming *mind ocean.* As Master Keizan reports, "He is now empty, bright, marvelous, vast."

Do not be overly impressed by this immense circle of one thousand years from Shakyamuni to Kumarata. This very circle which manifests through numberless eons in numberless universes abides here, right in the center of our awareness, where neither senses nor intellect can reach. This circle is located neither in ancient time nor in present time. It is never absent. This is the Old Friend whom we have known unerringly throughout all our previous lifetimes.

From this sublimely simple circuit springs the electricity of pure love and pure intelligence known as *sages* and *sacred traditions*. How can we picture such simplicity and fecundity? Imagine a bright blue river rushing in a circle, without original springhead or oceanic goal—pure dynamism, irrigating vast fields of civilization that spring forth without number, without multiplication.

closing poem

> Morning light
> through small window
> touches everything.
> Golden sun,
> our old friend,
> ever seeking, ever finding.

PLUM TREE DEEP IN THE GARDEN BLOSSOMS SPONTANEOUSLY

TRANSMISSION TWENTY
KUMARATA TO JAYATA

koan

Certain that his spiritual inheritor finally possesses full confidence in the unerring moral structure of the universe, the living Buddha now opens the door of transmission: "You have not yet realized that the moral structures of karma, coherent as they are, manifest only through the delusive sense of separation. The sense of separation results from subject-object consciousness, which in turn arises from primal ignorance. This web of apparent causality shimmers within the space of Pure Mind, the boundless expanse that experiences neither origination nor cessation. Pure Mind, free from agency or identity, is therefore free from any karmic results which may appear, whether superior or inferior. Pure Mind is dynamic, penetrating, yet essentially still. The moment you assimilate this truth, you will be exactly the same as all Buddhas throughout space and time. You will perceive the conditions called *good* and *evil,* as well as the unconditioned expanse beyond good and evil, as vivid yet insubstantial as dreams." Receiving and instantly assimilating these words of Light, the new living Buddha is completely awake. There is now only the primordial wisdom that all living beings always are.

comment

Raised in a devout Buddhist family in northern India, Jayata was insightful from an early age and especially gifted in teaching Buddha Dharma. To this very day of his enlightenment, however, he retains doubts about the precision, justice, and cosmic harmony of karma—the moral structure of the universe. His doubts become particularly intense whenever he honestly examines the chaotic surface of human experience. Perceiving this inner struggle, the

Awakened One first offers his successor a description of the astonishing continuity of moral causes and effects over vast periods of
time. Jayata's lifelong doubts are cleared. Buddha power pervades
the master's simple explanation, and the power of deep Dharma
understanding, humility, and receptivity pervades the disciple's
response.

Only from this basis of confidence in coherent karmic functioning can Kumarata invite his destined successor to Total Awakeness,
which reveals all karmic conditions as blossoming only within Pure
Mind, expressing only Pure Mind. This ultimate insight not only
awakens all beings, but actually softens, both for oneself and for others in the sphere of daily existence, the harsh results of negative
thoughts and actions performed during this life-stream and previous
life-streams. Through our practicing this way of transparency, a destined sword wound becomes a pinprick, and a destined pinprick
disappears entirely. Yet our karmic drama, however vivid and tangible, is neither external nor internal. It is the luminous play of Pure
Mind.

Nothing ever works out the way we want. Why should this become a reason for doubting the Buddha's revelation of universal
moral continuity? Master Keizan calls this doubt *ultimate stupidity.*
Disappointments and disasters actually serve to clear away our negative karma, by placing us in situations that we have placed other
living beings. Therefore trials should contribute to our confidence in
the teaching of karma rather than to our personal uncertainty. This is
not doctrine but experience.

The danger of spiritual delusion strangely increases when approaching the radiance of Pure Mind. We may attempt to take spu-
rious refuge in Pure Mind from the struggle and responsibility of
karmic conditions, thus creating a deceptive sense of duality—Pure
Mind here, karmic conditions over there. Whereas, if we open the
Eye of Nonduality and perceive Pure Mind clearly manifest as the
intricate display of karmic conditions that demand compassionate
action, we will be taking true refuge in the diamond teaching and
will be no different from any living Buddha.

The sage emphasizes neither the vivid blossoming of karma nor the radiant stillness of Pure Mind. They are not two. This is why rational discourse becomes inadequate as intimacy with reality progresses. Karma blossoms within the unthinkable profundity of Pure Mind. To express this more adequately, we could respond: *The plum tree deep in the garden blossoms spontaneously.* This is not mere poetic language or supposed Zen paradox, but an uncontainable explosion of realization. How wonderful! How wonderful!

The more the transparency of Pure Mind dawns, the more elaborate and precise the science of karma becomes. The more one appreciates karma as blossoming within Pure Mind, the more dreamlike or insubstantial karma becomes. Both sides are true. There is no separation.

Master Keizan's poem this morning kindly turns us in the right direction. He suggests that karma is a tree which grows in the open sky: "Its limbs, leaves, and roots flourish beyond the clouds." Karma is a tree without any ultimate rootedness. It draws nourishment directly from the cloudless sky of Pure Mind. Always remaining fully articulated, every vein on every leaf is clear.

The twelvefold, interlinking pattern of karmic conditioning is a continuous flow. If we mistakenly attempt to cut this flow, we appear to cut the flow of Pure Mind and our own intrinsic enlightenment is veiled. Thus we open up an apparent gulf between delusion and enlightenment, falsely placing ourselves either on the side of delusion or on the side of enlightenment.

Ignorance consists in halting and fixating on any single point in the seamless circuitry of karma. Even more dangerous is the misguided attempt to eliminate such circuitry entirely. Pure Mind flows as the whole circuit. As our ancient Japanese guide remarks: "It is neither impermanent nor permanent, neither conditioned nor unconditioned." Do not try to cut this flow, to grasp it, to eliminate it. Do not try to picture it or stand outside it. Limitless awareness is never limited by the subtly shifting shadows of karma. These shadows exist because of the wonderful play of relativity, yet they remain utterly insubstantial. Karmic structures are the white smoke of incense—drifting, spiraling upward, sensitive to every current of consciousness, dissipating spontaneously. O fragrance of enlightenment!

closing poem

> This human form
> is a Buddha
> with tranquil heart
> who dances and sings.

LAUGHABLE OLD SCARECROWS

TRANSMISSION TWENTY-ONE
JAYATA TO VASUBANDHU

koan

The twentieth successor of Shakyamuni effortlessly transmits Light: "I never pursue the path of evolution, so am not divided. I never venerate Buddhas, so am not self-important. I never practice quiet meditation, so am not passive. I never exercise discipline, so am not obsessed. I never impose limits, so am not limited. Simply abiding as its own true nature, my mind is already Total Awakeness." The twenty-first successor of Shakyamuni effortlessly awakens.

comment

Vasubandhu was an active Dharma treasure from his very conception. His mother, Supreme Adornment, dreamed about drinking a liquid jewel the night she became pregnant. The child was visited and honored by a liberated Buddhist sage while still within its mother's womb. Vasubandhu was ordained a Buddhist monk upon his own fervent request at age fifteen. Gradually, he became a teacher with a wide circle of students. They admired and trusted his impeccable Buddhist practice, which included study, meditation, debate, and careful monastic discipline. His name signifies *total practice.* Vasubandhu compassionately manifested this extensive spiritual wealth to the whole world.

Buddha Jayata, wandering through India demonstrating the Sudden Way, now enters Vasubandu's circle anonymously as a mendicant, dusty from the road. He first comments favorably to the assembled practitioners about the evident discipline and purity of their teacher, and then asks: "Vasubandhu is so pure, but will he ever completely awaken?"

"He is already awake," comes the indignant response from the assembly. With quiet intensity the Awakened One replies, not even glancing at Vasubandhu: "Your teacher is far from Total Awakeness. He can continue to practice strict disciplines and promulgate rigorous definitions for eons, but without Total Awakeness, these efforts will plant seeds of division, self-importance, obsession, limitation." Shocked silence. The senior disciple speaks: "What spiritual power have you accumulated, wandering sage, to enable you to evaluate our teacher?"

At this point, Jayata proclaims his radical realization, for which there is no limited self who pursues, venerates, meditates, disciplines, limits, or defines in any way. Through this absence of any *I practice, I realize, I teach,* the living Buddha unveils essential mind simply abiding as itself. Vasubandhu is delighted by these words of Light, which instantly disclose borderless, divisionless, flawless wisdom. To the amazement of his disciples, their teacher now rises to honor the old sage, thereby confirming himself as the inheritor of this Sudden Way, so greatly compassionate that it refuses to prolong the spiritual path.

There are three dimensions to the Buddha treasure: the Three Jewels of One Body, the Realized Three Jewels, and the Maintained Three Jewels. The *maintained tradition* includes teachers and students, scriptural study and debate, sacred Buddha images, ceremonial offering, and the various methods and levels of contemplative practice.

The *realized tradition,* by contrast, consists simply of the lineage of living Buddhas, an undivided stream of awakened masters extending in the realm of common historical record from Shakyamuni Buddha to the present. These awakened persons compassionately retain their conventional personhood by engaging in the *maintained tradition,* while remaining secretly free from any limited notion of pursuit, veneration, meditation, discipline, definition.

The *one body* is not even a tradition. Here there are neither Buddhas nor sentient beings. Within this realmless realm of transparent delight alone do the radiant words of Buddha Jayata really belong. From here alone springs the transmission of Light. To mistake the words of this *koan* as a call to eliminate the precious *maintained tradition* would be to eat only salt, rather than using it to season a meal.

But without the salt of *one body,* even the most nutritious teachings lose their savor and effectiveness.

To attempt to grasp *one body* with conceptual mind or even with contemplative mind is like grasping a whirling two-edged sword with bare hands. The only access lies through *maintained tradition* into *realized tradition. One body* has no inside or outside. It is suddenness. There is no approaching it or avoiding it. Without *one body,* there can be no *realized tradition* or *maintained tradition.* Without the fully conscious embodiment of *one body,* who is the living Buddha, all lineages, scriptures, and practices are laughable old scarecrows, ignored by birds, raccoons, and deer.

Master Keizan calls Jayata's *one body* teaching—or non-teaching—*the greatest secret.* Without awakening to this secret, practicing Buddhism is trying to make the blue sky rain flowers or trying to dig holes in empty space. "When there is nothing to want," proclaims our ancient Japanese guide, "this is called all-embracing awakeness." There is no desire here for enlightenment as a separate, personal event or even as a cosmic event. Remarks Keizan, with a living Buddha's great compassion: "There is not a single person who is deluded and needs to be awakened." There is only *one body.*

Keizan Zenji makes plain, however, the need to move through *maintained tradition* into *realized tradition:* "Those who are beginning must practice very carefully and arrive at the calm, peaceful, blissful realm." Arriving genuinely beyond practice and beyond non-practice, we will no longer be distracted by the arguments of various adepts who recommend particular procedures of contemplative practice or iconoclastic attitudes of non-practice.

Become so realized that at any moment you can stretch out for a nap, as Chia-shan describes the essence of the Sudden Way, for which there is no individual, separate, finite awakening. No one can imagine the persistence of the illusion: *there must be something more to do.* Its opposite, *there is nothing to do,* is not as common but is even more deceptive.

Awakening as *one body,* we will be like a person just finished eating and drinking who now stands before a sumptuous banquet. This is genuine tranquillity and happiness. Abiding in the fullness of *one body*, there is nothing to be sought. Now true Buddha activity can begin, inviting all conscious beings to the feast of their own essential nature. How are they able to arrive here? Only by trusting essential nature completely.

What closer friend can there be than essential nature? Sit alert, gaze straight ahead, and meet this friend right now as the living Buddha. Right here! Right in front of us! "Do not become distracted by beautiful patterns of frost on the gate," cries our Roshi Keizan. Come through the gate! Now, not later! Awaken as your own *one body* treasure!

There is no reason to doubt or distance these words of transmission. Mind abides simply as itself, through birth and death, eon after eon. There is no deviation from reality. Sings beloved Keizan with stainless wisdom: "Wind blows through great sky. Clouds appear from mountain caves. Religious life and worldly life—both irrelevant."

closing poem

> gilded Buddha image
> brown-robed master
> Zen hall of great sky

OCEAN IS MERGING WITH OCEAN

TRANSMISSION TWENTY-TWO
VASUBANDHU TO MANORHITA

koan

Destined successor passionately asks present Buddha: "What exactly is the awakeness of the Awakened Ones?" The enlightened response is immediate: "This awakeness is simply the essential nature of daily awareness." Another question arises spontaneously: "What is the essential nature of awareness?" The second response is swift and clear as the first: "It is the absence of any separation between sense organ, sense object, and sense consciousness." In the midst of ordinary experience, the new living Buddha is suddenly and completely awake.

comment

"What is the *bodhi* of the Buddhas?" This question is, in one sense, the most obvious question, because *bodhi*, or awakeness, is precisely what constitutes the awakened state, or *buddha*. But it takes great maturity to ask such a basic question with our whole being. We must advance to pure, simple, open beginner's mind, which nonetheless operates with the cumulative intensity of much practice, much aspiration.

The fact that two such rare questions are presented in a row shows the profundity of the destined successor. These are not to be viewed as automatic, logical, casual inquiries. Manorhita is the constant attendant of a living Buddha. There is no superficiality, mechanical thinking, arrogance, or ambition surrounding these two pristine questions.

The response to this ultimate questioning can only be to indicate *shunyata:* emptiness, indivisibility, indefinability. Only such an answer can provide the boundless space that such questioning demands—a space which has neither inside nor outside, neither closure nor openness, a space which is transparent continuity or harmony, not the absence of events. This is exactly what Master Keizan sings about in his closing poem, invoking the flavor, the subtle fragrance, the living breath of *shunyata*. The dictionary meaning of *shunyata* is emptiness. The actual implication of the term is absence of separation, emptiness of division or boundary, and therefore freedom from definition or identity. *Shunyata* is really a wonderful, tender, limitless embrace. Already complete. Pathless and goalless.

The *sense organ* is like the downward movement of a deep bow, the *sense object* like the upward or return movement of the bow, the *sense consciousness* like the *gassho,* palms touching, that constitutes the whole movement as a bow. Is there any separation between these three elements of bowing? Can we even claim that there are three elements? There is simply the continuous, graceful, timeless flow of reverence and gratitude. Are there any stepping stones or standpoints here? Is there anything separate to cultivate or to understand in this inseparability of function, form, and consciousness?

A certain Zen master used to begin all his talks, whether to advanced students or beginners, by describing a circle in the air with his hand. Does this indicate mere empty space, the total absence of perceiver, perceived, and perception? Certainly not. The circle indicates total continuity, continuous totality. This is awakeness!

Keizan Roshi warns us this morning that if we regard sense organ, sense object, and sense consciousness as false appearances, attempting to throw them away in order to achieve some static state of emptiness, the result will be ridiculous. To plunge into eternally unchanging emptiness is to fall into a nonexistent well. Cool, deep, dim, spuriously tranquil. Since such a place is nonexistent, it will be very difficult to climb out of it again. Instead, our kind Roshi advises us that sense organ, sense object, and sense consciousness should be like a living ocean merging blissfully with a living ocean, a living sky with a living sky. There is nothing left over.

Buddha Vasubandhu is not teaching here through *samadhi,* through any intense state of yogic concentration or absorption, but through our direct experience in the ordinary waking state. We are constantly involved in this daily awareness, this deep bow, this

graceful continuity of sense organ, sense object, and sense consciousness, We are instrinsically free from linguistically based,
imaginally constructed partitions or barriers. Right now, ocean is
merging with ocean, sky with sky, as we perceive whatever we are
perceiving. Sound is not *do-re-mi-fa-so-la-ti*. Experience is not *a-b-c-
d-e*. The expanse we call the universe is not composed of separate
objects—green ocean, blue sky, white sail, black rock. Nor are there
separate subjects—colorless, formless witnesses, hovering above
physical nervous systems like kites.

The breath of *shunyata* is always available, always overflowing the
cup of daily life, which is an ever-widening circle, an infinite circle,
always with the same indefinable center—the essential nature of
awareness. Here is the unobstructed summit of experience, Total
Awakeness. Arrive here easily and joyfully. No climbing necessary!

closing poem

> incense reaching
> corner touching
> wall seeing
> bell hearing
> blissful circling
> tender embrace

COME OUT OF THE SKY, YOU FIVE HUNDRED CRANES!

TRANSMISSION TWENTY-THREE
MANORHITA TO HAKLENAYASHAS

koan

Leaping suddenly over all preliminary words, the living Buddha, speaking in a gentle voice, generously reveals to his destined successor: "I am the inconceivable, inexhaustible treasure of Total Awakeness. Now you must receive this treasure, become this treasure, transmit this treasure to future generations." Simply by hearing these words of Light, the successor awakens.

comment

Haklenayashas entered the womb of his childless mother, Golden Light, after she dreamed of him standing as a radiant youth on the summit of Sumeru, the primordial holy mountain. Holding a golden ring, he cried out in this blessed dream: "I have arrived." As a boy of seven, eloquent in speech and uncompromising in conscience, the destined successor cleansed the local temple of degenerate practices. He became a Buddhist monk at twenty-two.

At age thirty, Haklenayashas visits Buddha Manorhita to inquire about the meaning of a strange omen, a flock of cranes that often follows him. The illumined sage interprets this way. "In a previous eon, you were a guide who led five hundred disciples into one of the mysterious palaces of the Nagas on the subtle planes. Knowing that few if any of your disciples were mature enough to receive the rich offerings of the Serpent Kings, you nevertheless brought them all, just to demonstrate the truth of nondiscrimination. You have been able to move consciously from one benevolent human birth to another, always manifesting as a spiritual guide who inspires many beings, but those particular five hundred disciples become birds, lifetime after lifetime. They fly vainly in emptiness, still unable to digest the powerful food of the Nagas, the Prajnaparamita, the radical teaching of open space. They have not been able to establish themselves on the true earth of the Dharma body."

His compassionate nature stirred by this revelation, Haklenayashas cries out with his whole being: "How can I liberate them?" At this pregnant moment, Manorhita calmly transmits the Light that already shines: "I am the unsurpassable treasure of Total Awakeness. Look at me! My very body is this treasure! Now you must consciously absorb, embody, and radiate it, just as I do."

Anuttara yoga tantra, the unexcelled diamond practice, unveils our supremely precious human body—here, now, and timelessly—as a living Buddha mandala. Material constituents are peaceful female Buddhas; mental constituents are peaceful male Buddhas; senses are male and female Bodhisattvas in blissful father-mother union; organs of action are fierce male and female Wisdom Warriors in mother-father union; the principal subtle nerve channels in the spiritual body are the primordial Buddha of the mandala and his radiant wisdom consort, Goddess Prajnaparamita. This is the Tantric experience of emptiness as this very body, not as the empty sky where the five hundred cranes are still flying. Such is palpable Buddhahood, the most sublime Dharma treasure. All Awakened Ones, along with persons who are irradiated by the Light of their Buddha transmission, can and must proclaim: "My very body is this treasure!"

The mother of Japanese Soto Zen kindly reveals this secret in his closing poem this morning. The great mountain he describes, piercing through even the highest clouds, is the Buddha body—that is, this human body, these organs and senses, these subtle channels of spiritual energy, unveiled as boundless magnificence. The mountain is deeply rooted beneath the thick clouds of *samsara*. Its snow peak, rising into *nirvana,* brilliantly contrasts with the blue sky. This Buddha body is not the same as the sky of emptiness, yet neither is this diamond body composed of atoms, molecules, cells. It is the rainbow body, so bright, sings our beloved Roshi Keizan, "its purity annihilates all conventional detail."

Living Buddhas move about on earth as this glorious body, but we can only see it from beneath the clouds. There actually *is* someone who attains enlightenment on earth, someone who lives enlightenment on earth, someone who tenderly and even rationally invites all beings to enlightenment on earth. Come out of the sky, you five hundred cranes!

closing poem

> Buddha body wakes,
> Buddha body showers,
> Buddha body eats breakfast
> on summit of Mount Sumeru.

WHATEVER MERITS I ATTAIN
DO NOT BELONG TO ME

TRANSMISSION TWENTY-FOUR
HAKLENAYASHAS TO ARYASINHA

koan

The destined vessel of Light approaches the Awakened One and proclaims with his whole being: "I am committed to attaining the Buddha way. What vows and methods must I adopt?" The living Buddha first empties the vessel entirely: "For one truly committed to the Buddha way, there are no procedures." Courageously, the successor enquires: "Then by what means can Buddha activity stream forth?" Light now transmits Light to Light: "Being busy or concerned with procedures is not Buddha activity. Performing nothing is Buddha activity. As Sutra teaches: *Whatever merits I attain do not belong to me.*" The new living Buddha is suddenly awake as the single wisdom of all Awakened Ones.

comment

After his Zen talk this morning is complete, Keizan Roshi opens the treasure of this *koan* with the key of his closing poem: "If you want to reveal the sky, do not cover it. Originally and always, it is unobstructed clarity." If you want to see, do not cover your eyes with cloth, hands, eyelids. The precious physical eyes are essentially bright and clear. They only need to remain exposed, uncovered. The wonderful merit of clear seeing does not belong to the eyes. *Whatever merits I attain do not belong to me.* The eyes make no separate claim. The eyes are not engaging in any contemplative methods in order to see, nor are they vowing to see or establishing altruistic motives for seeing. They just see. Naturally. Spontaneously. Joyfully. Unless one is very sleepy or ill, there is no sensation of struggling to keep the eyes open. Seeing eyes are open eyes, open eyes seeing eyes. After much meditative effort, one arrives at the effortlessness of direct seeing, not only with physical eyes but with the whole being. After drawing back the bow, simply release the arrow. It will certainly fly by itself.

Direct seeing reveals the unobstructed sky of Buddha activity. This seeing is not passive mirror reflection but dynamic ocean awareness. Do not cover this clear eye with physical seeing, much less with meditation halls, with religions, with the four bodies of the Buddha or the five levels of Buddha wisdom. Do not cover this oceanic eye with wanting to see or even with seeing. Roam freely as the open eye of reality, performing nothing, without routine procedure, and therefore remain at the constant service of conscious beings without any special form of doing or any special mode of being. This is not the common, selfish version of *performing nothing*. Even seasoned practitioners find this selfless *performing nothing*, moment by moment, to be extremely challenging. Yet without continuously realizing this freedom from self-structure and communal structure, not even one square inch of fully responsible Zen can be uncovered.

Shakyamuni Buddha and Dogen Zenji both speak about the experience of the enlightened person as similar to removing armor. How delicate the exposed eye—moist with tenderness, sensitive in movement, perceiving vast subtlety without any sensation of doing or performing! The enlightened person is all eye. Direct seeing is panoramic, yet responds to every changing frequency of light. It adjusts its focus many times each second, yet its field remains indivisible.

There is indeed a person who vows to see, who practices meditation in order to see, who longs to see the clear blue sky of nonduality in order to help all living beings awaken into their true nature. But the Sutra eliminates even this most intimate covering by proclaiming, *Whatever merits I attain do not belong to me.* There is actual spiritual attainment, but it does not belong to anyone. *Performing nothing* does not eliminate the rich procedures of Buddhist practice nor the whirling circles of the dervishes of Islam. Successor Aryasinha was thoroughly versed in non-Buddhist teachings. None of these ancient ways to expose the original eye belong to anyone and they are therefore ultimately not being performed by anyone. They are the spontaneous, loving activity of boundless seeing. Or, as dervishes would say, *the blazing, blissful unity of Pure Being.*

Nothing and no one can impede Buddha activity, which is simply seeing, seeing, seeing! Aryasinha, the noble lion, becomes a martyr, or witness to Buddha activity, at the hands of an enraged king. We will all meet the King of Death in one guise or another, but in his maturity, Buddha Aryasinha is actually executed. As the royal sword severs the living Buddha's beautiful head from his body, as he freely gives away the manifestation of being a Buddha, miraculous streams of milk gush forth. The beloved Muhammad once dreamed that milk was streaming from the crescent moons on his fingernails. Upon hearing this unusual dream, his companions asked for its interpretation. Concisely and intensely, the Prophet of Allah responded: "It is pure knowledge." This healing, nourishing, liberating stream of pure knowledge, or direct seeing, flows liberally from the awakened person, who no longer needs a head. Even when modern Chinese invaders cut the head from Tibet, destroying innumerable holy images both of flesh and of gold, a flood of milk gushed forth and filled the planet with knowledge.

Veda, Sutra, Torah, Gospel, and Quran are pure milk, borne in vessels of language and history. We drink the milk, not the vessel. The present Buddha transmits delicious Sutra milk, *Whatever merits I attain do not belong to me,* and the new living Buddha becomes a fountain of milk, even in his physical death as naked awareness—without armor.

closing poem

> Zen master Zen student,
> mutual gaze a single eye
> uncovering original brightness.
> "Now you can begin!"

ANCIENT SPRINGTIME MIND LIGHT

TRANSMISSION TWENTY-FIVE
ARYASINHA TO BASIASITA

koan

Living Buddha proclaims to destined successor: "Now I transmit the inexhaustible treasure of the eye that discerns everywhere only ultimate teaching. Guard this treasure well and all conscious beings will be awakened, both now and throughout time." Suddenly seeing through and thereby becoming free from all karmic causes and conditions, the new living Buddha receives the Great Mind Seal called *mahamudra*.

comment

The father of the young successor introduces his son, Sita, to the present Buddha, explaining that the boy was born with left fist clenched. This strange condition still persists. The Awakened One explains the hidden karmic cause. In a previous existence, Buddha Aryasinha, at that time a simple Buddhist monk, received a small crystal of Perfect Nondual Wisdom, offered to him by the Naga kings of the Western Ocean. The monk entrusted this priceless wisdom treasure to a certain young man named Basia, who guarded it with great loyalty. "Now give me back that original gem," the present Buddha calmly asks, and immediately Sita's left hand opens, for the first time since birth, releasing a clear stone. In this pregnant moment, the present Buddha decisively points the next Buddha toward the open door of Mahamudra, *the inexhaustible treasure of the eye that discerns everywhere only ultimate teaching.* Mahamudra dawns only when one lets go every precious treasure, both from this conventional world and from the Dharma realms, only when one melts and lets go every responsibility, no matter how sacred.

Keizan Roshi illuminates the teachingless teaching of Mahamudra in his vibrant Zen talk this morning: "Even though there are myriads of forms and thousands of basic categories, they are all simply the original Mind Light." Mahamudra is to abide continuously not only within but as this primordial radiance. This is neither meditation practice nor mental insight. It neither grasps conceptual and perceptual signs nor abandons them. It neither speaks nor avoids speech. Our ancient Japanese guide subtly alludes to Mahamudra: "Buddhas are essentially unawakened and sentient beings essentially undeluded." Why? Because there is no separate moment of awakening in the timeless, indivisible Mahamudra, nor is there delusion in the gloriously all-embracing Mahamudra. "No conscious being," Keizan Zenji remarks, "is fundamentally deficient of Buddhahood, nor are Buddhas superior in nature to conscious beings." Why? There is only *suchness, thisness, thatness, thusness.*

Mahamudra is a non-teaching because it has let go of the jewel of Buddha wisdom. There is no separate goal of Buddhahood, and therefore no separate path to such a goal taken by separate conscious beings. Even to chant the *Heart Sutra,* "no path, no wisdom, and no goal," is still instinctively to clasp the crystal of Prajnaparamita in our hand.

Buddha Aryasinha requests the newly unveiled Buddha Basiasita to guard well the incalculable treasure, Mahamudra, but not in any sense of defending it from intruders by keeping it locked or hidden away, for by its very nature Mahamudra always remains immediately accessible, fully revealed. No one and nothing can stain it. Guarding it means refusing to hold onto it, even by chanting the *Heart Sutra* or by sitting cross-legged with eyes half-closed.

On this wonderful morning in very early spring, with great kindness our Roshi Keizan unveils Mahamudra through the flash of his closing poem, where blossoming spring flowers and falling autumn leaves are displayed simultaneously. Both form and formless. Mahamudra, which he calls the king of medicine trees, "has no distinctive flavor." It is one natural taste everywhere. There is nothing distinctive or separate. This is the medicine that cures all notion of disease, all notion of *form* or *formless.*

Mahamudra is the universal *shikantaza,* the motiveless sitting recovered for Japanese Zen by Dogen Zenji. The whole universe is sitting, fully awake, beyond meditation. Pure and simple sitting, called *shikantaza,* need not refer to a cross-legged position or a focusless concentration so intense that one can stream with perspiration while sitting on a cold night. Universal *shikantaza* is beyond the categories *meditation* and *non-meditation*. It is not a state of stillness. Mountains, rivers, and Master Dogen are all flowing together timelessly. Mahamudra—plain, pure, and simple—is not a state at all, although it displays and embraces all states.

The California live oak always looks the same, but upon close examination, the tree can be observed simultaneously dropping away brown leaves and growing new green ones. Autumn leaves and spring blossoms on the same branch. Its gnarled bark and unpredictable shape also transmit the flavor of Mahamudra. After heavy rain, the trunk and limbs of the live oak turn deep black—reservoir of all color, absence of all color. Black dragon Mahamudra!

The nonduality treasure is one universal taste, neither ordinary nor extraordinary. We have proceeded together through twenty-five astonishing transmissions of Light, only now to experience the fullness of this *beyond teaching,* this *beyond meditation,* which is both beginning and end of every transmission, every transaction, every event.

The Awakened One gives the name Basiasita to the new master of Mahamudra, the new manifestation of universal enlightenment. The incarnation in the distant past as Basia and the present incarnation as Sita are not divisible. Neither is the radiant stream of living Buddhas prior to Basiasita in any sense divisible or even prior. Master and successor are utterly inseparable, as are past, future, and present. To awaken as this basic indivisibility is called *suddenly seeing through and thereby becoming free from all karmic causes and conditions.* Transmission is the deep black Mahamudra. Not twenty-five Buddhas, not two, not one. Mahamudra belongs to everyone.

closing poem

> ancient springtime mind light,
> original, before blossoms or leaves,
> shining, shining, bursting,
> blazing from bare limbs,
> blending with all, benefiting all,
> great mind seal Mahamudra

JUST A SELDOM FLOWERING CACTUS

TRANSMISSION TWENTY-SIX
BASIASITA TO PUNYAMITRA

koan

> MASTER: If you take the vow of home-leaving, what will you do?
> SUCCESSOR: I will do absolutely nothing.
> MASTER: If you take the vow of home-leaving, what will you not do?
> SUCCESSOR: I will not perform any ordinary thought or action.
> MASTER: If you truly leave home, what will you be?
> SUCCESSOR: Buddha activity, in all its plainness and intensity.

comment

Doing absolutely nothing is to be free from the notion of any independent self that initiates actions or receives the results of actions. It is to remain fundamentally notionless, while continuing to experience the daily sense of harmonious functioning and the authentic sense of accountability.

Not performing ordinary thought or action is to be free from the notion of any independent body or mind, while continuing to experience the coherent sense of thinking and doing. It is to be free from any notion of religious obligation, contemplative practice, or service to others, such as teaching, helping, or saving, while continuing to live the Mahayana life of appreciation and responsibility for all conscious beings.

To be pure Buddha activity is to manifest in a natural, effortless manner as transcendent wisdom, as Mother Prajnaparamita—ever clarifying, ever compassionate, neither active nor passive, invisible to the undiscerning eye.

The father of Japanese Soto Zen, Master Dogen, calls this bodiless, mindless, stateless way *gyo ji*, ceaseless walking. The character *gyo* is translated into English as contemplative practice or spiritual cultivation. But it means *just walking*—dynamic, simple, balanced, bare feet always in touch with the original ground consciousness. *Just walking* along the ever-expanding spiral of awakeness—continuously—is the Buddha way.

After completing his Zen talk this morning, Keizan Roshi illuminates the nature of Buddha activity with his closing poem: "The original ground is ordinary. Not even a blade of grass. No room for Zen." Consider the bare, packed earth at the village well, the village threshing floor, the village thoroughfare, the village dancing ground. This is the basic Mind Ground, always beneath the bare feet of the people, totally supportive, completely unnoticed. In such spirit, Jesus washed the feet of his disciples and asked them to make this primal gesture for each other, for the feet are in connection with the ground. "Become dust on the road beneath the feet of humanity," counsels a certain Native American sage.

Nothing grows from this Mind Ground. It is not like the bald head of the Buddhist monk that needs to be shaved again and again. Nothing wears out this basic ground. The ground consciousness is ultimate simplicity, ultimate functionality. Every moment of importance in the global village, our daily life, occurs on this ground— communicating, drawing water, threshing grain, expressing worship, feeling delight. It is like the ground beneath the Kaaba in Mecca or the Great Stupas in Sarnath and Bodhgaya, circumambulated ceaselessly by barefoot lovers of reality. But the Mind Ground is neither Islam nor Buddhism. Mind is not even the quiet sitting outside religion called *zazen*. *Zazen* is just a seldom flowering cactus that grows in deserted places.

Perform no ordinary thought or action. Not even Zen sitting or Zen walking, much less Zen teaching. Be the invisible ordinariness of the Mother Ground. Be plain, free from cultivation. Original Mind is the common ground for this borderless village called daily life, including beloved sentient beings in universe after universe. In this harmonious village, there is no essential distinction between deluded ones and awakened ones. There is no privilege or underprivilege in ground consciousness. This common ground is radiant as a full moon to those who have eyes to see. It belongs equally to all. It cannot be purchased, appropriated, conquered, subdivided. It is neither in front nor behind, neither developing nor regressing, neither internal nor external, neither gender nor neuter, neither self nor other, neither barren nor fruitful, neither lay nor monastic. The four elements, the five structures of personal awareness, the six levels of rebirth—none of them belong to this wonderful Mind Ground. Nothing grows from this bare soil, so there is nothing to be cleared away. Nothing to be planted, cultivated, harvested. Realizing this is truly to leave home, eon after eon.

closing poem

> bare feet on smooth floor
> walking walking touching
> basic ground everywhere
> support everywhere
> tender receiving caring
> invisible magnanimous
> Mother Ground

MOONLIGHT SWALLOWS MOON

TRANSMISSION TWENTY-SEVEN
PUNYAMITRA TO PRAJNATARA

koan

The Awakened One approaches a homeless youth whom he clearly recognizes as his destined spiritual inheritor, and throws open the door of Light: "Do you remember the ancient path?" The reply comes forth spontaneously, without thought: "I remember being with you in another eon, revered sage. You were silently radiating Mahaprajna, primordial wisdom, and I was chanting melodiously its ultimate expression, *Prajnaparamita Sutra.* Our present meeting is a mirror reflection of the previous one." Complete and instantaneous transmission is now confirmed by thundering silence.

comment

The master, whether approaching from East or West, is always the same primordial wisdom. Mahaprajna liberates each living being in a manner uniquely appropriate to that being. The successor is always a full expression of liberating wisdom, a beautiful human form of the *Prajnaparamita Sutra.* In the present drama of transmission, the Sutra of Nonduality is manifest as a nameless young man of twenty, orphaned and wandering since childhood, who calls himself by the name of anyone who offers sustenance.

Throughout both full and empty eons, master and successor are inseparable, like timeless mirror and timeless mirror image. One always attracts the other, inexorably, until the successor suddenly realizes again that they are not two. This *not twoness* is metaphorically called *the transmission of Light.* Such realization plunges the destined successor into the silent depth of Mahaprajna, which contains both *prajna,* transcendent insight, and *karuna,* boundless compassion, the skillful functioning of insight that spontaneously liberates all beings.

The notion that *prajna* relates to some peaceful absolute and *karuna* to some suffering realm of relativity is inaccurate. For Mahaprajna, there are not two dimensions called *absolute* and *relative,* either to be distinguished or not to be distinguished. For Mahaprajna, nondual insight and all-embracing compassion do not move in different directions. The *not twoness* which acts in the wonderful drama of transmission as *master* and *successor* is always completely awake. There is never anything lacking, never anything partial.

Looking back along the flowing stream of living Buddhas, we see only pure presence. This entire sacred history is just *you* and *me* in the companionship of nonduality. Master Keizan calls this timeless procession "golden needle and golden thread, without sharp point or sinuous length." There is only one seat for meditation. For *beyond meditation,* there is no seat.

Our ancient Japanese guide, who is precisely the same Total Awakeness that manifests as all living Buddhas, now sings a radiant wisdom poem: "Moonlight reflecting at bottom of clear pond is also brilliant in the sky." *Prajna* and *karuna* are the same brightness everywhere. Is compassion at the bottom of the pond and wisdom in the sky? Our beloved Roshi Keizan, full moon of Soto Zen, continues to sing: "The water, transparent and pure, reaches right to the sky." There is no separation between relative and absolute, water and sky, disciple and master, speech and silence. As Dogen Zenji once replied to a request to express Buddha Dharma in a single line: "It can never be stained." Stained by what? It can never be stained by twoness, nor even by oneness.

Our Roshi Keizan's closing poem this morning continues: "Even as countless sentient beings fill their vessels with this water, it remains fathomless—refreshing and clarifying all acts of consciousness, while in itself unthinkable." Pure *prajna* resides at the core of every act of perception and conception. Pure *karuna* abides at the core of every longing. There is no essential difference between Buddhas and sentient beings. They are just the harmony of *prajna* and *karuna.* Various intentions are the karmic water vessels, narrow or great. But the water, the limitless reservoir of Mahaprajna, remains indivisible, unknowable, silent. Such unparalleled silence, with which Buddha Punyamitra now embraces the newly unveiled Buddha Prajnatara, is not the absence of sounds or thoughts. This basic silence does not invalidate the function of various water-bearing vessels. This thundering silence is primal unthinkability. Not abstract or general. More concrete even than particularity.

Mathematical systems with their arbitrary axioms, as well as conventions of thought, language, social organization, and routines of perception—all simply draw a circle. They deal only with whatever is agreed to be within that circle. Hinduism, Buddhism, Judaism, Christianity, Islam are just more circles, valuable to human evolution as they may be. *Maha* means borderless. Mahaprajna erases every circle, every circumference, while leaving the center everywhere. All vessels are operative for drinking, cooking, washing, irrigating, offering.

Though the only seal of approval, or *inka,* received from his master is great silence, the successor is now given the name Prajnatara, one who compassionately bears *prajna* from past to present to future. Such a name is sheer play. For Mahaprajna, there is never any separate past, present, or future. There is only a transparent ocean of moonlight, loving and wise.

For Sufis, Allah alone is. Yet they continue to regard themselves and the entire creation as beautiful expressions of that Abyss of Love more primal than being, oneness, or essence. There is really no paradox here. Only by focusing on the conventional world, with its arbitrary circumferences and its dream of oneness and twoness, can we produce the appearance of some paradoxical, mystical journey beyond the world. The Awakened One is the person without paradox, without world, without beyond, without journey—filled with humor and responsibility. Here is the playful sage, standing comfortably, contentedly gazing. This white heron cannot be hidden, even in the brightest moonlight.

Comments Dogen, father of Japanese Soto Zen: "Since mind, which is all things, is completely moon, the all-inclusive world is the all-inclusive moon. Entire body is entire moon." Now the Great Sage takes another leap: "Moonlight swallows moon." The white heron now simply savors the inexhaustible moonlight into which even the moon of Buddha Dharma has disappeared.

closing poem

> Diamond thunderbolt father vajra
> is great compassion.
> Empty space mother moon bell
> is transcendent wisdom.
> But where is Mahaprajna?
> Ah, the tender smile of the master!

Though the Planet is Broad, There is No Other Path

Transmission Twenty-Eight
Prajnatara to Bodhidharma

koan

The present Buddha immediately recognizes the next Buddha, and probes for what he knows to be already there. The responses are immediate.

MASTER: What is completely without characteristics and therefore completely uncharacterizable?

SUCCESSOR: That which, while freely manifesting, never actually arises in the first place.

MASTER: What is most excellent, exalted, sublime?

SUCCESSOR: The innate clarity and brilliance of awareness itself.

MASTER: What is truly limitless and therefore without division or boundary?

SUCCESSOR: The very nature of reality, just as it is, moment by moment.

The young prince, while responding spontaneously, suddenly realizes the identity of his mind with the mind of the Awakened One, who confirms the transmission of Light with a subtle gaze.

comment

How wonderful to travel this morning from India to China, and from there to Japan and America. Eyes wide open. Whole being alert. So it is when we begin a great journey.

To this brilliant prince, who is a living, breathing wisdom jewel, Buddha Prajnatara gives the new name Bodhidharma, revealing that his karmic destiny is to bring the Great Dharma of Awakeness, or *bodhi,* to the distant land of China. This broad realm will serve as the door into global history.

Concealing his complete awakening and waiting patiently for the sixty-seven year transitional period his master foresaw, Bodhidharma finally travels to the land regarded as a mysterious, wealthy, and exotic world beyond the eastern horizon. The old sage originally advised the young sage: "Countless will be those who sincerely enquire about nonduality and actually come to full awakening in the land beyond the horizon. Though China is broad, there is no other path." In the fullness of time, Bodhidharma voyages toward the directionless East, always facing the rising sun of nondual wisdom, always facing the wisdom wall, always practicing the subjectless, objectless sitting called *zazen*. Arriving at Shao-lin Monastery, he continues to face the wall, literally and figuratively, never speaking about the teaching of nonduality, simply radiating *bodhi,* the Great Light of Awakeness. He is the perpetually rising sun of inconceivability, always balanced on the horizon of planetary history.

The sea voyage of Roshi Soyen Shaku from Japan to America in 1893 as our original Zen visitor is contained within this timeless moment when Prajnatara instructs Bodhidharma to leave India, the spiritual motherland, sanctified by the birth of so many living Buddhas. Each of these Awakened Ones has wandered aimlessly and unerringly in search of the successor, the destined vessel of Light. As the young prince proclaims to the old sage who is testing him: "Whenever beings acknowledge the Great Way, the treasure of Mind appears." This treasure is the living Buddha—always arriving wherever we are.

Never before this moment have the living Buddhas of India wandered beyond her sacred borders to transmit the treasure of Wonderful Mind. Now China and the whole planet become the motherland of Prajnaparamita, where living Buddhas recognize living Buddhas. Whatever becomes bounded territory, no matter how sacred, must dissolve its boundaries. Even Buddha Dharma is now opening its borders with other noble traditions—Hinduism, Judaism, Christianity, Islam, and many others—just as the borderline between *samsara* and *nirvana* was erased by the universal hearts of Mahayana and just as Tantric masters began to discover female Buddhas, both heavenly and earthly, eliminating gender hierarchy from our appreciation of awakening.

"Why did Bodhidharma travel from the West?" This has become an archetypal Zen question, indicating: "What makes you think Bodhidharma traveled anywhere at all? Who is there to travel? Where is there to travel?" But the Great Dharma of Bodhi, the radical teaching of perpetual awakeness, does indeed travel, while remaining perfectly still. It travels from moment to moment, from breath to breath, from West to East, and now from East to West. We are Bodhidharma, wandering into new eras, new breaths, new planetary spaces. There is no doubt the destined successors will manifest— great offering vessels, already bearing the plenitude of Light. This is not an existentialist journey, made poignant by doubt, disciplined by dread. This is the blissful, timeless journey of spontaneous transmission. The inevitable journey. The flowing breath of humanity. The full flowering of humanity.

Master Keizan's closing poem this morning kindly removes any sense of greatness, vastness, or heaviness from this archetypical journey of Bodhidharma, from our own journey. He sings a crystal song of enlightenment: "Without distinction, location, or border between inside and outside, all universes together are not as substantial as a single hair." As insubstantial as dark points that float before eyes under strain. To breathe in the entire universe and breathe out nothing, as one Zen master described his mode of prayer, is therefore not a tremendous feat. To travel from India to China to America, sailing with Bodhidharma across the open ocean, is not impossibly difficult or even amazing.

Remarks our ancient Japanese guide about this universal Bodhidharma, this Dharma of Awakeness that tenderly embraces all beings and all events: "Prior to the separation of heaven and earth, how can you distinguish sacred from ordinary?" This is the Great Way. The Original Way. The Undivided Way. Who would not wish to enquire about this natural, intimate, harmonious teaching of nonduality during our present planetary era? Countless are the persons who will awaken through the touch of this universal Bodhidharma, now traveling everywhere throughout our emerging global civilization. These suddenly awakening persons will be unconventional, intelligent, alert, undazzled by the blaze of inconceivability. Their differences in gender, education, culture, and religion will not be eradicated but celebrated. Though the planet is broad, there is no other path!

closing poem

> breakfast open rose old dog
> friendship among friends
> traveling traveling
> building good businesses
> pouring forth Dharma teachings
> no inside or outside
> motherland without end

ALLOW THE ENTIRE MINDSCAPE
TO BECOME A SMOOTH WALL

TRANSMISSION TWENTY-NINE
BODHIDHARMA TO HUI-K'O

koan

After remaining at the right hand of the Awakened One for eight years, destined successor proclaims to his great master: "I have finally put an end to conditions." The living Buddha sternly dismisses this attitude: "Such a state would be equivalent to death." The successor responds with diamond confidence: "It has nothing to do with death." "Can you prove that to me?" the fierce sage probes relentlessly. With ease, the new living Buddha replies: "I am clearly and continuously aware! Absolutely no words are adequate to express this clarity!" Satisfied that the transmission is full, Bodhidharma generously confirms it, revealing just a spark of his vast inner tenderness: "Be completely certain that such clarity is the very mind-essence realized by all Awakened Ones."

comment

Hui-k'o was born after intense prayers by his parents, who experienced wonderful light flowing into their room on the night of conception. The boy read extensively, experiencing disappointment with both Confucian and Taoist philosophy. He loved to wander through green mountain gorges. Eventually, he left home to become a Buddhist monk, avidly studying Sutras and engaging in rigorous concentration and meditation.

Hui-k'o leaves his original Chinese Buddhist master when the attraction of the rising sun from India, Bodhidharma, becomes a painful force throughout his body. He hears a mysterious voice: "This is no ordinary illness. Your very bones are changing. Do not become stuck here. Travel south." With the permission of his teacher, the young man migrates, drawn by the energetic presence of the living Buddha at the Shao-lin Monastery on Sung Mountain.

Hui-k'o arrives at the station of complete fruition by staunchly and strenuously practicing for eight years the wall-gazing instructions given by Bodhidharma, who himself performed only methodless wall-gazing *zazen*—year after year, breath after breath.

"Allow all mental conditions to become completely transparent, whether they appear external or internal," the old sage instructs the second Buddha Ancestor to manifest in China. "Do not even grasp mind with mind. Mind will then appear as a smooth wall. Gaze, gaze, gaze! This alone is truly to enter the nondual way." The entire panorama of phenomena is simply Mind. Why remain entranced by this panorama, which includes coherent personal and cultural experience as well as the chaotic surface play of events? Why continue to move through this panorama like fictional characters playing fixed roles in our own drama? Allow the entire mindscape to become a smooth wall, thereby coming to the end of cyclic experience. Reveals Bodhidharma about authentic wall-gazing: "If you try to continue straight ahead, you will not be able to move a single step." Until this point is reached, whatever wall one appears to encounter is just romantic projection.

Some persons dread reaching this final smooth wall. Others come more easily and gratefully to it, as it springs up in the form of daily events. This wall is the end of conditions, the end of our life lived as film or literary fiction. After accepting this mind wall, this wisdom wall, whether reluctantly or joyfully, one must assiduously practice wall-gazing for years before deep intimacy with Mind is attained.

Master Keizan, in both his Zen talk and his concluding poem this morning, uses a particularly potent phrase to indicate intimacy with Mind: *alert, clear, originally bright*. These words are not to be taken literally or even taken at all. As Hui-k'o responds to the probe of his master: "Absolutely no words are adequate to express this clarity!" This firm sense of inexpressibility is the incontrovertible demonstration the successor presents to his uncompromising guide. We must simply be alert clarity, original brightness, mind-essence. This essentiality is expressed moment by moment by all living beings throughout the borderless expanse of space and time, but is realized and actualized only by Awakened Ones, who become fountains of tenderness and intensity for all humanity, for all evolving mindstreams.

Master Harada of our contemporary era teaches that at least ten years of wall-gazing, *shikantaza* or *mahamudra,* are necessary before one experiences full intimacy. Wall-gazing is not just sitting in a *zendo* facing the wall. Wall-gazing is not sharp concentration, nor is it even contemplative method, for these are only paths to reach the smooth wall. All religions and their *koans,* all forms of suffering and aspiring, are long, precious roads to reach the wisdom wall. Yasutani Roshi, another contemporary Zen sage, reveals that during the process of realization, holes begin to open in this final wall. Gradually, it disintegrates or evaporates. This is not an actual transition. One simply sees that the wall was *wall-less* from the very beginning. *Originally bright.* Please do not turn this wisdom wall into an imaginary stone wall, into a silent, cool place to sit without distraction. Even the final wall can become a Cave of Demons.

The love that flows from living Buddha to living Buddha to all conscious beings is what melts the final wall. Bodhidharma's love is so fierce, so intense, that he continues to reject his successor's level of understanding, beginning from the first moment of their meeting. Arriving at the monastery near dusk, Hui-k'o is refused entry to the master's room and so stands outside his window for the entire night. There is a snowstorm. The disciple remains motionless, snow gradually rising to the belt of his robe, his tears of aspiration for all beings freezing on his cheeks. At dawn, he profoundly requests: "Please open your Dharma door of ambrosia and awaken sleeping beings everywhere." Bodhidharma scolds him through the window for lack of commitment to nonduality, and then ignores him entirely.

Yasutani Roshi explains that fierce compassion—so rare, even among spiritual guides—gives the disciple minimal instruction and no encouragement until the final confirmation of awakening. Bodhidharma incarnates this ferocity, which was necessary to open up the heart-mind of Chinese culture and the entire Western world. Hui-k'o finally severs his own left arm with a razor-sharp sword to demonstrate the seriousness of his commitment, thereby cutting through all the subtle obstacles that existed in China to the reception of the Dharma of Awakeness. Can we be this serious, here on the threshold of global civilization?

For thirty years as living Buddha, Hui-k'o conceals his exalted stature—sitting in wine shops, speaking street language, laboring among the people, even cleaning public latrines. Eventually, he manifests. After conferring the seal of transmission, the robe and bowl, upon his own successor, he peacefully accepts martyrdom, executed for heretical teaching by a maliciously misinformed imperial official. He is the second living Buddha in the revolutionary lineage of Shakyamuni to be executed. His pure death, releasing a flood of selfless wisdom energy, dissolves countless karmic obstacles to the harmonious spread of the teaching of Bodhidharma, the Way of Spontaneous Awakeness. Keizan Roshi teaches us to cherish Hui-k'o above the previous twenty-eight successors, although they are undifferentiable in essence, because without this first Western Buddha martyr, none of us Western barbarians from China, Japan, or America would have received the inconceivable transmission of Light.

After severing his own arm, thereby cutting the root of separate body and mind, Hui-k'o received his new name, Wonderful Potential for Dharma. Words are inadequate. We are not speaking here about *arm, sword, blood,* or *cutting motion.* May we cut away obstacles, our own and those of all beings in this global realm, with the clean, clear gaze of naked awareness—the sharpest, brightest sword. As beloved Keizan encourages us: "We have not come such a long way from Shakyamuni! There is nothing lacking in our present era! Never lose confidence!" Dogen Zenji offers even greater encouragement: "This is the moment when the one called *you* is actually Buddha Ancestor Hui-k'o."

closing poem

> Zendo floor, childhood memory,
> green springtime, open galaxy.
> Here is the wisdom wall.
> Swirling atoms of experience
> become still, fuse,
> melt in transparency.
> Such rare love
> in the dark eyes of the roshi!

DO NOT FALL INTO INERT MEDITATION

TRANSMISSION THIRTY
HUI-K'O TO SENG-TS'AN

koan

The future protector of the Buddha transmission humbly approaches its present protector. "This body is manifesting leprosy. I supplicate you, revered sage, to clear away my extensive negative karma." The Second Buddha Ancestor in the broad land of China vigorously gives life: "Bring me this negative karma of yours. Show it to me. I will clear it instantly." Entering deep concentration for several moments, the destined successor cries: "Though searching thoroughly for this karma, I simply cannot find it." The Awakened One now transmits the Sudden Way: "Your karma has always been clear. By approaching me with great sincerity, you have unveiled the Three Jewels—Buddha, Dharma, Sangha. The Buddha is Mind's original purity. The essential Dharma teaching is Mind's original purity. The Sangha, the community who realizes and spreads the truth of nonduality, is also Mind's original purity." The newly unveiled Buddha now receives a new name, Pure Jewel of the Enlightened Community.

comment

No details are known concerning the background of successor Seng-ts'an. Immersed in the unthinkable depth of Mind's original purity, he never spoke about his personal karmic causes and conditions. He never even mentioned his family name.

Keizan Roshi generously expresses to his Zen students the spirit of this *koan*. Rich meaning pours from his concise closing poem. Original Mind is absolutely empty of any independent or substantial self-existence, free from any internal division or external boundary. Neither negative karma nor positive karma leaves the slightest trace on Original Mind, which is what Buddha, Dharma, and Sangha really are. This Triple Gem is our own complete healing and illumination, as well as the liberation and enlightenment of innumerable living beings, right here and now.

Remarks Master Keizan about the Third Buddha Ancestor to appear in China: "After Original Mind manifested, his leprosy was cured." The rising sun of Mind's original purity dissolves the morning mist of causes and conditions. However, our kind Roshi Keizan also warns us about the proper manner of taking refuge in Original Mind: "Become intimate with the place where no trace of karma ever appears, but do not retreat or hide there!" Face and overcome every obstacle to universal conscious enlightenment!

After the transmission of Light, Buddha Seng-ts'an certainly does not retreat from the dangerous realm of negative and positive karma. Guided by a prophecy transmitted through Grand Master Bodhidharma and presented to him by Master Hui-k'o, the new living Buddha conceals himself deep in the mountains for more than ten years—moving constantly from place to place, teaching no one. Thus he avoids the virulent persecution of Buddha Dharma by a renegade emperor. Here is negative karma in its most extreme form, dealt with skillfully through foreknowledge, patience, obedience, humility, invisibility. The wandering sage even changes his personal appearance in order to protect the historical transmission of Total Awakeness.

At exactly the correct karmic moment, Buddha Seng-ts'an comes forth from the mountains into the conventional world, discovers his successor, and transforms the atmosphere of society. His final discourse is recorded under the title, *On Trusting Original Mind*. His words are astonishingly simple: "The Great Way is not difficult. It is simply to avoid accepting or rejecting." Did the living Buddha accept or reject the militant regime of the emperor during his ten years in the wilderness? In his skillfulness, he simply left no trace.

Master Keizan essentializes these teachings on Original Mind by the Third Buddha Ancestor: "What is there to accept or reject? There is nothing lacking. There is nothing in excess. You are already bright and clear. Investigate this most carefully. Do not fall into inert meditation and other forms of nihilism."

We will certainly be able to encounter the unencounterable, to receive the inconceivable Light of transmission. How? Look again! It has always been accomplished by Buddha, Dharma, Sangha. By Mind's original purity.

closing poem

> Life-taking edge:
> "It is not this! Not that!"
> Life-giving edge:
> "Where is it? Show it to me!"
> One bright blade
> with two sharp edges
> cuts through positive and negative
> with fierce compassion.
> "I cannot find it anywhere!"
> "From the beginning, it was clear!"

GLISTENING SERPENT NEVER ENTANGLED IN ITS OWN COILS

TRANSMISSION THIRTY-ONE
SENG-TS'AN TO TAO-HSIN

koan

The one destined to be the living Buddha for his generation now approaches the Third Chinese Ancestor: "Holy master, please demonstrate great compassion by pointing directly to the liberating teaching of emptiness." The Awakened One responds brusquely: "Who or what is imprisoning you?" Startled, this brilliant practitioner of Buddhist wisdom gazes deeply for a moment, and firmly replies: "No one and nothing imprisons me!" The old sage now points directly: "So why do you consider emptiness to be a *liberating teaching*? Why are you seeking liberation in the first place? Since no one is actually bound, how can liberation ever be demonstrated?" Total Awakeness alone is now manifest.

comment

This remarkable young sage is only thirteen when he receives the transmission of Light from Buddha Seng-ts'an. The boy was born from Prajnaparamita, the radiant black womb of nonduality. While growing up, he avidly sought and easily assimilated from many wisdom schools the teaching of emptiness, which was called, by un-realized Buddhism, *the teaching of liberation*. Keizan Roshi can barely contain his devotion and enthusiasm for the Fourth Chinese Ancestor, revealing that even among Awakened Ones, who are undifferentiable in essence, someone like this appears only once every thousand years.

By dissolving any notion of liberation that occurs at one particular time or another, which was cultural baggage from the popular Buddhist teaching of that era, Master Seng-ts'an opens his precocious young Dharma inheritor into timeless liberation, intrinsic freedom, the indivisible awakeness that shines evenly throughout past, future, and present.

From the very non-moment of this transmission, the newly unveiled Buddha manifests intrinsic freedom. For sixty remaining years, Tao-hsin does not sleep lying down, not from motives of austere discipline but because of the streaming presence of beginningless awakeness. There is no need for liberation. There is not even the possibility of some particular event called *liberation.*

The final teaching of Buddha Tao-hsin to his fourfold assembly— monks, nuns, laymen, and laywomen—is precisely the same truth which he expressed continuously through sixty years of Buddha activity: "All beings and events are already liberated, moment by moment. Keep only this teaching in the heart-mind. Pass on only this simple, ceaseless practice of pure presence to the precious future generations." After offering his last word, the old sage enters the silence beyond meditation and dies with eyes wide open. The glistening serpent is never entangled in its own coils.

Precisely one year after the diamond of Tao-hsin's bodily form is entombed, a sharp earth tremor occurs. The sealed door of the tomb opens, exposing the beautiful, serene, uncorrupted body, seated in *mahasamadhi,* exactly as it had appeared during his final breath. Only hair and nails have grown long. As Keizan Roshi comments about birthless, deathless realization: "The seamless tomb opens by itself. Everyday features are revealed as peaceful and mild." The devoted disciples hesitate to close the tomb again, realizing that their master, in death as in life, is still demonstrating the principle of timeless liberation, still teaching us, in Keizan's words, that we are "never imprisoned or bound up by life or by death."

The Zen talk of our ancient Japanese guide is particularly rich this morning, inspired by the immediate presence of the Fourth Buddha Ancestor, his tomb still wide open. Keizan Zenji shows that intrinsic freedom is neither body nor mind, neither delusion nor enlightenment. Subject, object, sleeping, waking—even sleeping mountains and waking rivers—are simply names and forms of our most intimate selfless awareness, playfully called the *selfless self.* In his closing poem, our guide proclaims that seeing and what is seen, hearing and what is heard, are nothing other than freedom, limitless awareness, boundless clarity.

Successor Tao-hsin realized, as we now realize with surprise, that the strong impulse to seek liberation is itself already the expression of timeless, universal liberation, which shines as natural, spontaneous, selfless awareness, as the core of our daily awareness. When seeking dissolves, finding dissolves. While still perceiving forms and hearing sounds in a normal manner, we now "blend the six tastes and discover something delicious where there is nothing, true form where there is no form." This is not paradoxical Zen discourse, but the most direct, sensible way of speaking. What is truly delicious is the modeless ground consciousness at the core of the six modes of relative awareness. What is truly beautiful is the formless form of the living Buddha.

Tao-hsin expresses timeless liberation not simply through ultimacy but through all dimensions of experience. Once a town was besieged. Buddha Tao-hsin instructed its inhabitants to chant the *Prajnaparamita Sutra* in an intensive manner. The invaders saw armed warriors by the thousands manifesting on walls and balconies, and they withdrew. Inhabitants, invaders, armed warriors, and skillful sage are all timelessly liberated.

How joyful and grateful we are to realize that our small efforts actually help to sustain this teaching of nonduality through decades, centuries, millennia! So many events conspire to distract humanity from the radical teaching of open space, freedom, emptiness—thousands of moments every day, disguised as divisiveness or indifference, disguised as challenges of conscience or even as the desire for liberation! Yet still we continue to chant, study, comment on sacred texts, light incense, offer flowers, cook, serve, clean kitchens, *zendos,* bathrooms. Devotedly, we pour clear water into offering bowls, create Buddha images sitting in silent meditation, endow land for temples. Drawn by our own spontaneous liberation, we perform these beautiful actions, preserving the context of Dharma for future generations. But only living Buddhas can unveil Total Awakeness at the core of every action, every perception.

The Chinese emperor threatens to have Tao-hsin decapitated. This would cut his Buddha transmission prematurely. The Awakened One, following the example of his own Grand Master's martyrdom, extends his neck serenely to the sword. The consciences of both emperor and executioner are awakened by this eloquent gesture of timeless liberation, which is not an expression of passivity but pure freedom. One cannot take pragmatic measures to protect Dharma, for such militant or compromising means would actually cut away the teaching of nonduality, something which no ordinary sword could ever do.

closing poem

> Timeless liberation
> blossoms spontaneously
> for hungry, lonely people
> in bare streets and dry fields.
> Sweet emptiness alone turns
> the waterwheel of compassion.

LIGHT CAN BE POURED ONLY INTO LIGHT

TRANSMISSION THIRTY-TWO
TAO-HSIN TO HUNG-JEN

koan

While walking along a remote mountain road, the living Buddha meets and instantly recognizes his destined successor, a homeless boy of seven. "What is your name?" the master probes. The reply is immediate and firm: "I am essence, not name." The playful sage asks the serious boy: "Does this essence which you are have a name?" "Awakeness," the child responds. The Awakened One now probes to the very depth: "Is awakeness your name?" The boy cries out: "I am nameless." In silence, the brimful reservoir of Light pours Light into this boundless diamond vessel. Only enlightenment shines.

comment

Light can be poured only into Light, essential awakeness into essential awakeness. Is there any basic difference between this illumined boy before transmission and after transmission? Of course not! After transmission, he is given the symbolic bowl, that is, he is enabled to pour the nectar of essential awakeness not only into his Dharma successor but into his whole generation. He is also given the symbolic robe, empowering him to invest not only his successor but all living beings with the gold brocade robe of Buddhahood. The boy's intrinsic enlightenment has now simply become supremely active.

The station of conscious Buddhahood is far more than the realization of nonduality. It is an infinite pouring forth to innumerable beings, to each one uniquely and intimately. But what exactly is poured forth? At their core of open space, essential awakeness is always clearly known by conscious beings. What needs to be poured? Light must be poured into Light!

Essential awakeness, proclaims our ancient Japanese guide, "remains exactly the same for the four castes—laborers, merchants, warriors, priests." Conscious Buddhahood alone dissolves the caste system, not only in India but in every culture. The living Buddha frees the entire universe from self-serving hierarchy and dependency. The Awakened One frees whatever manifests from appearing rigid or substantial. One can easily demonstrate that essential awakeness remains the same for five archetypal sacred worlds: Veda, Sutra, Torah, Gospel, Quran. And for three archetypes of direct transmission: Tantra, Sufi, Zen. With Master Keizan's own voice we can confidently proclaim: "All sentient beings are naturally immersed in timeless *samadhi*, the full expression of reality."

To accept the existence of delusion as some force that can impede or veil essential awakeness is itself the only delusion. And since there is no substantial delusion, there can be no moment of enlightenment, no crossing over some imaginary border out of delusion. Such is the vigorous spirit of the nameless boy's response: "I am essence, not name." No matter how deeply the master probes, this adamantine spirit remains clear on every level.

Keizan Roshi embodies this Zen spirit in his closing poem. Essential awakeness he calls *immense purity*, likening it to transparent water-moon-sky, neither divided nor marked by a single cloud. But even to call it *immense purity* could limit it. We might falsely assume the dark clouds that sweep naturally through the sky to be impurity. We might succumb to the temptation to posit *something else*. Freedom from *something else*, not absence of thought or sound, is what constitutes the wonderful silence of Zen.

An eighty-year-old Catholic priest learned to practice *zazen* from a Catholic sister who was trained in Japan under a contemporary Roshi. During his very first sitting, tears flowed from his eyes. Why? It was not the stillness of the body, nor the quietness of the mind, nor the sweet aloeswood incense. It was not a sudden increase in spiritual aspiration within a heart that had aspired ardently for more than sixty years. It was the absence of delusion everywhere. It was the light of Christ as all in all. It was the presence of essential awakeness, not simply within his own heart-mind but within all beings. It was immense purity without boundary. There was nothing else.

Zen is simply the demonstration of essential awakeness. Not crossing the legs and sitting on the cushion. Not teaching with paradoxical phrases and sudden gestures. Namelessness is what consitutes the primal ease and silence of *zazen*. Names are conventional boundaries, always shifting. The Fifth Chinese Ancestor never ceased practicing this nameless *zazen* from childhood to ripe old age, throughout a lifetime of intense activity. Buddha Hung-jen died immersed in this continuous, invisible *zazen*. His final words: "This activity is complete." Free from the slightest trace of passivity, dynamic *zazen* is always complete. Essential awakeness is always complete.

We must empty conventional names from our cup in order to fill it with the clear water of namelessness. We must become small children, remarks Jesus, to enter the Kingdom of Heaven immediately, here and now, to appreciate the essential awakeness which is our birthright, our true holy land. Small children know nothing of rules and protocol, metaphysics and theology. Nicodemus, a mystical rabbi, came to Lord Jesus Christ at night to receive transmission of the secret teaching. The Great Master told him simply: "You must be born anew." The newborn know nothing even of perception and conception. Hassidim who celebrate this secret openly wear white every Sabbath, the color usually worn only on Yom Kippur, the day of rebirth into oneness—annulling all boundaries, all names, all contracts, all conventions.

This exhortation to be born anew underlies the present *koan*. An ancient, pine-planting pilgrim, wandering across the face of a sacred mountain, approaches the Fourth Ancestor and requests: "May I receive your transmission?" Buddha Tao-hsin replies tenderly to this illumined sage: "You are so venerable in age that were I to transmit Dharma, you could not teach it very long. Come back again. I will await you."

The pilgrim takes leave and soon meets a spiritually qualified young woman, who is washing clothes in a river. "May I receive lodging for the night?" the adept humbly requests. Feeling intense love for this old sage, she smiles and nods. When she returns home to ask her parents, she is already miraculously pregnant and the old pilgrim is dead. She is eventually driven from her home in disgrace and lives independently by spinning thread. When the child is born, she leaves it beside the river for seven days. Returning, the young mother sees her infant, who has not been swept away by the rushing current, protected by two large birds and two wild dogs. He is healthy and radiant. She begins to nurse him. They live as homeless beggars. Because of the strange countenance and unknown origin of her child, she cannot find even menial work. The boy is called *nameless one* by his mother and by the villagers, since no one knows the name of his father. Yet certain persons, gifted with inner sight, can discern in this swiftly evolving child many signs of spiritual greatness.

When he is seven years old, *nameless one* meets Buddha Tao-hsin walking along a mountain road. The Fourth Ancestor immediately recognizes that old planter of prayers and pine trees, whose facial structure was so distinctive, and asks the boy his name.

The old pilgrim was born anew to plant living Buddhas. He emptied himself of names by becoming nameless. Each Buddha Ancestor must be born anew as his own destined successor, and each successor born anew as Shakyamuni. Each of us is born anew for this ultimate awakening. Why should we be essentially different from the ancient sages? In this process of spiritual rebirth, there is no father. The only mother is limitless awareness, Prajnaparamita, Mother of the Buddhas. This is the transmission of Light, the reincarnation of Light. The Light remains exactly the same, shining as very different faces in different cultures. It is instantly recognizable to the sage.

As our beloved guide Keizan declares during his Zen talk this morning: "There is a name that is not received from the father, that is not inherited from the patriarchs." Our real name is *awakeness*. Born anew without father, born anew without patriarch, spontaneously born from the radiant blackness of wisdom's womb, we are namelessness. We are neither this body nor the next body. Neither past, nor present, nor future. Neither *I* nor *you*. Neither birth nor death. Neither Indian, Chinese, Japanese, or American. Do not be fascinated! Be fundamental!

closing poem

> Early summer morning,
> gentle rain falling,
> Zen temple locked, waiting,
> friendly dog inside barking,
> welcoming,
> no practitioner appearing,
> nothing to do but return home,
> laughing.

WOODCUTTER REALIZES INSTANTLY HE IS A DIAMOND CUTTER

TRANSMISSION THIRTY-THREE
HUNG-JEN TO HUI-NENG

koan

Fifth Chinese Buddha Ancestor enters at midnight the dusty shed where rice is hulled and polished, and asks his hidden successor: "Is the rice white yet?" The unlettered laborer responds: "Yes, perfectly white! But the husks have not yet been sifted from the grain." The Awakened One immediately strikes the stone mortar three times with his Zen staff. The new living Buddha responds appropriately by shaking the sifting basket three times. Walking to the master's private chamber and entering it as his own place, the rice-husker now manifests as the Sixth Buddha Ancestor.

comment

Since childhood, Hui-neng supported himself and his mother by cutting firewood, working hard and living with complete concentration and absorption. Coming into town from the forest slopes one day, carrying a large bundle of kindling, he hears a man chanting from the *Diamond Cutter Sutra*. One line strikes like lightning: "Think and perceive freely, without imagining the support of any underlying physical or metaphysical basis." The woodcutter realizes instantly that he is a diamond cutter. All Sutras become transparent to him. Hui-neng asks where the man received instruction in this wonderful Sutra. The lay practitioner, who is simply out buying wood, replies: "From the living Buddha, Hung-jen." This is the initial call from master to destined successor.

The illiterate laborer now appears different to outward eyes, though inwardly he has always been essentially the same. His face shining like the sun, the rustic begins to share his spontaneous knowledge, always seeing right to the core. Dharma students bring subtle questions about the Sutras, and Hui-neng elucidates the spirit of each passage perfectly, without being able to read. An old temple is restored by earnest practitioners, both lay and monastic, and woodcutter is installed as revered teacher.

Although many are inspired by these teachings, Hui-neng is not drowned by adulation. Sensing the subtle inadequacy or incompleteness of his own realization, he escapes the crowds and retires into the wilderness. Here, a certain Zen master recognizes his innate greatness and advises him to visit the present living Buddha, sealed by the very mind of Bodhidharma. "Who is this living Buddha?" "Hung-jen." Once again, the successor hears the potent name of his destined guide, and this time travels at once to the luminous presence, the aura of completeness, which always surrounds the full embodiment of Shakyamuni Buddha's enlightenment.

The Fifth Buddha Ancestor immediately recognizes the Sixth, yet with polite formality enquires about his background and motivation. Proclaims the rough-hewn sage: "I do not want to discuss Sutra. I want to be Buddha nature." The sublimely subtle master replies with the humor of the absurd: "People from your part of the country have no Buddha nature." This pregnant remark begins the process of removing hulls from rice, the hulls of Buddhist understanding and Buddhist aspiration from the kernel of essential awakeness. The accomplished Zen master immediately sends his hidden successor, not to Sutra hall or meditation hall, but directly to the small rice-hulling shed, isolated on the forest slope behind the monastery. The Great Sixth humbly works here without interruption for eight months, husking and polishing during both waking and dreaming.

Sensing that Hui-neng is ready, Buddha Hung-jen now stages a drama of the absurd. He urges the seven hundred monks under his guidance to compose verses of realization, announcing that the time has come to hand over the bowl and robe of succession. The senior monk, brilliant and broad beyond all his Dharma brothers, is the obvious one to come forward. He is nowhere near ready, but the playful master is pushing. The head monk enters the chamber of the Awakened One repeatedly, but is overcome by trembling and cannot deliver his poem, sensing its inadequacy. This happens fourteen times in three days. Finally, he decides to inscribe the verse on a wall of the monastery at night, anonymously.

In this poem, the rice has not yet been hulled, much less thoroughly polished. However, when these lines are discovered the next day, the master praises them with concealed irony. He even makes all the monks memorize and recite them. How else will he get his message to the illiterate laborer who works, eats, and sleeps in the rice-hulling shed?

Hearing this poem being recited by a monk coming to get fresh rice for the kitchen, Hui-neng asks about it and hears that Buddha Hung-jen will probably pass his venerable bowl and robe to its author. With the simple, courteous manner of a country man, Hui-neng remarks, "It is fairly good but not quite there," knowing inwardly that the author of this poem remains hopelessly confined within the hulls of the Sutras. The worker monk shouts insultingly: "O uneducated rice-husker, what could you know about the spiritual level of our head monk, who obviously composed these lines? You are even elevating yourself above our abbot, who has proclaimed that if future generations practice in accordance with this poem, they will achieve excellent results."

Clear that Total Awakeness cannot possibly be connected with *achieving results,* heart-mind stirred by this confrontation, the illiterate sage invites a young servant, who is literate, to accompany him on an adventure after midnight. The boy inscribes Hui-neng's alternative lines on the wall beside the head-monk's verse. The hidden sage holds the lantern steadily as the boy draws black characters on the white wall.

This second poem is not an improvement on the first but its complete refutation. The process of wiping away dust from the mind-mirror, advocated by the head monk, is replaced by brilliantly polished white rice—*no separate mirror, nowhere for dust to collect.* The next morning, the new poem is discovered and the advanced practitioners in the monastery, including the senior monk, are struck by its supremely confident, self-manifesting, self-luminous spirit. However, Buddha Hung-jen, master of Zen theater, now dismisses the second poem as mere intellectual play and personally erases it, kneeling before the crudely shaped characters with soap and scrub brush. That night the Awakened One secretly visits the rice-hulling shed, bows to the sage whom he knows must be the author of the second poem, and the final act in the play of transmission occurs.

Of course the rice is brilliantly white! Hui-neng has become the Prajnaparamita Sutra beyond letters, transcendent wisdom without any hulls. There is no separate mirror, no separate emptiness, no diamond to be cut, no diamond with which to cut. This astonishingly profound successor already knows the next step. The rice needs to be sifted in order to become nourishment for all living beings. The absolute task, the open space beyond religion, has been demonstrated by the mortar. The fusion of absolute and relative— that is, to prepare and serve delicious hot rice to the people—must now be demonstrated by the sifting-basket. How nutritious nonduality!

One living Buddha strikes the stone mortar, like a bell, expressing empty space and its resounding revelation, the emptiness of emptiness. The other living Buddha, laughing, shakes the bamboo sifting-basket, expressing skillful means, liberative art, active compassion. The illiterate laborer, covered with rice dust, now enters the elegant abbot's chambers as the Sixth Chinese Ancestor. Wisdom and skillful means have united, generating a living Buddha after eight months of gestation. Ramakrishna was born in a rice-hulling shed in Bengal. He used to say: "No one can realize Truth, which is utterly simple, without becoming utterly simple."

As our ancient Japanese guide reveals in his closing poem this morning: "While sifting clouds, silver moon suddenly appears." A new living Buddha graces the landscape with gentle radiance. This full moon is called *the unsurpassed, supremely subtle, most intimate, completely miraculous eye of transmission.* It has no beginning and no end. This is the thirty-third drama of pouring Light from one vessel into the next without spilling a single drop. The Light remains innately clear, complete, and fundamental in every moment, in every movement. This Light of transmission, essentially nameless, nevertheless opens the treasury of eighty-four thousand skillful Buddha teachings, including sixteen Bodhisattva stages, ten transcendent perfections, nine vehicles, and the ways of gradual and sudden enlightenment. But Light must be transmitted to each generation for the teachings to live and breathe.

The Fifth Buddha Ancestor now sends the Sixth into temporary hiding, knowing that the formal succession will be jealously contested, because Hui-neng is an illiterate layperson, not an educated monastic. He has never even once practiced *zazen* in the meditation hall. Hui-neng's very life could be in danger. The Great Sixth will hide among tribes of hunters in remote mountain ranges for ten years before coming forth to present his incomparable teaching.

Maintaining the selflessness of discipleship, Buddha Hui-neng now prostrates before his master, Buddha Hung-jen. Bearing the antique robe and bowl, emblems of the complete transmission from Shakyamuni, Hui-neng peacefully walks down the mountain path in the deep silence before first light, personally escorted by Hung-jen. At dawn, he prepares to board the ferry boat across the misty river, requesting his master to return to the monastery. Hung-jen maintains the sweetness and inseparability of their relationship by taking the boat across together and returning alone. Between living Buddhas, fervent devotion, continuous guidance, and intimate friendship function gracefully in the mode of nonduality. This crossing the wide river together mysteriously opens the whole world to Buddha transmission.

From this day on, the Fifth Buddha Ancestor no longer presents Zen talks on his mountain. The servant boy has confessed the authorship of the second poem. The search for Hui-neng has begun. The era of the Great Sixth has dawned, an era of inconceivable spiritual intensity and resulting spiritual acceleration.

Inspired by the burning example and direct presence of Hui-neng, Keizan Roshi cries out to his monks and to all humanity: "Through infinite good fortune, we meet together today. You have not yet completed your awakening. Your life is slipping away. Why wait until tomorrow? How long can you hang on to Sutra knowledge and imagine that any limited study or limited experience can express what is limitless? Hanging on to my Zen words is a terrible waste of time."

Remove the husks of ignorance and knowledge! Sift the rice of Mahayana! Cook it effortlessly in the vast, boiling pot of the modern world! Without wasting a single grain, serve life-giving nonduality to all conscious beings!

closing poem

> Powerful prayer beads in one hand,
> strong hand of my consort in the other,
> method and wisdom melt together,
> tears pouring down
> with generous morning rain.
> This may be the day
> I have been waiting for.
> "Don't plan anything,"
> comments the master.

HOW CAN ONE SEW
IF THE NEEDLE REMAINS
SHUT IN THE CASE?

TRANSMISSION THIRTY-FOUR
HUI-NENG TO CH'ING-YÜAN

koan

The destined successor earnestly approaches the Sixth Chinese Buddha Ancestor. "How can one avoid becoming stuck in some stage of spiritual development?" The fiery sage responds like lightning: "What stage have you attained?" With equal swiftness, the mature practitioner replies: "I have not even begun to consider the Four Noble Truths." The Awakened One now removes the final veil from the new living Buddha: "What stage will you ultimately reach?" His innate enlightenment now completely revealed, the successor laughs and responds: "If I never begin, not even at the beginning stages, how can I end at any stage? What stages can there be?" The old sage confirms the transmission of Light with a steady gaze.

comment

Successor Ch'ing-yüan has been a Buddhist monk since an early age, immersed in the perfect refuge of the enlightened teachings and the enlightened community. His level of spiritual certainty is so profound that he keeps silence during all the discourses and debates on Buddha Dharma which he attends. He is a brimful vessel.

Yet the moment he encounters the Sixth Chinese Ancestor, who has removed the husks and even the subtle colorations of Buddhism from the rice of essential mind, this serious monk senses the subtle arrogance of his own certainty and stability, of his continuous absorption in silent practice. Ch'ing-yüan becomes intensely concerned that he has been frozen into some stage of spiritual evolution. He may even have fallen into what Master Keizan calls *the deep pit of liberation* or, even more dangerous, *the demon cave of clarity,* thereby extinguishing the precious longing to go further, to be truly free, to extend compassion boundlessly. Asks Keizan Roshi: "How can one sew if the needle remains shut in the case?"

One glance at the naked flame of the Great Sixth serves to melt this long established personal sense of certainty. Not intellectually but with intense longing, successor asks living Buddha: "How can I escape from this insidious sickness of my Dharma body, my subtle arrogance of attainment, my feeling of being silent and complete?"

This living needle case is opened by the sudden bolt of energy, *What stage have you attained?* Then with the deep probe, *What stage will you ultimately reach?*, the sage reveals enlightenment from the successor's naked awareness as a Buddha image spontaneously manifests from uncut stone. The responses of the successor are not premeditated. Not even for a second. They are completely surprising. To everyone.

We must simply never begin. We must not submit reality to our assumptions of states and stages. The First Noble Truth, that egocentricity is suffering, cannot be relied upon ultimately, for both suffering and ego are empty of any substantial self-existence. The Second Noble Truth, that analyzes the cause of suffering, is therefore also provisional, not applicable to ultimate realization. The Fourth Noble Truth, the existence of an objective, definable path to the cessation of suffering, is also mere metaphor, not meant to describe reality in any ultimate sense. Only the Third Noble Truth, *nirvana*, the total absence of egocentricity throughout beginningless time, can be said to express what is real.

Nirvana is clear sky. As Master Keizan remarks: "Right from the start, there are no boundaries in the sky. Can you place stone steps there?" There are no stages of open space, no bridges or paths or steps to open space. There are no possible boundaries or definitions anywhere—not even temporary, provisional, metaphorical. "Right from the start!" cries out Keizan Zenji, startling us into awakeness.

We must never conceptualize ourselves as beginners, first contemplating the Four Noble Truths and then gradually establishing a hierarchy of meditative practices, until we attain the status of advanced practitioners, ending in some special realm or experience called *universal emptiness,* where we gain some status called *enlight-enment.* Our kind Master Keizan transmits the words of Lord Buddha from the inexhaustible treasury of Mahayana wisdom: "Precisely because practitioners postulate emptiness and establish practices to attain it, they do not see clearly. For living Buddhas, there are no practices and no realm of universal emptiness." There is nothing concealed or revealed.

"What stages can there be?" proclaims the new living Buddha, no longer heavy and serious, as he is swept into the uprushing bliss of awakeness. This bliss belongs to all persons in the present moment as the molten core of their own conscious beingness, but they dissipate it by channeling it into routinized perception and stages of development, into narrow or broad systems of understanding that strain to produce and sustain both personal and communal certainty and security.

Any sense that we hold a final or even a provisional solution—knowing exactly what it is, how it is, how it should be—must dissolve. A certain modern Japanese master responds with pleased surprise to every   affirmation by his Zen students: "Thank you! That's how it is!" Another contemporary master often responds: "This is another wonderful way of looking at it!" These enlightened responses are offered with encouraging sweetness, not with the studied irony of those who consider themselves to be completely realized and the views of others to be merely partial. Even the most subtle sense of self-satisfaction must disappear into laughter.

Keizan Zenji's closing poem this morning illuminates the disappearance of self-satisfaction and self-perpetuation. It contains two images. The first is the flight of birds that leaves no trace. Zen teachers often refer to the turtle that sways slightly as it walks across the sand, with the result that its tail erases its tracks. Yet, they point out, the tail itself is leaving another track. As long as there is any erasing, or self-effacing, some subtle mark will be made. Without the slightest effort, the bird simply makes no tracks in the sky.

The tail of the turtle is the verbal expression of emptiness. To affirm universal emptiness is what Keizan Roshi calls *Dharma attachment.* Our way, right from the start, must be the sky. Not the teaching of emptiness, which remains indirect. Only direct sky! As our ancient Japanese guide remarks: "Look carefully! This clear sky is brighter than the rising sun!"

Sky is not empty. The blue sky is full of soaring birds and clouds, the black sky full of stars. This apparently stable earth is really deep in the sky. Every breath flows from sky into sky. Every thought arises and disappears in the mind sky. Sky neither moves nor stands still. Everywhere we look is sky, sky, sky!

The second image in Master Keizan's poem is the path of radiant darkness. "How can you look for stages here?" he asks. This is the Cloud of Unknowing cherished by Christian mystics. An infinite cloud, brighter than the rising sun of intellect, so bright that it appears radiantly dark. The Third Chinese Buddha Ancestor once offered a major discourse. Its principal meaning was contained in an ideogram which can be understood to indicate an unspecified, indescribable way. A way through open space. A pathless path of radiant darkness. No definitional light is cast, yet our steps are firm and well-guided.

May we take this path of beautiful darkness with the ease of a soaring bird. This path consists of freedom, the open space of indefinability. This *dark path,* as Master Keizan calls it, is never the same, never foreknown, unique for each culture, for each person, for each step, for each breath. This path is not mapped, not mappable, not even encounterable, yet runs true. There are no practices or stages here. We can never even begin the *dark path* with any such preconceptions. There is no provisional teaching. Only unspecified ultimacy. As Keizan Roshi remarks confidently, causing our own confidence to surge: "There will be an unexpected realization of alert knowing, not received from someone else or somewhere else."

What about suffering sentient beings, all of whom have been our mothers during some eon of beginningless time, all of whom are now our mothers? How does this open space, this radiant darkness, help them? Simply by being the transmission of Light, living Buddhas are tangibly serving all conscious beings, lifting them into their arms just as tenderly as Mother Theresa of Calcutta holds the dying, who are actually enacting pure life and whom she perceives as pure

Christ. Verbal teachings of compassion are no more ultimately reliable than verbal teachings of emptiness. We must come direct.

The *dark path* manifests boundless love and freedom. Where? Right here in the contentious atmosphere of daily life—monastery, marketplace, family, psyche. The Great Sixth warns his successor: "Since receiving the robe of transmission, I have run into so much trouble. There will certainly be more contention in later generations."

Without needing to generate any special motive of compassion, the left hand comes to the aid of the right hand when it runs into trouble. This dynamic oneness and mutuality of our two hands, beyond meditation and premeditation, is the actual, moment-by-moment experience of emptiness as subjectless, objectless compassion. This perfect mutuality and inseparability of our two hands is beyond any verbal teaching, yet we all experience it clearly. As Keizan Zenji confirms, speaking from this wonderful realm of mutuality, free from division: "Ordinary experience is nondual wisdom." *Right from the start!*

closing poem

> Open space walking.
> Why move forward?
> Why not move backward?
> In every direction?
> Radiant darkness
> leaves no trace.
> Beautiful darkness.
> My father's face
> in the face of the master.

RIDING EFFORTLESSLY ON A LARGE GREEN TURTLE

TRANSMISSION THIRTY-FIVE
CH'ING-YÜAN TO SHIH-T'OU

koan

MASTER: Where are you from?

SUCCESSOR: From your own original monastery.

MASTER (raising his white horsetail whisk): Does *this* exist in the monastery?

SUCCESSOR: Not in any monastery, nor even in the sacred land of India.

MASTER: Since when did you go to India?

SUCCESSOR: Only if *I* went to India, would *this* exist there.

MASTER: Outrageous statements are not enough. Tell me more.

SUCCESSOR: You cannot rely on me to say it all. You must say part.

MASTER: I am not refusing to talk. I just feel concerned that after me, no one will really be awakened.

SUCCESSOR: Future successors will certainly be awakened, but they may be unable to express it.

At the moment these words come forth, living Buddha strikes destined successor with his ceremonial whisk. The vessel of Light suddenly awakens beyond every level of awakening, empowered to express Total Awakeness fully for all future beings.

comment

There is no way to strike a hard blow with a whisk. The ancient master swiftly flicks the long white horsehairs, mounted on a black lacquer handle. The movement is sudden and graceful, the touch of the blow delicate. The supercharged intensity of the destined successor is melted. His fierce atmosphere of awakeness which, in the words of Keizan Roshi, "could easily demolish heaven and earth," is transformed from storm to calm. Realization can now express itself easily and fluidly, like the long tail of the whisk.

As Buddha Ch'ing-yüan discerns from the very first moment, his spiritual inheritor is experiencing difficulty with the free, generous expression of awakeness which perceives enlightenment everywhere, not just in the realm of transcendent realization. Successor Shih-t'ou is subtly and unconsciously blocking the flow of Total Awakeness with his bold statement: *Where I am, awakeness is!* Such an attitude is not incorrect but incomplete. Yet the successor does instantly recognize the white whisk raised high as the realization of nonduality, which cannot be found in the hierarchical formality of any monastery or at any sacred place of pilgrimage, where the stubborn tendency to seek ever elsewhere is reinforced. This highly evolved practitioner also recognizes that the only living Buddha is *this,* whether one uses the name Ch'ing-yüan or Shih-t'ou, or the name of the master they both share in common, the Great Sixth, Hui-neng.

However, the successor does not yet recognize the deep mystery of the dynamic whisk, which is both Shakyamuni raising the flower and Mahakashyapa smiling. It is movement, not stillness. The fluent expression of awakeness, the subtle smile of Mahakashyapa, is sadly missing from this successor. His mind is as inert as the wooden handle of the whisk. It needs to achieve the luminous aliveness of the white horsehairs.

Through the compassionate skill of Dharma dialogue, the Awakened One leads his destined successor, in just a few moments, over a vast course of spiritual maturation. The whisk moves unexpectedly, completely alive. Light is transmitted and the new living Buddha unveiled. With delightful humor, Keizan Roshi calls this form of Buddha activity "whacking the tall grass and scaring the snakes away." These poisonous serpents are bold affirmations of self-realization.

Strangely enough, the possibility that Shih-t'ou might not be able to express or transmit awakeness was so thoroughly reversed by this blow from a mere bundle of horsehair, that the new living Buddha eventually writes the powerful poem, *Identity of Relative and Absolute.*

These condensed verses are chanted even now in Japan, some thousand years later, within countless Soto temples during the morning service. In certain places, the chanting monks make their formal procession in a whirling pattern, much like the fluidly moving whisk, called *fu-tzu* in Chinese, *hossu* in Japanese.

This Dharma utterance of Buddha Shih-t'ou, *Identity of Relative and Absolute,* is a consummate expression of the awakening beyond every level of awakening. Now it is also being chanted in Western languages across the globe. It presents, clearly and darkly, the unspeakable relation, or non-relation, between *hossu* raised high in stillness and *hossu* that strikes and transforms. As Shih-t'ou sings in this song of supreme maturity: "To encounter the pure absolute is not yet enlightenment." This line is a comment on his own state of subtle fixation when he first encountered the *hossu* of his master raised high.

The gracefully moving *hossu* sings this timeless Zen song through his lips. The lines continue to flow, describing the mature perception that arises after the master's tender blow.

> Relative fits absolute
> as box its lid.
> Absolute meets relative
> as two arrows
> touch point to point
> in the empty blue sky.
> Apply no criterion!
> Neither absolute nor relative!
> Simply perceive!

Where can we find these two formidable arrows? Now even they have disappeared. It is not the rich lacquer box, nor its beautifully illuminated lid, but its empty space which is useful for holding the incense of compassionate wisdom. It is the open sky which permits the arrows to fly.

Ever since childhood, this very intense successor was fearless. As a boy, he fiercely opposed the ritual animal sacrifice performed to propitiate demonic forces by tribes of hunters in his native region of

China. He became a novice at age thirteen, just before the Great Sixth died, and received some instruction directly from him. After the demonstration of physical death by the Sixth Chinese Buddha Ancestor, Shih-t'ou sat in such relentless solitary meditation, for such long periods, that he often appeared dead. He indeed experienced Great Death. He lived on a stone terrace and was called the Stone Monk. This earth-shattering, heaven-shattering realization is what manifests in the present successor as unshakable confidence. But such boldness creates rigidity, which is not appropriate for a mature Zen sage. Great Death without Great Resurrection is copper waiting to be transmuted into living gold.

Shih-t'ou now abides in bliss as perpetual springtime awakeness. How? Only by coming into the presence of Buddha Ch'ing-yüan, spiritual inheritor of the Great Sixth. Only by receiving the tender blow from the living Buddha's *hossu*. On the night after his awakening, the newly unveiled Buddha dreams that he and the Great Sixth are riding effortlessly on a large green turtle. This marvelous creature swims freely in a deep blue mountain lake, the water of self-luminous awareness. So it is that the Great Sixth transmits his entire being—free, undivided, clear—down through the line of his destined successors to all those who gather around them throughout time. Thank you! Thank you!

closing poem

> Just by sitting and looking,
> you are raising
> the horsehair whisk.
> Now you strike.
> Such delicate motion!
> Of course! It has to be this way!
> Laughing,
> I feel the ancient *hossu* in my hand.

PLANTING FLOWERS
ON A SMOOTH RIVER STONE

TRANSMISSION THIRTY-SIX
SHIH-T'OU TO YAO-SHAN

koan

Destined successor approaches Buddha Ancestor and reports: "I comprehend the twelve basic Sutras that clarify all manifestation. Yet I long to receive the radical transmission by which master points directly to Mind, allowing disciple suddenly to realize Mind's nature and thereby become a living Buddha." The Awakened One responds: "No step-by-step understanding will work. The sudden approach will not work, either. Nor will any combination of the two. Now what are you going to do?" Stunned, the successor stands speechless for a few moments. Before he can gather any thoughts whatsoever, the uncompromising sage sternly sends him to visit the mountain of Master Ma.

Entering the more gentle atmosphere of another unique disciple of the Great Sixth, the aspirant once again requests direct pointing at Mind. Master Ma replies: "Only the One Mind raises these eyebrows and blinks these eyelids. Sometimes gestures occur, sometimes not. It makes no difference! Now what are you going to do?" Flooded suddenly with omniconscious Light, the successor melts into a deep bow.

MASTER MA: What glimpse have you received that causes you to bow so profoundly?

SUCCESSOR: When standing before Buddha Shih-t'ou, it felt completely different. Like a mosquito attempting to penetrate an iron ox.

MASTER MA: Through the wonderful kindness of Shih-t'ou, you are awakened. But now you must become refined!

comment

Ardent monk from age sixteen, sensitive scholar of the Sutras and careful practitioner of monastic discipline, Yao-shan is experiencing a spiritual crisis. He feels no direct, conscious connection to Buddha nature, to the elusive essence of his own mind. After receiving from these two sages in concert the transmission he longs for so intensely, he serves Master Ma for three years as intimate attendant. Finally perceiving completeness in the destined vessel, Ma-tsu questions him about his daily awareness, and Yao-shan replies: "I am the snake that shed its skin. Only one bright, clear reality remains." The master joyfully confirms this to be the refinement he has been waiting for, proclaiming: "Mind-essence now consciously pervades all your thoughts and actions. There is no dimension in your entire being where it does not shine. Go to a sacred mountain and teach. Why? Because mind-essence is inseparable from all suffering and aspiring beings. Do not hang around your home monastery and do not indulge in the illusion of benefiting the world by staying alone. Build a big boat! Carry people to True Mind!"

Successor Yao-shan now returns to visit his root teacher. Buddha Shih-t'ou also confirms his completeness, after the destined successor finally answers the basic question, *What are you going to do?* This very same question was posed by both his benefactors, for there is no division or contradiction in the way of awakening. The enlightened response, *nothing at all,* comes unexpectedly. While the new living Buddha is sitting relaxed in the Dharma hall, old Shih-t'ou suddenly confronts him.

MASTER: What are you doing?

SUCCESSOR: Nothing at all!

MASTER: Then you are sitting in idleness.

SUCCESSOR: Sitting in idleness would be doing something.

MASTER: What kind of nothing are you doing?

SUCCESSOR: Not even all sages from human history can say.

MASTER: Because speaking is not related to it.

SUCCESSOR: Neither is keeping silent related to it.

MASTER: Not even room for a needle to enter.

SUCCESSOR: Planting flowers on a smooth river stone.

The two guides of this successor were spiritual father and spiritual mother, one fierce, the other gentle and playful. Both were wonderfully kind, skillful, patient. They waited for the long gestation period of Sutra study and formal meditative discipline to take its course and for the sharp pangs of labor to begin. After coming forth from his mother, Ma-tsu, in intensive labor, it takes the successor three years to remove the placenta, to shed his skin, his habit of bowing and meditating. How compassionate and committed each living Buddha must be to unveil the diamond body and diamond mind of the successor!

Usually, one master acts as both father and mother, wielding both life-taking sword and life-giving sword. In this unusual case, the roles were assumed by two sages. As a result, Yao-shan is considered by Keizan Roshi to be the most marvelous among living Buddhas in teaching skill. Buddha Yao-shan brings forth several incomparably great beings, both monastic and lay persons, from his small, spare, rigorous monastery. Some say that his austere simplicity of life is what limited the number of his students, but it was really his affinity with his spiritual father—the impenetrability of his teaching. "One Mind has no eyes or ears," he used to comment to his disciples. Such austerity is much harder to endure than cold, sleeplessness, hunger. Not many flowers can put down roots into pure stone, but their blossoms are the most amazing ones.

In secret, intimate relationship with these hardy disciples, Buddha Yao-shan becomes like his spiritual mother, Ma-tsu—playful, gentle, eyebrows dancing. Hence these aspirants flourish and come to exalted realization. His is a truly vast monastery, a fully enlightened community, much more extensive with its twenty students than monastic institutions of thousands.

How much sweet nectar should master offer disciple? How many obvious hints? How much encouragement? Will the disciple become like domesticated cactus, receiving too much water and growing into unnatural forms? The more uncompromising and impenetrable the teaching, the more compassion is actually being displayed. This is the *wonderful kindness* that Ma-tsu ascribes to Buddha Shih-t'ou.

One Zen master gave almost no Dharma discourses. After a

particularly long silence of many months, his students sincerely requested his words. Entering the Dharma hall, he bowed to the ex-
pectant disciples, turned, and left. This is the father mode in all its
hidden tenderness. The inconceivable, impenetrable Dogen Zenji is
the father of Japanese Soto Zen. Generous with clear elucidation,
Keizan Zenji is its mother.

The teaching of the father, Shih-t'ou, is that nothing works, nothing opens. The teaching of the mother, Ma-tsu, is that everything
functions, everything reveals. Father speaks from absolute silence,
mother manifests glorious relativity—the dance of eyebrows, stars,
branches and banners in the bright wind. Standing before the iron
ox, the great monolith of *nothing works,* the successor already becomes enlightened. All his words and concepts suddenly and utterly
gone, he is lost in the ungraspable. As Keizan Roshi helpfully remarks about that silent moment: "Even though he was not yet aware
of it, right then and there Yao-shan became a true human being."

Unveiled by the gently rising eyebrows and humorously blinking
eyelids of Master Ma, that original awakeness which belongs intrin-
sically to all beings now begins to move through the destined successor, to refine him into a living Buddha who is fluid, alive, expressing
everywhere, every way. Father is ineffable Mind, mother the graceful
expression of Mind through existential gesture. The offspring of this
union can only be a new living Buddha. Encountering One Mind is
not yet complete awakening. We must become conscious, fluent, refined gestures of One Mind—raising eyebrows, blinking, teaching.
As Master Ma makes clear, sometimes gestures occur, sometimes
not. Sometimes water is still, sometimes in waves. Sometimes father,
sometimes mother. It makes no difference. Water is water. Light is
light. *Now what are you going to do?*

Keizan Roshi, greatly inspired this morning by the presence of
Buddha Yao-shan whom he describes as "particularly sublime in his
relationship with students," prefaces his closing poem with the remark: "Shall I add to the truth of this *koan?*" These are strong words.
A new level is going to be revealed. "The One Mind that raises the
eyelids and blinks," sings our ancient Japanese guide, "is always

entirely active, vibrant with infinite life." How astonishing! There is no still water, no silent deep, no separate absolute. In Tantra, this mysterious dynamism is called the unsurpassable father-mother union. Bliss void.

closing poem

> Sitting in vast awakeness is father,
> standing at bell sound is mother,
> walking through fields
> of inexhaustible perspectives,
> is their playful child.
> White walls turning, turning.
> Gestures of One Mind.

SAME WIND BLOWING
FOR A THOUSAND MILES

TRANSMISSION THIRTY-SEVEN
YAO-SHAN TO YÜN-YEN

koan

The living Buddha asks a wandering monk who appears at the monastery one day: "Where have you practiced?"

SUCCESSOR: Twenty years under Pai-chang.

MASTER: What does he teach?

SUCCESSOR: He usually says: "My expression contains all hundred flavors."

MASTER: What is that total expression, neither salty nor bland?

The monk hesitates to make any statement. During this moment, the Awakened One breaks through: "If you remain even slightly hesitant, what are you going to do about the realm of birth and death that stands right here before your eyes?" Becoming more bold, the destined successor replies: "There is no birth and there is no death."

MASTER: Twenty years with the wonderful Pai-chang have still not freed you from habitual affirmation and habitual negation. I ask you again plainly, what does Pai-chang teach?

SUCCESSOR: He often remarks: "Look beyond the three modes of looking. Understand beyond the six modes of understanding."

MASTER: That kind of instruction has no connection whatsoever with actual awakening. What does he *really* teach?

SUCCESSOR: Once Master Pai-chang entered the Dharma hall to deliver a discourse. The monks were standing expectantly in straight rows. Suddenly the sage lunged at us, fiercely swinging his large wooden staff. We scattered in every direction. At full voice, he then called out: "O monks!" Heads turned and eyes looked. Pai-chang asked gently: "What is it? What is it?"

MASTER: Thanks to your kindness today, I have finally been able to come face to face with my marvelous brother, Pai-chang.

Ignited by these words of deep appreciation, all sense of distance vanishes. The mirror reflection disappears into the original. There is only Total Awakeness.

comment

Yün-yen is not a superficial practitioner. He enters the monastery of the living Buddha confidently, streaming with fragrant realization, after twenty years of immersion in companionship with a great Zen master. This special atmosphere around Yün-yen is what attracts Buddha Yao-shan to inquire immediately about the practice of the unknown traveler.

Yün-yen, fully trained, has been sent forth by his original guide to wander freely and thereby to blossom spontaneously into awakeness. His intense devotion to Master Pai-chang's teaching is the final veil over boundless clarity. Thus the living Buddha goes directly to this point: *What does Pai-chang really teach?*

Yün-yen is not merely repeating his master's words. He has realized the spirit of Pai-chang's teachings, which he reports carefully and selflessly to the Awakened One, hesitating at first to make any statement at all that would limit the richness of what he has received. Only the non-teaching, *What is it? What is it?*, has Yün-yen overlooked. Why? Because it is more subtle than the subtle, more essential than the essential. Under the relentless probing of Buddha Yao-shan, the submerged memory of this non-teaching arises from early in his discipleship. Remembering the fierce swinging of the heavy wooden staff, Yün-yen suddenly becomes sensitive again to the dangerous realm of birth and death which, from an absolute point of view, he has mistakenly dismissed. *What is it? What is it?*, spoken twice, almost in a whisper, clears away both absolute and relative. This is what our ancient Japanese guide calls "releasing the handhold on the rock face and leaping from the precipice."

Through the re-emergence of this precious memory, this Zen seed planted in the mindstream of the destined successor, Buddha Yao-shan encounters Pai-chang, whom he has always longed to meet. Through the present Buddha's profound response, *I have finally been able to come face to face with my marvelous brother,* the new living

Buddha sees the secret face of nonduality that has been hidden from him during twenty years of earnest study, deep meditation, intimate companionship, and partial enlightenment experiences. The karmic causes and conditions of the destined successor demanded these twenty years. No living Buddha wastes time in transmitting Light. It simply could not have been transmitted earlier.

There is nothing particularly noble about practicing hard for twenty years. Awakening occurs instantaneously, and the period of preparation, whether long or short during this lifetime, disappears into the blaze of awakeness. *I and all conscious beings have always been awake!* The role of disciplined practitioner, with devotion to the teachings and love for the teacher, so useful along the path, is the most difficult veil to remove.

Master Keizan calls this encounter of the grateful Buddha with his elusive brother Pai-chang, "the same wind blowing for a thousand miles." Light appreciates Light directly, without needing to make some arduous journey through valleys and across rivers. Some twenty years later on a distant mountain, the fragrant wind of Pai-chang's *What is it? What is it?* touches the cheek of Buddha Yao-shan. As the bright face of the Awakened One standing before him, the successor now encounters the face of his original master, and instantly awakens as the faceless face behind all faces.

Yao-shan and Pai-chang, brothers born from Mother Prajnaparamita's womb of nonduality, represent the Zen lineages which eventually become Soto and Rinzai. This jubilant encounter between them, through the kindness of successor Yün-yen, is the demonstration that these two great lineages share a single inner face. This very same face of naked brilliance, untouched by the innumerable masks of doctrine and cultural conditioning, is recognized and shared by adepts of all wisdom traditions. Meeting a realized Sheikh of Islam, we can proclaim: "Thanks to your kindness today, I have finally been able to come face to face with the marvelous Muhammad."

As during this historical era of Chinese Zen, so today in the modern world, there exists great spiritual dynamism. There is much traveling between lineages, sharing among traditions. Day by day, in secret refuges of high aspiration all over the planet, precious experiences of recognition between different lineages of the One Light are being ignited. Mutual recognition between mature Hindus, Buddhists, Jews, Christians, Muslims and others—those who have removed the veil of exclusive devotion to the teachings and exclusive love for the teacher. The surprise is really no surprise. One face!

Keizan Roshi concludes his talk this morning: "May I try to express this principle more concisely?" He now proceeds to improvise a poem which recreates, in another mood entirely, the spirit of Pai-chang's startling Buddha activity in the Dharma hall.

> Lone bark
> sails by itself
> down moonlight river.
> Turn and look!
> Tender reeds along the bank,
> not even swaying in the current.

Pai-chang enters the hall as this lone bark, moved only by the current of limitless awareness. There are no other boats here, because only the awakened sage can sail free, far out upon this insubstantial moon river. The poem's turning point, *Turn and look,* is parallel to the shout of the master, *O monks,* which caused the spontaneous turning of heads and eyes, an action unconnected with any step-by-step thinking, any habitual affirmation or negation. The tender reeds are disciples standing in rows, newly growing in the ancient river of awakeness, not even swaying in the powerful yet gentle current that whispers continuously: *What is it? What is it?* The primordial non-teaching is always here, flowing around us. Because of its great subtlety, we do not even sway, do not even notice.

After genuinely assimilating their formless spirit, why continue to be obsessed with the forms of various wisdom traditions? Why remain in the realm Buddha Yao-shan calls *habitual affirmation and negation?* Every possible statement, no matter how exalted, remains in this conventional region of affirming and negating, describing and analyzing. Only the infinitely open question without answer, *What is it? What is it?,* can by itself sail free.

closing poem

Black predawn fills
with something like moonlight.
This delicate radiance,
where does it come from?
Cat scratches at zendo door
and goes away.
No way to enter here!

Sound of Wood Preaching Deep Underwater Words

Transmission Thirty-Eight
Yün-yen to Tung-shan

koan

SUCCESSOR: Who can discern nonsentient phenomena preaching Buddha Dharma? Who can hear ancient stone walls proclaim nonduality?

MASTER: Only by going beyond sentience can one hear the pervasive, primordial preaching carried on by nonsentient phenomena.

SUCCESSOR: Can you hear it?

MASTER: Were I presenting it now, you would no longer hear my human presentation of Buddha's teaching.

SUCCESSOR: I do not wish to listen to your presentation of Dharma if it obscures the sound of all phenomena proclaiming Dharma.

MASTER: If you cannot appreciate my teaching, how will you hear the universal teaching flowing from every direction? They are not two!

SUCCESSOR: Now I am awake! How wonderful! The proclamation of nonduality by all phenomena occurs simply through phenomena appearing as phenomena. Before, listening with conventional hearing, I could not hear the sound of the inconceivable. Now, listening with Wisdom Eye open, inconceivability speaks eloquently, everywhere.

SUCCESSOR: That is precisely how it is.

comment

Continuously renouncing conventional experience, successor Tung-shan is on fire with a certain *koan* promulgated by the National Teacher of China. A monk once asked this prominent sage: "What is the Mind of the ancient Buddhas?" He replied: "Fences, walls, roof tiles, and pebbles." The monk was shocked and asked: "Can nonsentient phenomena preach Dharma?" The National Teacher replied: "Certainly the nonsentient preaches—continuously, vigorously, eloquently." "What is the scriptural basis for this assertion?" demanded the monk, lost in his own conceptual mind. The National Teacher responded courteously that no master would ever propound teachings out of harmony with the glorious scriptural record of Buddha's words, and then quoted from the *Avatamsaka Sutra*: "Worlds preach, sentient beings preach, and all phenomena of past, present, and future preach Dharma."

Destined successor Tung-shan has deeply inquired into this *koan* of the nonsentient, both within his own depth and under the guidance of several realized masters. With his entire being, he longs to hear this primordial preaching of nonduality from all directions, throughout all dimensions. By one of his guides, Tung-shan is finally sent to the living Buddha, and the present conversation takes place, following the lines of the National Teacher's *koan*. At one point, to maintain the parallel, Tung-shan even asks Buddha Yün-yen for the scriptural basis. The Awakened One chants in reply a verse from the *Amida Sutra*: "Streams, birds, and trees all praise Buddha and teach Dharma."

Why is the successor awakened by this particular conversation and not by all his previous study and contemplation concerning primordial preaching by nonsentient phenomena? Because his longing to hear universal cosmic praise and to experience universal cosmic enlightenment needed to mature through many causes and conditions. Tung-shan began this intense inquiry as a young boy studying the *Heart Sutra*. Once, when he reached the line, *There is no eye, ear, nose, tongue, body, mind,* he touched his face with one hand and remarked to his teacher: "I have eyes, ears, and nose. Why does the Sutra suggest they do not exist?" The Sutra scholar sensed potential greatness in this remark, which already alludes to the preaching carried on by nonsentient eyes, ears, nose, and tongue. He sent the boy to a Zen master. Tung-shan's long path unfolded gradually. When the young man reached twenty, he became a Buddhist monk, holding his vows, his renunciation of self, in a powerfully uncompromising manner.

Why does Tung-shan attain completion during the present encounter, after so many years of aspiration, practice, assimilation? Why is it only now that he can cry out the same *Now I am awake! How wonderful!* that Shakyamuni proclaimed beneath the Bodhi Tree upon receiving the teaching of nonduality from the nonsentient morning star? Simply because Yün-yen is the living Buddha and Tung-shan his destined successor. Not just the words of the National Teacher or the words of Buddha Yün-yen, but every moment of this and previous lifetimes have made such complete awakening possible. Tung-shan first awakened when he touched his own face as a young boy. The rest is inconceivable deepening.

Were someone to ask me the scriptural basis for this teaching, I would look to the *Prajnaparamita Sutra in 8,000 Lines*: "All phenomena are awakened sages who have put down their burdens by realizing that no burdens were ever put upon them in the first place." The fences, walls, roof tiles, and pebbles mentioned by the National Teacher have put down their burdens in this radical manner, as have the eyes, ears, and other physical sense organs of young Tung-shan or the morning star of Shakyamuni. Having put down burdens, one naturally sings praises. Realizing that there are no burdens in the first place, we hear all phenomena proclaim nonduality and demonstrate Total Awakeness.

This morning Master Keizan extends his generosity beyond all conceivable limits. Perhaps it is because this particular transmission, although undifferentiable in essence from other transmissions of Light, represents the beginning of the profound Soto Way. The syllable *to* of Soto points to the primacy of Buddha Tung-shan, the first full moon of the Soto lineage. States Keizan Zenji, without ambiguity: "Because he understood the true nature of the nonsentient, Tung-shan generated the extensive Soto tradition." More than a thousand years after this thirty-eighth living Buddha, this radiant full moon Tung-shan, the Soto Order remains the most extensive manifestation of Zen in Japan, and has arrived in the West as a gentle rain of spiritual plenitude, slowly soaking the thirsty soil of the modern world. Soto is the primordial preaching of a rain that falls quietly, almost imperceptibly. The soil is completely soaked with Buddha nature.

What is meant by *nonsentient*? Keizan Roshi saves us years of misguided contemplation: "People usually think what is *nonsentient* must be fences, walls, roof tiles, and pebbles. But that is not what the National Teacher's reply is really indicating." The key is found in the monk's original question: "What is the Mind of the ancient Buddhas?" By mentioning the *nonsentient,* the National Teacher is pointing directly to primordial Mind, not to rooftiles or stone walls. In Tibetan Tantra, this primal space is called *the one supremely subtle fundamental innate mind of clear light.* Zen masters call it *the subtle consciousness which has no connection to thinking yet remains keenly aware.* This has nothing to do with some romantic notion of pebbles preaching sermons in rushing streams. Zen is not a religion of earthly nature but of Buddha nature, the Light that always shines. Yet what appears to us as earthly nature is Buddha nature as well. Cries out the living Buddha: *They are not two!*

The characteristics of sentience are reaching, striving, feeling, grasping, thinking. Primordial Mind does not engage in any such activity. Mind is the pure potential for sentience, infinitely more sentient, or keenly aware, than sentient beings, who are veiled by innumerable conditions, primarily the supposed separation between subject and object. Therefore, the playful National Teacher speaks about Mind as the nonsentient, because Mind does not run in search of experience, any more than a tile or a pebble does. Here *nonsentient* really means *supersentient.* This supremely subtle awareness, free and clear from any of the busy workings of consciousness or sentience, is what preaches Buddha Dharma, while appearing as moss-covered rocks, as venerable Sutras, as brown-robed Zen masters.

This keen awareness, this pure alertness or openness, Keizan Zenji describes as "the One who appears magnificently—very bright, never dark." Mind is the primal proclamation of Buddha Dharma by all phenomena. Why? Because primordial Mind manifests as all phenomena. Simply to manifest is to preach Dharma. Manifestation is already nonduality. It is certainly not this mouth that preaches, nor this pen, nor this Buddha image, nor these rain-drops. It is primordial Mind—invisible, actionless—that preaches continuously, effortlessly, from all directions at once.

The Mind of the ancient Buddhas is calm and radiant, here and now. It is the full moon always shining, neither sublime nor ordinary. Do not try to hear its primordial preaching with these two ears or to think about it with this linear mind. Do not try to establish categories or abolish categories. "Listen with Wisdom Eye open," as Tung-shan was inspired to say at the moment of Great Awakening.

Primordial Mind is inconceivability. A strangely powerful inconceivability that opens, plays, transforms, awakens. It is tangible, not abstract. Direct, not indirect. Utterly unconnected with any thinking process, Mind is nevertheless clear and distinct. Preaching compassionately through all phenomena, simply by revealing itself as all phenomena, Mind remains perfectly still, like the emptiness of an infinite jar, impossible to fill. An emptiness which is not merely passive but actively receptive, wonderfully creative. Yet primordial Mind never labors at any task. It does not even exist, because it is more primal than existence, more pristine than original being or original non-being. We can never distance ourselves even slightly from primordial Mind. Can Mind ignore Mind?

Keizan, mother of Japanese Soto Zen, kindly elucidates: "By revealing everything and being revealed by everything, including the croaking of bullfrogs and the sound of earthworms, it preaches keenly and ceaselessly. It makes one raise the eyebrows and blink. It makes one walk, stand, sit, lie down, become confused, die here and be born there, eat when hungry and sleep when tired. All this functioning is the *nonsentient* preaching Dharma." What a marvelous contemplative life: ceaseless Zen talk and Zen walk, continuous Zen sitting and Zen breathing, always overflowing with inexhaustible tender compassion, the honey of Mahayana. This is not only our life but the life of the entire universe.

When Tung-shan, now unveiled as the next living Buddha, leaves the monastery of his master to wander in search of his own destined successor, there is still a faint hesitation in his being. On parting, he asks Buddha Yün-yen: "After you disappear from this earth and people begin to ask me about your core teaching, what will I say?" Yün-yen pauses imperceptibly and then softly intones: *Just this! Just this!* At this moment, the successor hesitates. The old sage perceives it and warmly encourages Tung-shan: "You must be extremely careful and thorough in realizing *Just this!*"

Traveling on foot through green mountains, pondering *Just this!*, Buddha Tung-shan, while wading across a clear stream, suddenly perceives the reflection of his own face in the swiftly flowing water. His subtle hesitation evaporates, and he is now prepared to accomplish the transmission of Light. He sings in quiet ecstasy:

> Why seek Mind
> somewhere else?
> Wandering freely, I meet
> my own true nature everywhere,
> through all phenomena.
> I cannot become it,
> for it is already me.

The Mind of the ancient Buddhas appears as stone walls, stream-smoothed boulders, clear Sutra verses, unique human faces. But is this reflection really something other than the original? Of course not! Both original and reflection are *just this*. Here is the very depth of inconceivability. Taste it! Smell it! Touch it! See it! Hear it!

closing poem

> While expressing this koan
> with human tongue,
> I hear the fish-shaped
> wooden drum,
> whole beats throbbing,
> passing easily
> through floors, walls, doors,
> the sound of wood preaching
> deep underwater words.

WHOLE BODY POURS WITH PERSPIRATION

TRANSMISSION THIRTY-NINE
TUNG-SHAN TO TAO-YING

koan

The First Soto Ancestor invites the second full moon of Soto into his private chambers and inquires in a penetrating manner: "What is your name?" Without any hesitation, the brimful vessel of Light responds: "Tao-ying." With a joyous smile the old sage asks: "What is your name beyond all stages of evolution, beyond all states of realization?" The next living Buddha replies with great clarity: "Speaking from beyond all perspective, Tao-ying can no longer say *I am Tao-ying.*" With intense enthusiasm the Awakened One proclaims: "This is precisely the same spirit with which I responded to my own guide. Thanks to you, beloved friend, my way of fullness will expand past all horizons."

comment

The present transmission makes clear that Light always flows in both directions. There is a secret equilibrium, mutuality, and even equivalence between one living Buddha and the next. But here the innermost secret is revealed. There is really no Great Awakening. Tao-ying is already total Tao-ying. The successor does not cry out in ecstasy. It is the master who experiences bliss, offering profound gratitude to the successor. Buddha Tung-shan identifies completely with his successor, rather than encouraging the successor to identify with him. *This is precisely the same spirit with which I responded to my own guide.*

Even as a young monk, Tao-ying had no taste for those Sutras which provisionally acknowledge limitation. From his birthless birth, he was always the full moon. He encountered various Zen teachers, manifesting for them his attitude of effortless fullness, free from any notion of path or cultivation, and was always recognized by them. Once during their intimate friendship, Buddha Tung-shan pushed his destined successor toward the provisional acknowledgment of some spiritual path, some process of gradual evolution. "If there were no path, how could you have come to me?" probed the old sage. Tao-ying replied instantly: "If there were a path separate from enlightenment, we would never have met." Great ones meet only as the light of the full moon.

The subject of this *koan* is relative and absolute, *name* and *beyond name*, both dimensions being equally profound, equally original. The first question in this Dharma dialogue unveils the depth of Tao-ying's realization of relative truth. The living Buddha already knows his successor's name. *What is your name?* is a form of relentless probing. The response of one previous successor to this very question was *I am essence, not name.* Yet Tao-ying does not, even subtly, take refuge in the essential realm. He remains just Tao-ying. This is what Keizan Roshi calls his *great functioning.* He remains totally and nakedly focused in the relative realm of compassionate activity. This is why the old sage smiles joyously, knowing that his successor will spread the teaching of unobstructed fullness everywhere. This is how Soto Zen remains vibrant today in the entirely different worlds, Japan and America. From the moment that one sits on the round cushion in simple *zazen,* the universe, while remaining just the universe, is already the full moon of nonduality, floating peacefully in the black sky of Mother Wisdom.

The central question of the present Buddha to his successor, therefore, is the first one. *What is your name?* The radically simple response, *Tao-ying,* free from any absolutizing tendency, causes the master to smile, confirming his successor's awakening. Even before posing the second question, relating to absolute truth, Buddha Tung-shan already accepts Tao-ying as an Awakened One. In his response to the *beyond name* probe, Tao-ying still playfully mentions his relative name: "Tao-ying can no longer say *I am Tao-ying.*" Once more we see his great functioning, his intimate, tender, humorous connection with the karmic careers of all beloved beings, even when he is referring to the wordless transparency beyond stages, states, structures, events.

As a sage so deeply identified with relativity, Tao-ying's compassion is intense, even revolutionary. Once his master quoted a *koan* which concluded: "There is no Maitreya in the celestial realm or upon the earth." Tao-ying fiercely responded: "If there is no Maitreya in heaven or on earth, then what is the meaning of the name Maitreya?" Again, Tao-ying's emphasis is on *name,* immanence, not on *beyond name,* the transcendence toward which this Maitreya *koan* is directed. The Sanskrit name Maitreya derives from the verbal root that indicates love and friendship. Just in order to emphasize ultimacy as open, substanceless expanse, how can one insist that there is no Maitreya, no love and friendship, in heaven or on earth? This is unacceptable to Tao-ying. When the living Buddha receives this answering probe from his successor, *Then what is the meaning of the name Maitreya?,* his Zen seat quakes and his whole body pours with perspiration. As Keizan Roshi points out, such an event is rare, both now and in the distant past. Usually the master makes the successor sweat, not the other way around. Buddha Tung-shan greatly celebrates this reversal of roles. As Keizan comments about their relationship: "Here there is no difference in level between questions and answers of master and disciple." Exclaims the living Buddha happily about his successor: "Not one thousand sages, not even ten thousand sages, will be able to restrain him." Tao-ying's enlightened compassion that reveals relativity itself as the full moon, the plenitude of awakeness, will be forever victorious over every form of projection, limitation, superstition. Effortlessly victorious. Pervasively victorious. Later, on Tao-ying's own Dharma mountain, both lay and monastic practitioners in great numbers gather and awaken.

Each sacred tradition holds together *name* and *beyond name* in a unique manner. In ancient Jewish tradition, the ultimate Name can be spoken only once a year by one person in the empty space of the most inner sanctum. Thus *name* merges with *beyond name,* and is ultimately lost there. Saints and sages often incline more to one side than to the other, experiencing a personal predilection for *name* or for *beyond name.* Tao-ying demonstrates both relative and absolute in fullness, because for him they are not two. On one side, he is simply *Tao-ying.* On the other, he is *Tao-ying can no longer say.* This appearance of the relative name, *Tao-ying,* on both sides, indicates the unique Soto approach. Relativity is already Total Awakeness. It does not need to be merged into some other experience of ultimacy.

Before offering his closing poem this morning, Keizan Roshi pauses to ponder. The elegant verse comes forth by itself:

> Never has reality been bound
> by *name* or *beyond name*.
> How can one speak
> of here or beyond?

Precisely because reality is beyond name can we say that neither *name* nor *beyond name* can characterize it. Certain masters of Zen lean toward *beyond name* for their basic mode of expression—not to absolutize but rather to emphasize the equivalence of *name* and *beyond name*. In the Soto teaching of immediate fullness, however, great functioning, or Great Compassion, is a fusion of *name* and *beyond name* coming from the unexpected direction of *name*.

If *name* and *beyond name* are not two, we cannot even speak of union or fusion. Beyond all stages of spiritual evolution, here is Tao-ying calmly reporting: "Tao-ying can no longer say *I am Tao-ying*." Is he here and beyond? No. There is no *here*, no *beyond*. This is what Keizan Zenji hints at during his discourse: "It is extremely difficult to reach this realm." Our guide is not referring to some other, vastly higher realm, but to the unreachable realmlessness of great functioning. When the successor caused his master's sacred seat to rock and his venerable body to sweat, as Keizan says, "Tao-ying put his great functioning into motion." This *hereness* beyond *here* and *beyond* shakes the universe and immediately awakens all beings as living Buddhas.

Sometimes Zen teachers speak of great functioning as *nonaction*, but this simply means *superaction* or Buddha activity. An intensely spinning top appears perfectly still. The greatly kind and friendly Soto sage breathes in *beyond name* in order to breathe out *name*. This very breath is illuminating wisdom and healing compassion. This is our own precious life-breath. Day and night, we meditate upon it!

closing poem

> Manifest the universe
> as a teapot and pour hot tea
> from the spout of your finger
> into the cup of my bare hand
> without spilling or scalding.
> Sit, stand, walk, bow
> as gentle Soto rain—
> falling, falling.

PREGNANT JADE RABBIT ENTERS PURPLE SKY

TRANSMISSION FORTY
TAO-YING TO TAO-P'I

koan

The living Buddha enters the Dharma hall and remarks to the assembled practitioners: "If you wish to attain a limitless result, you must become a limitless being. Since you already are such a being, why become anxious to bring about any such result?" Upon receiving this transmission of boundless clarity, the master's attendant and destined successor, standing at his right hand, awakens as the Original One.

comment

Tao-ying transmits to Tao-p'i. Great Way transmits to Great Way. Tao to Tao. There is nothing entering here from the outside. Buddha Tao-ying is very firm about maintaining this radical simplicity. He admonishes: "You monks speak too much. You vomit words. The thoroughly awakened person becomes still as a fan in winter. Moss grows over the lips. This silence involves no effort at restraint. It is a natural expression." Not a vow of silence but an awakening to nonduality. Nothing new. Nothing outside. Nothing other.

Later, as living Buddha, successor Tao-p'i used to say, when engaged in radiating the plenitude of Soto Zen: "If you seek the Great Way from someone else, you will wander further and further away from it." We already are the Great Way, the Original One. To seek elsewhere for this One would be as absurd as avidly searching for our own head. Only someone drunk, insane, or wandering through contemplative states would do that. Therefore, the path of spiritual cultivation, in all its forms, is a kind of drunken insanity. We strive desperately to enter certain *samadhis*, certain states of concentration or absorption, in order to attain what we already are. Buddha Tao-p'i playfully refers to this imaginary and absurd process: "Pregnant jade rabbit enters purple sky."

During his Zen talk this morning, the motherly Keizan treats with gentleness and kindness this strange disease of anxious or ambitious seeking: "Even though you are mistakenly looking for your own head, this very process of looking around is itself your head." We never get away from our own head, no matter how peculiar our thinking may become. There is not a single moment when we are not the Original One that we are and that all beings are. The diamond with infinite facets.

To elucidate this transmission of Light, Master Keizan, Fourth Ancestor of Japanese Soto, quotes Dogen Zenji, First Ancestor of Japanese Soto: "Who am I? I am the one who asks who I am." We are not some separate entity or distinct set of relations which can be designated *I am*. We are the Original One who asks *Who am I?* The One whose asking alone constitutes its own limitless awareness. We are not statements: *I am this, I am that.* We are the single, infinitely unfolding question, *Who am I?* This unique question can never receive any finite response and never expects any finite response. We are this boundless clarity, free from answers, free from doctrine.

As our beloved guide hints in his closing poem: "Seeking it with empty hands, one returns with empty hands. When fundamentally nothing is acquired, one actually acquires it." We should consider this verse carefully. There is indeed authentic seeking, but it is a completely open seeking, with open hands, not a seeking which attempts to grasp or cognize some object imagined to be the goal of seeking. In this nondual sense of seeking, we definitely must seek the Great Way. To rely on anyone or anything other than our own immediate awareness—to rely on any religion, on any form of thinking—would be to lose touch with the intense intimacy we already have with the Original One, the unexpected intimacy of identity. There is also genuine spiritual evolution, but this is a spontaneous, natural unfolding, without pushing or presupposition. It is not our habitual form of acquiring, by which something else or something new is taken into ourselves and then called our own.

Keizan Roshi mentions the incident of a Zen master who sees one of his mature students coming to visit. The illumined sage immediately enters his room and shuts the door. Although he has noticed the sage retire, the student possesses enough confidence to approach the door and knock firmly. From inside a thunderous voice is heard: "Who is it?" Just as powerfully, the disciple responds with his own name, Liang-ts'ui, and at that moment is fully awakened. Our own names, even though they function in the world of convention, are also names of the Original One who asks the limitless question, *Who am I?* We are intimate with this Original One moment by moment, naturally, even when responding to our personal name. The enlightened Liang-ts'ui then throws open the door to his master's private chambers and exclaims: "How wonderful! You cannot deceive me any longer with such notions as *teacher, disciple, practice, enlightenment.* If I had not come to offer respect to you this morning, I might have wasted my whole life studying Sutras and going through the motions of monastic discipline." We must come to our guide with deep, loving respect, but all notions of *coming* and *going* will eventually dissolve in the presence of this intense light with a human face. Such is the untransmittable transmission.

Sutras basically teach non-self. Clear, brilliant, ever-present awareness, or Original Self, bears no resemblance at all to the imaginal self-entity clearly refuted by the Sutras. The Sutra teaching of non-self is therefore extraneous to that Original Self. Non-self is the teaching, whereas Original Self is the reality behind the teaching. If we seek Total Awakeness somewhere else or from someone else, even from the noble Sutra teaching of Lord Buddha, we will wander farther and farther away from it.

Keizan Roshi exclaims in the ecstasy of awakeness: "Throw out *right* and *wrong!* Do not depend on others or even get involved with them!" Is this nihilistic teaching? Must we reject Sutra study, guidance from the master, meditation, compassionate action? Certainly not! How could the Great Way become negative or exclusionary? All these activities are perfect expressions of the Original One, but we must live as the Original, not as its reflection. Keizan Zenji reveals that Original Self shines brighter than the sun. It remains pristine as newly falling snow. It has never been absent, not even for an instant. Even our strange anxiety about finding it is simply an expression of this brightness, this alertness, this vividness, this purity. The practice of *zazen* and the sacraments of other wisdom traditions are simply limitless awareness approaching itself, appreciating itself, being itself.

Original Self alone shines as the play of the senses. As conscience, it clearly illuminates *right* and *wrong,* inspiring us to study Sutra teachings and engage in moral disciplines. But we are Original Self, not definitions or disciplines or sense experience. We are this inexhaustible radiance without boundary. This delicate, perpetual dawn. This alone is to be realized.

The Original One is not *no one.* When the successor is awake, he or she is a living Buddha, not *no one.* The contemporary Zen teacher who signed his letters *no one special* was nonetheless not *no one.* Master and successor are two names for the same Original, which is not infinite absence but infinite presence. There is never any actual lack or blindness, only imaged lack and imagined blindness. Upon awakening, we know this without even a breath of anxious hesitation.

Advises our kind and careful guide: "Do not sit alone, immobile, without thought of self or others, without mind at all, unconnected with living beings." This is Master Keizan's clear warning against nihilism. The Original One is wonderfully active compassion, intimate with every detail of existence. Never mindless. Let us not indulge in some romantic or aesthetic notion of Zen as flowers, grasses, mountains, rivers. Calling out our own names, let us be this primal radiance, this living Buddha in loving identity with all beings. Right now! Ours is Living Buddha Zen.

O sisters and brothers, be soaked with that bright awareness, like walking for hours through a rain so gentle as to be imperceptible. Do not push. That creates a downpour in which life-giving water carries away topsoil rather than impregnating it. Keep palms open. Keep *Who am I?* open. Simply by being complete, spread Soto extensively. No words are necessary. Nor is there any final horizon. Remember

the sage of eighty years, with many experiences of Great Enlightenment behind him, who proclaimed: "Only now am I beginning to
act according to what I see."

closing poem

> Pushing toward the Original One,
> filled with *I am that One,*
> standing too abruptly,
> walking through the zendo artificially,
> so much karma, so much conditioning.
> "Just let it unfold," says the master.
> Ah, gentle rain falling!

ALL IS GREAT PEACE FROM THE VERY BEGINNING

TRANSMISSION FORTY-ONE
TAO-P'I TO KUAN-CHIH

koan

The destined successor, already well seasoned, boldly addresses the living Buddha: "Ancient sages say, *I cannot love conventional conceptions and mundane appearances.* Revered master, what do you love?" The Awakened One replies: "I am those ancient sages and have been so from the very beginning." The successor awakens as Original Awakeness, and lovingly embodies the full moon way.

comment

Awakeness is always the basic fact of consciousness itself, existence itself. Enlightened teachings from all traditions point to this surprising fact, as surprising as it is incontrovertible. Soto Zen encourages practitioners to abide solely as this naked fact of awakeness during their long study and practice of Buddha Dharma. Be Original Awakeness from the very beginning! Be a living Buddha! This is the round Soto moon that never wanes.

We must not simply be aware but beware, through constant vigilance, of falling in love with conventional conceptions and mundane appearances. Even the exalted terms that point directly, such as *Soto Zen* or *Great Way,* can become mere convention, mere stipulation. This is adding gold chains to iron chains. The common terms *male* and *female,* for instance, are conventional designations, unrelated to the basic fact of awakeness. *Self* and *other, sentient* and *nonsentient*— such correlative terms indicate divisions that do not exist at all for Original Awakeness. If one becomes obsessed with cultural and personal routines of thought and perception, all forms can become blindness, including the beautiful golden Buddha or the precious human form of the master. For the sage, however, all forms are the clear eyes of freedom.

Even advanced contemplative experience of formlessness can create subtle conceptual conventions. By falling obsessively in love with formlessness, one becomes a demon in a dark cave, as our ancient Japanese guide sternly reminds us. If we become enamored with no-mind, we will be reborn after biological death into one of the tranquil formless realms. After abiding there for eons without experiencing active compassion for suffering beings, we will eventually fall into the narrow realms of embodiment that result from avoidance or denial of compassion.

"What do you love?" asks the profoundly compassionate successor, who loves all beings truly by seeking the complete and immediate enlightenment which includes them all. The master's reply reveals the existence of this enlightenment *from the very beginning.* He identifies completely with the perennial sages of humanity who *cannot love conventional conceptions and mundane appearances,* thereby implying that what he does love is uncommon, extraordinary, spontaneous reality. He loves reality by being reality. This indescribable reality has always been reality. There was no moment during which Buddha Tao-p'i became reality, any more than there was a moment when reality became reality.

Our generous Roshi Keizan clearly points to reality in his closing poem which, as he advises us, should be received by our intuition in the same mode that we experience ourselves before we project any physical body or any physical world.

> Light of mind-moon,
> colors of eye-flower—
> pure brilliance, wonderful splendor.
> They shine forth simultaneously
> beyond any conception of temporality.
> Who can appreciate them truly?

This inexhaustible reality to which and as which all Awakened Ones awaken is simultaneously mind-moon and eye-flower, simultaneously absolute and relative, simultaneously still, formless radiance and the colorful play of appearances. There is no trace of our habitual conception of time here, nor our common conceptions, *form* or *formless*. The eye-flower world, astonishingly diverse, is fresh and clear as a rainbow. Elusive as a rainbow, it is transparent play. Never opaque, substantial, solid, cold. The mind-moon is round. Total. Nothing missing. No multiple dimensions.

Our ancient Japanese guide indicates that Extraordinary Reality has nothing to do with the ordinary physical body as we habitually conceive and then perceive it. Nothing to do with ordinary subject-object consciousness, conditioned by cultural and personal conceptions of individuality and polity. Nothing to do with habitual conceptual oppositions between dreaming and waking, delusion and enlightenment. What could be more conventional than our notions of purity and impurity? Is the moon pure or impure?

Keizan Roshi cries out: "Who can appreciate this extraordinary awakeness-world, this rainbow world of timeless play? Who can experience extraordinary compassion, extraordinary beauty? Who can love truly?" Infatuated by its own convention of no-mind, false Zen might respond: "There is no one to appreciate it and nothing to appreciate." Such a perverted view, masquerading as true non-view, is no less than a capital crime committed against humanity. It not only fatally confines the misguided practitioner within the Demon Cave, but attempts to attract others into this dark imprisonment, made all the darker by considering itself enlightened.

Who actually exists—in the most extraordinary sense of existence—to appreciate this mind-moon-eye-flower? The countless living Buddhas. With ecstatic wisdom, successor Kuan-chih proclaims: "Their singing can be heard for ten thousand miles, celebrating Great Peace." Keizan Zenji expands: "There is not a speck of dust for ten thousand miles. Where are clever officials and fierce generals now? There is only singing, singing. All is Great Peace from the very beginning."

This uncommon, unexpected singing is heard clearly across ten thousand years, ten thousand eons. It is sometimes called *uninterrupted Dharma transmission*. The singers are diamond beings, celebrating nonduality. Every living being joins the chorus with its own natural tone. Throughout extraordinary mirror space and extraordinary rainbow time, mind-moon and eye-flower are one. The conventional terms *absolute* and *relative* simply melt away like mist into the powerful sunlight of this non-numerical oneness. Every unique style of every empowered lineage within every sacred tradition sees by mind-moon-eye-flower, enjoys mind-moon-eye-flower, awakens as mind-moon-eye-flower.

The Sufi lover is intoxicated with selfless love for the Beloved. The Zen sage intensely breathes Great Peace. Sometimes they reverse roles. What a wonderful play of colors! To erase these colors with some abstract notion of transcendence or essence would be destructive. Even murderous. Let members of all spiritual families blossom uniquely. Let earthly species evolve uniquely. Let subtle and heavenly beings praise uniquely. Let Divine Names resound uniquely. All is mind-moon, ever at play as eye-flower. Moon-flowers everywhere! Calls out Keizan: "Here is where you must arrive!"

closing poem

> cold autumn dawn
> burns sky clear
> so many trees
> and colors
> unaccountably
> my heart is singing
> singing

DEEP INTIMACY AND EVEN DEEPER INTIMACY

TRANSMISSION FORTY-TWO
KUAN-CHIH TO YÜAN-KUAN

koan

The destined successor, background unknown, is functioning as attendant to the living Buddha, carrying his ceremonial robe. As they stand together in the Dharma hall, the attendant opens for the master this venerable patchwork robe. The old sage turns and whispers: "What is really going on beneath this robe?" The successor, deeply prepared for the transmission of Light, remains poised in silence. Intensely, the master continues to whisper. "To study and practice the Buddha way without reaching what is beneath the robe creates the greatest pain. Please, ask me the question." The successor repeats the sage's words: "What is really going on beneath this robe?" With almost no sound, the Zen master responds: "Deep intimacy!" Immediately, successor awakens as living Buddha, places the ceremonial robe over the shoulders of his master, and performs three prostrations of gratitude, abundant tears soaking his own upper robe.

MASTER: You have now greatly awakened. But can you express it?
SUCCESSOR: Yes!
MASTER: What is going on beneath this robe of transmission?
SUCCESSOR: Deep intimacy!
MASTER: And even deeper intimacy!

comment

Many spiritually gifted students from the next generation come to the newly unveiled Buddha, Yüan-kuan, and he always expresses, sometimes with tears, this ever-deepening intimacy. But he never puts it into words directly. It is too intimate for words. One aspirant even asks the original question: "What is really going on beneath this robe?" Yüan-kuan instantly responds: "None of the awakened sages can reveal it!" Unless it reveals itself, in its own intimate way, what is profoundly intimate can never be spoken, demonstrated, or expressed.

Keizan Roshi gives a passionate Zen talk this morning, illuminating the inexpressible, inaccessible, yet indispensable nature of true intimacy. "Even if you obliterate your meditation seat with tireless sitting, even if your conduct is immaculate, even if your eloquent Dharma teaching astounds heaven and earth, causing flowers to rain miraculously from the blue sky, even if you annihilate all thoughts and emotions and your body becomes like a dry tree, even if you never lose mindfulness though confronted by disasters, even if you die while sitting in *zazen* and appear to have gained liberation—if you have not reached true intimacy, it is all without value." This Bodhisattva hymn to intimacy, *mitsu* in Japanese, is the same as Saint Paul's hymn to selfless love, *agape* in Greek. "Even if I speak with the greatest human and angelic eloquence, even if I possess prophetic powers and esoteric knowledge, even if I experience the complete faith that can move mountains, even if I renounce all my possessions and allow my body to be burned alive—if I do not truly love, I am nothing but the din of crashing cymbals."

To reach true intimacy is called by Zen sages *to clarify the One Great Matter.* This is what Jesus calls *the one thing needful,* referring to the intimacy of Mary Magdalene with her master, washing his feet with her tears and drying them with her long hair. She is the summit of spiritual intimacy, for both men and women. As the Gospel reports: "She never ceased kissing his feet." This true intimacy, which never ceases for a moment, which does not care about convention, which cannot be spoken, this *mitsu* which is intensely private and sensitive, this nakedness, described in Japanese as *gen,* as subtle and mysterious, is nonetheless a thorough clarification, a vast clarity. Keizan Zenji hints at this in his closing poem:

> The water is diamond clear
> right to the bottom,
> its clarity the pearl that shines
> without cutting or polishing.

As one glides in a small boat over clear water, the deep sand bottom seems so close. We sense it in our whole body as intimacy. There is nothing particular to see on the bottom. It is simply this clarity and intimacy which inspires us and gives us joy as we gaze into the depth, feeling that we could gaze forever. We expect obscurity in deep water. When we encounter transparency instead, our entire mode of perception is subtly transformed.

There is nothing that needs to be done to make the water clear, to cause the pearl to shine. No cutting or polishing. No study or meditation. Consider an intensely blue sky, without a single cloud intervening. In intimacy, there is nothing intervening, neither subject nor object. As contemporary American Zen Master Tetsugen elucidates: "Intimacy is what remains unnoticed. The fish is truly intimate with water. It breathes water, it swims through currents, it rests only on water, it becomes a perfect expression of water. The fish is not even aware of the water." Saint Paul points to God as "the One in whom we live, move, and have our being."

These are life-giving images. Raising the life-taking sword of Zen, we can say that true intimacy is like the flames of a wildfire meeting a man-made wooden structure. They gradually interpenetrate. The situation is greatly intensified by the powerful wind of longing. Flame and wood become so intimate, they complete consume each other. Conventional structures and revolutionary fire are both reduced to ashes beneath the clear blue sky.

The factor of intensity in this fire of intimacy is very important. Master Keizan pointedly warns us "not to give in to a life of peace and tranquillity." We must not settle down in the comfortable house of our cultural body or in the beautiful temple of our religious contemplation. Our ancient Japanese guide continues: "You must stand on the peak of the highest mountain and walk on the floor of the deepest ocean. Then you will begin to be filled with life." True intimacy is blazing life. Not routinized existence. Not the defensive structure of personality or society. Intimacy is infinite life, living breath by breath.

On fire with intimacy, Keizan Zenji describes *clarifying the One Great Matter* as the spontaneous functioning of all Buddhas, who encourage and empower sentient beings to express their innate awakeness, their pure aliveness that extends far beyond the boundary of biological sentience. The Great Matter is therefore inseparable from Great Compassion. We become lovingly intimate with all consciousness, and live intimately the life of all that lives. Separate, substantial subjects and objects are consumed.

Our generous guide warns: "Even if innumerable living Buddhas were to approach you, offering clarification of the One Great Matter, their inconceivable spiritual power alone could not awaken you. This way of awakening cannot be passed on to children or received from parents. You must awaken to it yourself. Now! In this very moment!" The authentic taste of awakening is intimacy with our own true awareness, our own true depth, our own true body which is, as Master Keizan remarks, open space, without fixed form. Pure water, clear to the bottom. This inimitable taste, *our own,* does not result from isolating some personal subjectivity. The life of every insect is *our own.*

This act of clarifying the One Great Matter has nothing to do with escaping or dismantling karma, whether personal or collective. It has nothing to do with countering the negative impact of the degenerating age in which we now live. It has nothing to do with cultural or religious differences between the Buddhist lands of India, Sri Lanka, China, Tibet, Mongolia, Japan, Korea, Burma, Thailand, Cambodia, Vietnam, and America. Without attraction or repulsion, without reasoning, without seeking, gaze directly into intimacy. Now what? Gaze deeper!

closing poem

> eyes wide open
> gaze straight
> into dawn zendo
> so intimate
> no subject or object
> eyes close part way
> chin drops toward chest
> intensified gaze
> rests on floor
> intimacy deepening

THE VERMILION SAIL IS SO BEAUTIFUL!

TRANSMISSION FORTY-THREE
YÜAN-KUAN TO TA-YANG

koan

The one destined to be the Sixth Soto Ancestor approaches the living Buddha: "Where is the ultimate place of Shakyamuni's enlightenment? Where is the formless *bodhi-mandala*?" Pointing to an ancient scroll on the wall beside him, an icon of the female Buddha, Kuan-Yin, the master remarks simply: "This is the exquisite work of scholar Wu." After intense silence, the successor prepares to speak. In this pregnant moment just before articulation, the old sage rises suddenly from his meditation seat, clasps the disciple by the shoulders, and fiercely whispers: "Here is form! Where is no-form?" Receiving the full transmission of Light, the successor awakens into living Buddhahood.

comment

Dedicated monk since age eighteen, unsurpassable student and debater of Ultimate Meaning Sutras, Ta-yang, traveling here and there to test his own realization, comes to his destined master with both Sutra knowledge and transcendent wisdom. But he has not yet encountered the *bodhi-mandala,* the actual place of Shakyamuni's enlightenment. He is expecting it to be formless. The living Buddha, by pointing out the subtly smiling Kuan-Yin, is attempting to show Ta-yang his own true face, just as the original Soto Ancestor, Tung-shan, saw his own true face mirrored in a mountain stream. But Ta-yang is not quite ready for this direct pointing. Even the great Tung-shan had to leave his monastery and his enlightenment experiences behind before he could see his own personal face as Buddha's facelessness, before he could encounter transparent form itself as the *bodhi-mandala,* the matrix of awakening.

The destined successor starts to reply to his destined master from the level of Sutra knowledge that distinguishes *form* from *no-form*, that seeks a formless *bodhi-mandala* apart from this wonderful mandala of living forms that we see and that we are. Mercifully, the old sage stops Ta-yang at the moment before articulation. This very moment is his own true face before he is conceived, before conceptuality. The dimensions *form* and *no-form* are not separated here—not by the distance of a single atom, not by the play of a single concept. His master's intense countenance, so close to his own, becomes the compassionate mirror, Mother Kuan-Yin. Naked awareness. The successor is awakened suddenly from his metaphysical dream of *form* and *no-form*, just as we would awaken from sleep if someone clasped us vigorously by the shoulders.

MASTER: You are awake! Say something!

SUCCESSOR: I am not avoiding speech. I only hesitate to form words because someone may write them down someday

MASTER (laughing): What you have just said will be engraved in stone.

Whatever is written down is now suspected by Ta-yang to be part of formal Sutra knowledge, including such fabrications as *form* and *no-form*. The successor has indeed awakened from his dream of separating various realms, enumerating various categories, debating various positions. The playful sage is reassuring him here that it does not create obscuration to express realmlessness or inconceivability by means of written and spoken words. Even engraving his present comments in stone will not reintroduce any conceptualization. The new living Buddha is now free to move in any direction, through what may appear as speech or silence, form or no-form. He is free to use spoken and written words to encourage awakening in others, without generating the faintest imprint of self and other. Sutras and Tantras have now come alive—breathing, walking, talking, standing, sitting, eating, eliminating, washing, sleeping, waking, meditating.

Buddha Ta-yang exercises this spiritual freedom immediately by uttering a poem. The last line is most suggestive: "Black bird, released at night, soars clothed in snow." Even the ultimate experience of formlessness—the black bird, released from the cage of conventional conception, flying freely through impenetrable midnight darkness of transcendent wisdom—will still be clothed in the radiance of form. There simply is no separation between *form* and *no-form*.

In the spontaneous verse which overflows from his mother heart this morning, Keizan Roshi generously offers another image.

> Mind-mirror hangs high
> yet reflects structures clearly.
> The vermilion sail is so beautiful!
> It can never be the subject of a painting!

The infinite mind-mirror is not an empty mirror. It brims with beings, structures, and events that bubble up out of its spaceless, timeless clarity as from a clear mountain spring. Yet if one tips this mirror, nothing pours out of it. The so-called realm of forms, bright sails moving on the river of space and time, is really formless. No painting can truly represent these darting sails, filled with fresh wind. Even scholar Wu's magnificent painting cannot represent Kuan-Yin. She is suchness. She is pure presence.

This awakening to transparent form is called *seeing without eyes, thinking without mind.* Here is the place of Shakyamuni's enlightenment. Here is Bodhi Tree and morning star. The dynamism of seeing, hearing, holding, and discriminating continues, but there is no substantial form. There are neither senses nor objects of senses within this mirror. Ah, the beauty of these rainbow sails! Vermilion, royal blue, bright as snow in sunlight. Even the amazing art of scholar Wu cannot touch the spontaneous calligraphy and iconography of all lives, all sacred traditions. Our own true face now shines from the infinite mirror of Mind. We are the Mother Buddha, subtly smiling.

The new Soto Ancestor now speaks from the spiritual mood of the perpetual full moon: "The brimful vessel can be turned upside down and still it does not empty. There are no living beings that are hungry." Hearing these words, Buddha Yüan-kuan proclaims joyously to the newly unveiled Buddha Ta-yang: "Tung-shan's tradition will flourish because of you!" The Soto emphasis is that every being and every environment is already perfect and complete, although this completeness is ungraspable, this perfection ineluctable. The Light of transmission is not missing from any stream of awareness, not even for an instant, for this Light simply is awareness.

Rinzai Zen is for aristocratic Samurai warriors. Soto Zen is for peasants. For the whole people. For all beings. There is no trace of elitism here. This is why Soto can spread widely, across every social and religious border. It unveils the intrinsic fullness of all persons, all conscious streams. Soto is not a means to an end, not a path to a goal. Yet this full moon way never dilutes our precious Mahayana compassion with complacency. It only increases our active concern for beings who are starving—starving to know that they are never deprived of their own intrinsic completeness. This full moon way only increases our Dharma activity to reveal to all beings their own plenitude of beingness, their innate reality prior to the apparent arising of form and no-form, body and mind. *There are no living beings that are hungry!* How brightly shines the sixth Soto moon!

What robbery to imagine that only Zen masters experience enlightenment! What crime against the freedom and dignity of humanity! We are all mothers, pregnant with limitless awareness, giving birthless birth, moment by moment. And what absurd claims are made for *no-form* and *no-mind*! Shall we roll up the beautiful scroll painted by scholar Wu? Shall we eliminate brilliant sails from the river? Shall we erase the Sutra of the morning star?

closing poem

> Kuan-Yin smiles
> as sail, sky, sea—
> pouring, pouring
> from a vessel
> never empty

Zen Master Dreams of Raising a Green Hawk

Transmission Forty-Four
Ta-yang to T'ou-tzu

koan

Yuan-chien, acting as representative of the previous living Buddha, instantly recognizes the long-awaited successor and asks him to re-live the following moment from the life of Shakyamuni. An advanced non-Buddhist practitioner once approached the Awakened One and inquired: "What is the reality that is neither speech nor silence?" In response, Lord Buddha manifested through his very being the pristine purity of a cloudless sky. The practitioner was thoroughly awakened, bowed in gratitude, and acknowledged: "You have lifted the veil of my delusion and allowed me to enter."

For three years, the destined successor remains immersed in this vast response of Shakyamuni Buddha. One morning, the teacher perceives the preparedness of the student and requests him to present the spirit of this *koan*. The great practitioner gradually comes forth from the state of profound immersion which has become perfectly natural to him. Just as he is about to speak, the teacher raises his right hand, palm outward, and covers the mouth of the student. Filled with the Light of Shakyamuni's transmission, the new living Buddha is completely awake and performs three deep bows.

comment

Successor T'ou-tzu was such a remarkable child that he left home at age six to live in a monastery, receiving full monastic ordination at fourteen. Buddha Ta-yang senses the presence somewhere in China of his great successor. However, unlike their Indian counterparts who go wandering in search of the successor, the Chinese sages simply wait on their sacred mountains for the destined Dharma inheritor to arrive. As a consequence, Ta-yang passes away before meeting T'ou-tzu in any literal, physical manner.

Before dying, the Soto full moon entrusts his old leather sandals, his self-portrait, and his tattered robe to a brilliant Rinzai teacher, Yuan-chien, requesting him to give these empowered objects to his genuine successor, whenever that highly gifted person should arrive and become deeply awakened.

This teacher, who entirely understands and appreciates the perpetual full moon approach, calls the presence for several years in his Rinzai monastery of the Seventh Soto Ancestor *a golden phoenix lodging in a dragon's nest*. Phoenixes and dragons, although very different in behavior and habitat, are equally powerful, magnificent beings. Keizan Roshi insists that there can be no division of inferior or superior among the five schools of Zen in general and the two great lines of Soto and Rinzai in particular. Dogen Zenji did not want to hear the term *Zen* used to label and thereby subdivide what he simply called the Buddha way. How can the awakening into transparent selflessness be infused with *my school* and *your school, sudden* and *gradual*?

The fullness of Shakyamuni Buddha is present in the transmission to his forty-third successor, Ta-yang. Why should the fullness of Buddha Ta-yang not be present in his transmission to successor T'ou-tzu through the intermediary teacher, Yuan-chien? We are seated face to face with Shakyamuni Buddha during each of the fifty-two transmissions of boundless clarity presented by Keizan Zenji. Why hesitate to accept the present transmission as coming face to face to Buddha T'ou-tzu from Buddha Ta-yang, even in the master's physical absence?

By participating intimately in this *denkoroku*, this record of the transmission of Light, we are also face to face with beloved Master Keizan. He is sitting before us this morning as brown-robed Tetsugen Sensei, born in America, eighty-first generation of Shakyamuni's transmission of the single Light. Some seven hundred years that appear to separate us from our ancient Japanese guide have melted away like morning mist before the irresistible sun. Can Shakyamuni, Keizan, and Tetsugen possibly be of two minds or three minds? How can there be the slightest twoness in the flow of an authentic transmission of nonduality, a transmission which does not distinguish past, present, or future, which does not separate master and disciple?

Strangely enough, T'ou-tzu is awakened in precisely the same manner as his Buddha Ancestor Ta-yang, further confirming the karmic destiny that links them, further demonstrating that Dharma transmission is not a patchwork of limited human efforts, no matter how sincere, but the pure current of Shakyamuni's original enlightenment, uninterrupted by the limitations of society or personality, essentially untouched by the factor of historical accident. The transmission is of indubitability. It is without beginning, middle, end.

Both living Buddhas, Ta-yang and T'ou-tzu, were silenced just as they were on the verge of speaking about the unspeakable, and instead were unveiled as unspeakable reality itself. An awakened sage can, of course, speak about the unspeakable. Effortlessly. Briefly or at length. We encounter such Buddha speech constantly in our study of Dharma transmission. But first there must be the clear realization of identity with that reality unrelated to speech or to silence. As Master Keizan elucidates: "If you cannot say reality is anything at all, how can you say it is silence?"

The present transmission is even more intimate than in the case of Ta-yang, whose master rose from his meditation seat to clasp the shoulders of the disciple, preventing him at the very last moment from speaking. Yuan-chien simply raises his open palm before the successor's lips. Less than one arm's length between them. No reaching. No word spoken. Just a concise gesture, accomplished easily, right where one is. But this silencing motion, in both instances, is extremely swift. The awakened sage must catch the precise instant when the inner silence, or preparedness, of the successor is spontaneously coming into speech in order to affirm itself as silence, coming into form in order to proclaim itself formless. The answer is going to be correct. But still it must be cut off, exploded, dissolved. Otherwise, it will stand in our way as the correct answer. Only cloudless sky allows us to enter.

Even the most sublime concentration must be removed, along

with the slightest trace of habitual perception. The lay master Vimalakirti, after playfully debating and refuting the *correct answers* of Lord Buddha's direct disciples, is faced by Wisdom Deity Manjushri, who completely rejects all verbal expression and recommends ultimate silence. Vimalakirti, who is a living Buddha, dismisses with a gaze even this divine teaching on silence. There is only the radiant black womb of Prajnaparamita, Mother of the Buddhas.

Shakyamuni does not present silence as his answer to the query of the advanced non-Buddhist, for this aspirant is clearly inquiring about *the reality that is neither speech nor silence.* The Awakened One manifests the borderless, traceless sky of nonduality. Lord Buddha's response is not, strictly speaking, a response at all. It is stillness beneath ocean waves, roots beneath splendid blossoms.

Through this sudden gesture, the outstretched palm of his compassionate guide, T'ou-tzu in turn awakens beyond speech and silence, whether they are viewed as opposites or correlates. Buddha Tou-tzu awakens as perpetual plenitude.

Both singing and keeping still, Keizan Zenji offers his closing poem this morning: "Only birds can fly over the sharp outline of the mountains against the dawn sky. Who can walk along a sharp sword edge?" Yet when the birds reach the peaks, they find not a sharp line but a vast landscape, range after mountain range, covered with pine trees, filled with rushing streams. When someone actually reaches the realmless realm—*not speech, not silence*—this sword edge provides plenty of space to walk comfortably. Even to dance or run in all directions. Here are leather sandals, self-portrait, and Zen robe of *plenty space,* transmitted without any particular words, without any particular meditation.

Successor T'ou-tzu began as a youth with rigorous training in *abhidharma,* the metaphysical analysis of experience into its subtle components. Then he advanced to the study of the *Avatamsaka Sutra,* the consummate presentation of the cosmic wholeness of experience. One day, while contemplating the Sutra phrase, *essential nature of mind,* the destined inheritor intensely questioned how Dharma transmission can come through words and letters, through reasoning, through intuitive thinking, or through any form of concentration or contemplation.

Finally entering the Zen mountains, he encounters Yuan-chien waiting for him. On the very night before the successor arrives, the Zen master dreams of raising a green hawk. Although itself the colors of forest and rice field, this bird's natural habitat is the colorless sky of self-luminous awareness.

T'ou-tzu is asked immediately by his Rinzai teacher to enter deeply into Lord Buddha's nondual response—the cloudless sky. He remains waiting for three years within this boundless expanse. Finally, one bright morning, both speech and silence are momentarily suspended and the new living Buddha awakens beyond light and darkness, beyond relative and absolute. The green hawk leaves the green mountain, never to touch down again.

closing poem

> "Will the transmission be broken?"
> Soto moon never sets!
> We are always face to face!

I AM TERRIBLY ASHAMED TO BE CALLED THE HEAD OF THIS MONASTERY

TRANSMISSION FORTY-FIVE
T'OU-TZU TO TAO-K'AI

koan

The one destined to be the next vessel of Light approaches the living Buddha of his generation and boldly asks: "The words of ancient Buddha Ancestors have become commonly accepted, like ordinary tea and ordinary rice. Is there any special delicacy to attract new generations to the teaching of nonduality?" With even greater boldness, the Awakened One replies: "Do you imagine that the power of a living emperor to declare laws in his own kingdom depends on what emperors of ancient history may have once declared?"

The successor immediately sees the truth of radical presence, radical freedom, radical unrepeatability. He opens his mouth to express this truth in an appropriate way. Like a flash of lightning, the old sage swings his *hossu*. The long white horsehairs of the ceremonial whisk gently brush the lips of the successor. Smiling, the master comments: "The moment you consider any partial expression, you are subject to thirty blows!" The disciple, now totally awake, bows in profound gratitude, ceases to be a disciple, turns and walks away.

"Have you finally reached the realm of no doubt?" the playful sage calls after him. Without pausing or looking back, the new living Buddha places his hands over his ears.

comment

This is the third transmission in a row where successor is prevented by master from offering an insightful answer, and is thereby awakened from the partial to the complete. Whatever verbal response is offered, no matter how profound, will inevitably remain a partial expression of nonduality. To keep silence is also only partial. No wise words should come forth from the mouth, nor should wonderful

Dharma words be allowed to enter the ears. This is the nondual silence beyond speech and silence.

The implication of this *koan* is that Buddha expression must be fresh for every generation. Teachings never heard before. Nothing common or stale. No servile reliance on the words of ancient scriptures, the declarations of ancient emperors. But these revolutionary new expressions must be cut away with the Zen sword just before they manifest, unveiling instead Original Awakening, plain and simple. Following this timeless moment of awakening, any words whatsoever can be used, traditional or not. Or no words need be used. The everyday life of the sage becomes the deepest teaching. No brilliant philosophy. Ordinary tea and ordinary rice are fine.

There are three kinds of Dharma words: revealed Sutra, inspired commentary on Sutra, and direct response to reality. All three should be carefully chewed by the practitioner, reduced to essence, swallowed, and thoroughly digested. This creates a balanced diet. When fully assimilated, these three modes of expression will come forth as the very being of the sage, as the confident declarations of a living emperor. This approach does not favor silence over words or words over silence. What is really meant by silence is to be uncluttered by partial expressions. Spiritual completeness is self-authenticating, free from any obligatory reference to master or tradition.

This blow from the Zen whisk which, along with Zen stick and Zen staff, is a sacramental form of Buddha's body, is not punishment. It is not even some signal to remain silent. It is the most intimate gesture of confirmation: "You are already full and complete. You have been so from beginningless time. You and I are the same body of the Buddha. There is no need for any partial expression. In fact, there is no possibility of any partial expression. At the center of the sun, there is neither night nor day."

The mouth is an especially intimate part of the person. Here the *hossu,* the Buddha's long hair, touches the lips of the successor in a mysterious gesture of identity. The Eighth Soto Ancestor, Tao-k'ai, is thus confirmed as living Buddha, as conscious fullness. The all-embracing presence and open freedom of humanity is Buddha. Elucidates Keizan Roshi in his closing poem this morning:

No powder for this face.
There is no imperfection.
Completely natural appreciation
for the most sublime ornament,
our own humanity—
jade bones filled with light.

Reality is a perpetually full moon without the slightest stain or flaw. Fully awakened humanity is the most beautiful expression of reality. The one fundamental innate Mind of Clear Light shines through the translucent human form. Humanity simply is this diamond clarity, this round Soto moon. Even our flesh and bones are luminous. The appreciation of this basic fact is natural and spontaneous. A beautiful sunset or sunrise does not need to be called *beautiful* or called attention to in any way. Words like *enlightenment* or *Buddha nature* need not be applied like cosmetics to this flawless face. Jade manifests its own inner lustre. Should we lacquer it gold?

The newly unveiled Buddha Tao-k'ai becomes more and more mature in the limitless expanse of the Great Way. He does not care about green meadows and bright streams, meditative states and eloquent teachings. His widespread recognition as an enlightened sage appears to him merely like summer dust that irritates the eyes. He does not care about the external form of his monastic community. Sometimes small, sometimes large. The living Buddha makes no special effort to attract the new generation. The monks always eat the same rice gruel, nonduality, one bowl a day. More practitioners, more hot water. How unexpected the manifestations of Great Compassion!

Tao-k'ai cries out to the residents on his mountain: "Do not follow the example of this unrefined person. I am terribly ashamed to be called the head of this monastery. I am wasting the precious energy of this place with my lack of genuine commitment. When anyone mentions the sublime Buddha Ancestors, I look for a place to hide, until I realize they have given me no place to hide."

Keizan Roshi is so inspired by this ecstatic humility, this total effacement of any Dharma claim, that he breaks into his own Zen talk this morning with an unusual personal cry: "I am prematurely teaching this great Soto transmission. I am unqualified. My way of life is not luminous. How could I dare to give a Zen talk of even one sentence, even one phrase?" This is what Keizan Zenji elsewhere calls "being without an atom of pride or self-satisfaction." One is reminded of the present Dalai Lama's words: "I am a simple Buddhist monk. Even in my dreams, I appear as an ordinary monk, never as Dalai Lama."

This empty-handed attitude is not a form of unhealthy self-abnegation but is an adornment of true Dharma practitioners and living Buddhas alike. They are immune to even the slightest self-inflation, either by words coming forth from their lips or words entering into their ears. Buddha T'ou-tzu is no stranger to this attitude. Immediately after enlightenment, he was asked by his master: "Have you now wonderfully awakened to the most subtle functioning?" T'ou-tzu replied: "If I had this *wonderful awakening* you speak about, I would instantly vomit it out!" This spontaneous response of self-effacement, not artful or artificial, is inseparable from genuine awakening, and is tested for by an authentic master right away. It could be called an appreciation of our naked humanity, our precious jade bones.

True nakedness is enlightenment. Remarks Keizan Roshi: "If you think about *mind-essence* or *Buddha nature,* you begin to look elsewhere and ignore your own naked being." He warns us against lovely mystical phrases—*it is entirely self-revealed, it is naturally bright.* Attractive as such words may sound, they will only inflate the sense of self-importance and imprison the spirit. Describing glib Zen—based on partial glimpses of oneness, elevated language, and enigmatic gestures—our ancient Japanese guide comments dryly: "Even were I to deal you not just thirty blows, but strike you continuously during lifetime after lifetime for ten thousand eons, it would be difficult for you to escape from such plotting and scheming." Each fascinating Dharma teaching is a new plot, each new level of *samadhi,* or absorption, a new scheme. No wonder awakened sages are allergic to putting this powder on their faces!

The longing to be true to every Awakened One who has come

before, to demonstrate complete enlightenment as complete humility, is not some obsessive tendency to emulate or to become a lifelong follower. To be a follower is merely a ploy of the ego to keep itself alive, no matter how noble or humble followership may sound. To envision the sacred footsteps of previous Buddhas clearly is to come eye to eye with them in the gaze of identity. We can only honor ancient Buddhas by standing unveiled as present Buddhas. Our kind Keizan Roshi assures us: "Despite the terrible dissipation of Dharma energy and Dharma effort in these degenerate modern times, you will occasionally be able to see a wild tiger prowling through the marketplace. Perhaps you will even find a priceless gold coin beneath your cap."

We can actually encounter the living Buddhas of our generation, these tigers who make no distinction between remote mountain and busy city. And perhaps, through this encounter, we may even awaken as timeless gold, as radiant value beyond evaluation. Confesses beloved Keizan, speaking from his Mahayana mother heart: "This is my intense prayer and deepest aspiration for you all!"

closing poem

> China, one thousand years ago.
> Master hands over to student
> his living Zen stick, Buddha's body,
> casually, in the vegetable garden, remarking:
> "There is someone who does not carry."
>
> Today it happens again.
> Basement zendo, America.
> Same stick, same master, same student.
> Same one who does not carry.

Now Melt Away Like Wax Before the Fire!

Transmission Forty-Six
Tao-K'ai to Tan-Hsia

koan

Destined successor asks living Buddha: "What is the single phrase transmitted by all Buddha Ancestors throughout space and time?" The Awakened One replies sternly: "If you imagine that you can encounter the timeless radiance of transmission as any phrase or as any gesture, you are burying the moon deep under ground." Through the kind intensity of his master, the successor suddenly meets his own Original Light, directly and completely. He now shines as the ninth Soto moon.

comment

The Light of transmission is always flowing, mind to mind, beneath diverse cultural landscapes composed of phrases and gestures. Buddha Ancestors differ widely in temperament and method, but they transmit one boundless clarity—without direction, dimension, division, demarcation. This is pure mind-transmission. Since there is only Mind, any sense of passing down or handing over some wisdom or some energy is inappropriate. Can the moon's reflection in the lake shine light on the great mountain? All Zen phrases and Zen gestures are merely reflected moons. We must encounter their true source. Only self-luminous awareness—the moon which remains always full—constitutes transmission. It is the complete awakening from our personal and communal dream of countless reflections. Transmission is described by Master Keizan as "the one genuine place to which all must return." There is no place where this *one genuine place* is absent.

No destined successor is ever awakened by the brilliant word or sudden gesture of the living Buddha. The precise word or precise gesture is necessary, but it does not actually cause the awakening. How could Total Awakeness be caused? How could timeless awareness come about at a certain moment? The living word-gesture opens the ripened consciousness by gaining its complete attention, but the transmission is already flowing within Mind. It is pure mind-transmission. There is no actual line of succession. No drama of living Buddha after living Buddha. Mind-transmission is always complete.

Living Buddha Zen presents this original mind-transmission directly. To buttress our understanding and our courage temporarily, we may call it Shakyamuni's experience beneath the Bodhi Tree. But such supports naturally fall away. The crescent moon, with its two points, melts away when the moon is full. To view transmission as flowing from one mind to another mind is still to view the moon as a crescent. The planet earth of our *skin, bones,* and *marrow* is still obscuring the clear view of a moon that is always by nature full, causing it to appear two-pointed.

This melting into transparency of physical body and social body—this melting away even of the deep levels of realization, symbolized in Zen talk by skin, bones, and marrow—is the necessary preparation to the full moon rising. The earth does not disappear. It simply turns. It gets out of the way. All phenomena, while remaining in play, turn and are suddenly out of the way. Various word-gestures help to accomplish this turning, and then melt away, as all other opacity now melts away. It is like the senses melting away during the stages of physical dying.

The transparency of limitless awareness is the only clear sky where this full moon can manifest. Keizan Zenji comments about the experience of universal melting away: "This is not an event that many practitioners know about. It is not a teaching revealed to one and all by our Soto lineage." It is an open secret, concealed only by its complete transparency.

Right now, skin, bones, and marrow—every layer of being, including essential being—are disappearing and the full moon is appearing. This moon of self-luminosity is not rising. There is no horizon for it to rise above. Horizonless awareness alone is this wonderful moon. No phenomenon is annihilated. All is moon. There is not even a microscopic grain of sand, not a single separate being or event, on this infinitely sensitive full-moon eyeball. Seeing all, all is seeing.

Burying the moon deep under ground is to allow the earth of conventional perception to rotate and plunge the moon of nonduality beneath the horizon. What strange shadow theater! Our common earthly experience must become transparent. Then all is moon. This realization Master Keizan calls the oneness of absolute and relative, coining the term *nonempty emptiness.* Empty plenitude. Emptiness that is completely full, completely active, completely compassionate toward all living beings. As our motherly guide Keizan Zenji points out, we will never be able to use up this inexhaustible compassion.

We cannot really say *full moon.* Where is half moon or crescent moon that needs to become full? Yet the term *full* remains appropriate to indicate that we are not presenting some primordial absence or nonbeing. This poison of nihilism is sometimes perversely extracted from the beautiful flower of Buddha Dharma. No mere empty sky will ever experience enlightenment.

The radiant human form is full moon. The face of the master, like a round mirror, is full moon. The diamond lotus position of Shakyamuni, sitting as Total Awakeness beneath the Bodhi Tree, is full moon. The *zazen mudra*—left palm face up above right palm, thumbs lightly touching—is full moon. The *hara,* center of spiritual gravity below the navel, is full moon. Mother Wisdom, Prajnaparamita, is full moon. Her radiant black womb is full moon. All beloved sentient beings, called mother beings by Tibetan commentators, are one full moon. The deep Zen bell is full moon, its round sound full moon. Even the simple round meditation cushion is the full moon. Only fullness. Only plenitude. Why interrupt our moon-viewing with an imaginary horizon of Zen phrases or Zen gestures, any more than with a mountain of Sutras? Now melt away like wax before the fire!

This morning there is an exchange between the eighty-first and eighty-second generations of Shakyamuni Buddha's transmission.

SENSEI: You look fresh.

STUDENT: It is the week of the full moon of Buddha's enlightenment.

SENSEI: When is the actual full moon coming?

STUDENT: It is here! The full moon of Soto!

SENSEI: Ah, the twin moons, Dogen and Keizan!

STUDENT: There can be only one moon. But on the waves of the ocean, there are millions of moons.

SENSEI: Dogen Zenji locates the entire moon in the depth of a dewdrop.

STUDENT: That is why I can aspire to be the full moon, although my depth is that of a dewdrop compared to the moon of Shakyamuni.

SENSEI: Pure mind-transmission is not enough, although Zen moves primarily in that direction. You need the phrases and the ceremonies. They are somehow even more important than the invisible transmission!

STUDENT: That is why Dogen Zenji became so moved, almost to tears, when he was shown the ancient written document of Dharma transmission in the Chinese monastery he was visiting.

SENSEI: You will see that, too.

STUDENT: Thank you, Sensei.

Master Keizan illuminates invisible mind-transmission in his closing poem:

> Great wind of transparency
> circles the earth silently
> and shakes the planet with its power.
> Who can pick up this wind
> and show it to you?

This blissful circular wind is self-luminous awareness, the life-giving atmosphere within which all beings experience being alive, while remaining unaware of its great power as the very source of beingness. Only a living Buddha can raise this flower and show it to us, mind to mind.

closing poem

> Word-gestures and body-mind
> blown away by great wind,
> a full moon sits on the cushion,
> breathing, gazing,
> now standing, walking,
> bowing, talking,
> never waxing or waning,
> setting or rising.
> Shine on, shine on Soto moon!

YOU HAVE TAKEN A STROLL
IN THE REALM OF SELF-LUMINOSITY

TRANSMISSION FORTY-SEVEN
TAN-HSIA TO WU-K'UNG

koan

Sensing the approaching moment to transmit Light, the treasure holder asks his inheritor: "What is the self-luminous awareness more primordial even than a cosmic eon completely empty of phenomena?" The disciple begins to respond from his profound Buddhist knowledge. The master flashes like lightning: "I see you are still involved in creating noise! Take a journey!" The humbled student treks to a distant mountain peak, experiencing there a great sense of spaciousness and silence. Returning, he stands before the Awakened One, who looks him over carefully. Laughing, the living Buddha now forcefully claps his right hand against the left shoulder of the destined successor who, unable to open his mouth, is suddenly awakened beyond spaciousness and beyond silence. "At last you know self-luminosity directly," comments the old sage. The new living Buddha bows with deep joy.

comment

Although the successor has delivered brilliant lectures on the *Lotus Sutra* since age seventeen, we know Wu-k'ung was not awakened until this sharp blow from Buddha Tan-hsia. In later years, as prolific founder of monasteries and teacher of the imperial family, he used to say: "When I was slapped by my master, all my cleverness disappeared." How amazing that *cleverness*—pride in religious and philosophical thinking, pride even in contemplative experience—survives so long in this sincere and profound aspirant. Coming back from his open space meditation on the mountain peak, Wu-k'ung may have been indulging in what Keizan Roshi calls *the usual mis-*

take: "When some persons hear *more primordial than an empty eon,* they mistakenly think there is no self, no other, no before or after, no origination or extinction, no beings, no Buddhas." Our ancient Japanese guide calls this immature experience of emptiness *scheming and plotting.* There is nothing truly primordial about it. From such nihilistic reading of self-luminous awareness develop the most prevalent forms of pseudo-Zen. As Master Keizan describes these misguided practitioners: "They are convinced that if one utters a single word, one distances oneself from primordial nature, or if a single thought arises, one is turning away from primordial nature. They become like ghosts without a genuine body." Intoxicated by this same *cleverness,* Keizan warns, some practitioners talk poetry or paradox about mountains, rivers, moon, clouds, water. Others engage in flamboyant behavior, as if this were realization.

What a blessed and powerful blow finally drives the last vestige of *cleverness* from the successor, unveiling him as an empty vessel, instantly filled with Light! Keizan Roshi describes this state of complete receptivity as having no skin, "becoming utterly stripped and exposed like the sky." The transmission comes spontaneously, but not from someone else, not from somewhere else. Remarks our guide: "You will not need to look for power elsewhere." We will experience pure decisiveness, without the faintest hesitation. This is the self-luminous awareness which remains unwavering, even during empty eons. In fact, innumerable eons disappear in a moment before the face of self-luminosity.

How sensitively attuned master must be to successor! This blow from the strong right Buddha hand, explains Keizan Zenji, "sweeps away the way of the world and the way of Buddha simultaneously." But this direct touch would not have been effective before the trek to the mountain peak, where Wu-k'ung "perceives the ten directions free from any obstructions and the four cardinal points standing gateless right before him," as our mentor expresses it. The mandala of pure awareness is thus prepared. Now the living Buddha must appear at its center. But not some other living Buddha! This empowerment process is facilitated by the master, who breathes intimately with the disciple. *Take a journey!* the inbreath. *Smack!* the outbreath.

The next morning, Buddha Tan-hsia openly proclaims in the Dharma hall the awakening of his successor, warning the monks: "The subtle secret of master and successor cannot be contained in a heart only one inch deep." Now we witness the former master accepting confirmation of his own realization from the former disciple. Newly unveiled Buddha Wu-k'ung comments to Buddha Tan-hsia: "Your remarks in the Dharma hall this morning did not fool me!" "What did my words express?" the old sage asks, smiling. "I can see you have taken a stroll in the realm of self-luminosity," the young sage responds, and instantly leaves the monastery. This is pure play—eye to eye, filled with laughter. Awakened successor almost always moves away from Buddha Ancestor in order to express Total Awakeness uniquely.

Master Keizan's closing poem this morning is invaluable. He sings about a clear stream, originating from a dark, deep, icy mountain spring. This secret springhead will never permit travelers, that is, transmigrators, to plumb its depth or even to discover its location. The stream is awareness as it flows through the valley of human existence—quenching thirst, irrigating fields, even powerful enough to smooth stones and cut through mountains. But the invisible spring, the primordial nature of awareness, has no point of access and no function other than its own spontaneous bubbling forth, its own self-luminosity.

In some sense, spring and stream are the same. At least they are inseparable. However, although all sentient beings, all travelers, perceive and participate in the valley stream, only Awakened Ones come to know the secret, self-manifesting mountain spring. They arrive here instantly, not by climbing down some deep gorge, but by awakening as this spring, as this unexperienceable source of all experience. These words disappear as they are written!

closing poem

Eyes on floor
during walking meditation,
cleverness evaporating.

Late afternoon light
in the master's room
is plain gold,
his brown robe
sweeps away pretension.

Sweet sounds arise
from evening chanting:
"May all karma be resolved
and the mind-flower blossom
in eternal spring."

Dark Side of Moon
Infinitely Vaster than Bright Side

Transmission Forty-Eight
Wu-k'ung to Tsung-chüeh

koan

Discerning the fullness of time, the Awakened One addresses his longtime attendant, whom he secretly recognizes as the destined successor to living Buddhahood for the next generation.

MASTER: How are you looking at life these days?

SUCCESSOR: *Just this!*

MASTER: Not quite enough. Say more.

SUCCESSOR: *Just this* is the fact.

MASTER: I did not say it was not the fact. But what extends beyond?

SUCCESSOR: *Just this* already includes what is beyond.

MASTER: Then tell me what is beyond. Express it completely!

successor: It cannot be put into words.

MASTER: You are still far from awakeness.

SUCCESSOR: Please, revered master, you express it.

MASTER: Ask me.

SUCCESSOR: What extends beyond?

MASTER: *Just non-this!*

The new living Buddha instantly shines as the non-Light of the non-transmission, awakening all beings into non-awakeness.

comment

For years his attendant practices deep awareness unceasingly, day and night, but only now does Buddha Wu-k'ung discern the appropriate level of preparedness, the ability to go completely beyond.

Just as there is the Awakened One who is Thus Gone, so there is the *non-Thus non-Gone non-Awakened non-One*. Tung-shan, sublime opener of the Soto way, discovered this amazing fact and called it the *beyond Buddha.* By various Zen masters, it is referred to obliquely as the *path beyond,* and was previously regarded as a special refinement of realization. Tung-shan's unique calling was to make the *beyond Buddha* central and primary.

The *beyond Buddha* is like the dark side of the moon which, given the nature of the solar system, will never turn in our direction, will never be illuminated for us, even by all-pervasive sunlight, will never enter into the realm of our natural perception. But we know with certainty that the dark side is there. It is implied by the bright side. It grounds the bright side.

Another analogy for *beyond Buddha* is anti-matter. Although now commonly accepted, this notion shocked physicists of an earlier generation. Tung-shan was like a radical physicist who saw implications far beyond what other adepts of his own era could see.

Keizan Roshi gives the following example. The person awake to *Buddha* is sitting on a beautiful green mountain top, surrounded by clouds, certain that the ultimate realization has been reached. Suddenly, the clouds part briefly, revealing a much larger peak looming behind the first. It is an extension of the mountain, not other than the mountain. This dark, mysterious, inaccessible peak, seldom if ever glimpsed and never climbed by even the most advanced mountaineer, is the *beyond Buddha.*

The bright clarity of Buddha nature is incomplete without this obscure, primal non-nature. Master Keizan explains to his Zen students that by affirming *just this,* the successor "falls into the secondary and the tertiary." The primary reality is *just non-this.*

Imagine the dark side of the moon as infinitely vaster than the bright side. The living Buddha describes this boundless black light as the fundamental ground, from which no absolute sphere or relative sphere ever emerges in the first place. This is called *the way of no traces from the beginning.* In this sense, it is the way of *non-awakening,* because this truth has never been awakened to or transmitted by any sage. All we can perceive in Dharma history is the transmission of Light from living Buddha to living Buddha. This is the bright moon. The inexhaustibly mysterious dark moon, although really central, is only hinted in the historical record. The dark moon has no charac-

teristics or manifestations such as fullness, brightness, sentient beings, or living Buddhas. It is the death of Buddha, the death of the
path, the death of realization, not to mention the death of earth,
heaven, and hell.

What do you think of it? It cannot be thought about! Why? It is
infinitely closer than thinking or looking. Sings newly unveiled Buddha Tsung-chüeh: "It will not submit to the gaze of a single sage, or
even a thousand sages." Yet the *beyond Buddha* can and must be expressed for awakeness to be total, to be *non-awakening,* to be boundless, to be completely beyond and free.

Untouched by any analogy, such as our example of the moon's
dark side, *beyond Buddha* totally embraces *Buddha.* The black light is
already the core and matrix of the bright light. The black light is so
bright it is dark. There are not two sides of light, not even two poles.
There is no surface, no depth.

How to express this? Consider the mantra of Buddha Avalokitesh-
vara, who is unfathomable compassionate awakeness. *Om mani
padme hum. The jewel is embraced by the lotus.* The jewel is the bright
moon, Mind or Buddha. Concentrating on it, we barely notice the
dark, rich, profound recesses of the lotus, which are the *beyond Buddha.* Yet only within the folding and unfolding petals of this mysterious darkness can the jewel be found. Jewel and lotus are always together. We must learn to remove our gaze from the brilliance of the
jewel, dissolve our meditative concentration entirely, and merge
with the fragrant darkness of the lotus, the *beyond Buddha,* experiencing as our own its utter profundity—essentially free, completely
beyond, liberated from all partial notions such as clarification, realization, awakening.

As we contemplate the twin moons of Japanese Soto, Dogen Zenji
appears as the dark moon—impenetrable mystery, deep lotus, *prajna,* transcendent insight, illuminating the way but never casting any
light upon itself. Keizan Zenji appears as the bright moon—revealer
of secrets, shining jewel, *upaya,* skillful communication, compassionately pointing out every detail. The bright moon, with luminous
kindness, is now pointing to the dark moon!

Dogen Zenji's radiant darkness does not conceal. He always advocates the way of expression. Without thinking about it, without describing it discursively, without relying on any conventional Zen gesture, express it! Reveal it! We must express realization through our very pores, like sweating, or through our very heart, like weeping or laughing. As Master Wu-k'ung suggests to his successor: "If you cannot express it, you are still far from awakeness."

Keizan Roshi confirms in his closing poem this morning that no words can describe or thought penetrate the *beyond Buddha,* just as no thick iron wedge can separate the planks of a wood floor laid down by a master Japanese carpenter. Walking on the floor, sitting on the floor, prostrating on the floor, sweeping the floor—these activities alone can express its floorness. Why clumsily attempt to take apart what cannot be taken apart? *Buddha* and *beyond Buddha* are one. Bright and dark are one. Express fluently what is beyond expression simply by taking the *path beyond*!

closing poem

> Eyes open, bright moon.
> Eyes close, rich black light.
> Brilliant Buddha diamond
> merges in dark mystery.
> Fragrance, fragrance,
> fragrance!

WHY HAVE I NEVER ENCOUNTERED THIS MYSTERY BEFORE?

TRANSMISSION FORTY-NINE
TSUNG-CHÜEH TO HSÜEH-TOU

koan

Living Buddha enters Dharma hall and proclaims to the assembled practitioners: "Awakened Ones have a secret body, not a secret verbal teaching. But this hidden body is not hidden to Mahakashyapa, who smiles, nor is it essentially concealed from the gaze of any living being, for it shines always and everywhere, a full moon in a clear autumn sky, totally naked, unobscured."

The moment he hears these words of Light, the successor begins to weep profusely. Shattering monastic decorum, he cries aloud: "Why have I never encountered this mystery before?" After the completion of his discourse, the master invites this monk into his private chambers and inquires: "What has caused you to weep so intensely?" Destined successor replies: "The hidden Buddha body is not hidden to Mahakashyapa!" Remarks the present Buddha to the newly unveiled Buddha: "You were predicted by the ancient sages." Only boundless clarity now shines.

comment

Our kind Roshi Keizan presents the essence of this mystery in his closing poem, which points directly to "our indestructible hidden body, empty and bright." This is the secret of Tantra, the secret which Living Buddha Zen embodies in its own unspoken way. The diamond body, not mentioned by Sutras and therefore previously unencountered by the successor, is forever completely present. It is complete presence. This diamond body is not the seed of Buddhahood, slowly growing within all sentient beings, but the complete body of self-luminous awareness, the complete Buddha body. This is why we can aspire to manifest as living Buddhas during our present lifetime. Otherwise, the natural process of spiritual evolution into Buddhahood—the growth of the *tathagata garbha,* the embryonic Tathagata, or Awakened One, within our mindstream—will take not only several incarnations but one billion lifetimes of concerted contemplative practice and self-sacrificial service. The gestation period for a living Buddha prescribed by Mahayana Sutras is three Great Eons.

The destined successor weeps, and then cries out with uncontainable ecstasy: "Why have I never encountered this mystery, this inconceivable blessing? We can manifest the Buddha body here and now for the instantaneous awakening of all beings. What utterly unexpected Dharma teaching is this?" This teaching, or better this revolutionary fact, is not essentially secret but is always and everywhere fully revealed. This is what constitutes its supremely revolutionary character. Yet it remains self-secret. Only when the proper level of preparation has been reached does the open secret of the Buddha body dawn on awareness directly. How? Through the recognition by our awareness of its own inexhaustible self-luminosity.

We will never encounter this root fact of the Buddha body by reading Zen and Tantric texts, although it is richly alluded to on every page. The appropriate preparation cannot be brought about by study or even by meditation. Only through blissful and startling companionship with the living Buddhas of past and present, who are undifferentiable presence, will this awareness of the Buddha body dawn, accompanied by spontaneous tears and laughter.

Master Keizan speaks playfully about the diamond body of self-luminous awareness as a faceless, timeless wanderer. "Even if you think you see forms and hear sounds, it is not actually your physical eyes seeing or your physical ears hearing. It is this one faceless fellow who is accomplishing it all, both perception and objects of perception."

Our true body is this diamond body, not the biological instrument, the social envelope, or the various karmic tendencies that shape them. Keizan Roshi calls this body *bright light existing only brilliantly.* Elsewhere he alludes to it as *sheer alertness.* The diamond body is infinite aliveness—pure, total, simple—enlivening every cell of our physical body and every strand of our personal and communal consciousness. It is inconceivably more sublime than existence, and shatters any nihilistic notion of non-existence. The diamond body is not destroyed, even when all universes are destroyed at the end of the cycle. This ontologically transparent secret body is such a profound mystery that, as our ancient Japanese guide ruminates: "Even living Buddhas themselves do not know exactly what to make of it." Accurately speaking, it is neither *light* nor *dark,* for these terms are logical correlatives, and there is nothing to which the diamond body can be correlated. Certainly not to some distinct, substantial entity called *diamond body.*

Master Keizan now offers some subtle instructions about encountering and living as our true body, which is everywhere, always whole and perfect. We will get a precious glimpse of this Buddha body, concealed only by its own utter transparency, by becoming a cloudless blue sky. But this is only a glimpse. We cannot rest here. When kindling fire by rubbing two sticks together, eventually one sees a puff of smoke arising. One cannot stop complacently at this point, or flame will never burst forth. Becoming empty sky is only the stage of seeing smoke. Our intense, continuous, uninterrupted gaze of nonduality must be sustained, smoothly and powerfully, until we see a moon so full it fills the sky from horizon to horizon. This is the compassionate Buddha fire that instantly consumes the limitations of all beings. Now we have truly kindled the liberating and illuminating flame!

The diamond body, empty of substance, is pure presence. Never absence. It is a sun as large as the entire universe, yet is beyond any description such as *universal* or *brilliantly shining.* It resides comfortably within each breath, each heartbeat. This hidden body of self-luminosity has existed from beginningless time, but cannot be encountered within the conventional realms of *time* or *existence.* Great aspiration must be generated to encounter it directly, without any subject encountering any object. As Master Keizan remarks, this nondual encounter does not depend upon sitting cross-legged on *zafu* and *zabuton,* any more than it depends upon croaking like a bullfrog on a lily pad. It has no correlation with the conventional categories *lay* or *monastic, male* or *female.* Only deep, burning tenderness toward all beings and aspiration for their full awakening is effective, because such complete empathy itself is the diamond body, which hears, sees, weeps, and laughs as all life. The term *diamond* does not mean cold or hard. Quite the opposite!

Universal aspiration alone brings about the bright death of partial understanding, exploding every encapsulated atom of personal and cosmic experience. The body of universal aspiration orients directly to the Original Source by awakening immediately as Source, everywhere present. Such presence!

The delicacy of the Buddha body has flowered in the destined successor since childhood. Once, while washing a wound on her small son's hand, his mother asked Hsüeh-tou how he received the wound and whether it was causing him pain. The young boy simply responded: "My hand is a Buddha's hand." The Buddha body is not supernaturally invulnerable. It feels intimately the suffering of living beings everywhere, calling and drawing them home to their ever-present Source. O precious human body! O gate of mystery always open wide! Thank you!

closing poem

> O beings of one body
> from one source,
> family of consciousness,
> angel, animal, human,
> homeless wanderers
> coming home to
> timeless awareness,
> please realize
> Total Awakeness now!

In the Last Few Hundred Years, No Spiritual Guide Like Me Has Appeared

Transmission Fifty
Hsüeh-tou to Ju-ching

koan

Living Buddha remarks to destined successor: "Your request to become head cleaning monk will be honored when you tell me how what is never soiled can be cleansed." During the course of more than one year, the old sage asks the ardent practitioner this same question several times. On each occasion, the young contemplative is unable to emerge from immaculate silence. Finally perceiving the pregnant moment, the master admonishes: "Become free from cleanness and clarity! Move forward out of silence like a cartwheel rolling out of a deep rut!" Through these potent words, open space opens. After several days of intense, indefinable forward motion, the Light of transmission suddenly shines.

SUCCESSOR: Revered sage, I can now respond.

MASTER: Speak immediately!

SUCCESSOR: I am what is never soiled. There is no more impulse
   to clean or clear away.

Before these words even leave the successor's lips, the Awakened One strikes a light, playful blow, dissolving the final verbal imprint and confirming Total Awakeness. The new living Buddha—sweat of power and completeness streaming copiously from his entire body—performs a deep bow and goes to clean the monastery latrine.

comment

Ju-ching abandoned his deep study of Buddhist philosophy at age seventeen and fervently took up Zen. For years now, his silent sitting has been stainless. He calls his practice "crushing the diamond teaching throne."

Ju-ching cherishes the most intense longing to cleanse every impurity from the life of the monastery and from the careers of all living beings. He burns with the aspiration to clear away all obstacles, including even their faintest karmic traces. It is this subtle Dharma disease, accurately diagnosed by Buddha Hsüeh-tou, which drives successor Ju-ching to request the position of head cleaning monk. But the old sage recognizes this as a fruitful sickness, filled with great promise for the clarification of the Buddha way throughout the entire future of humanity.

Here is a great vessel of pure intensity, pure commitment, who must now fill spontaneously with Original Light, untouched by any assumption concerning the need for spiritual cultivation, free from any obsession to purify, to clear away, to become still or silent. The Great Way is neither engaged nor disengaged. The aspirant must awaken as ever present, ever perfect Core Reality. This is the full moon way, so radical that it takes one year of continuous attention for successor Ju-ching, a rare being even among living Buddhas, to assimilate it.

The more intense our Mahayana aspiration to heal, protect, and enlighten all beings, to place them in the bliss of nondual awareness, the more arduous it is to assimilate this revolutionary fact of completeness. Through our own intimate beingness, all beings already shine as the never waning full moon, Total Awakeness, illuminating the boundless space of primal purity we call the universe. Yet the more arduous the spiritual struggle, the more vast its fruition.

Courageously dissolving his deep drive to cleanse—to clear away impurity and other karmic obstacles—this new living Buddha paradoxically becomes a tremendous force for the purification of Zen tradition during his generation. Through his uniquely illumined Japanese successor, Dogen Zenji, Buddha Ju-ching will also purify Zen in Japan, Zen in America, and the Zen of the emerging global future.

For China and the broad earth, Ju-ching presents the panorama of Soto completeness, joining it with intense Soto sitting, unstained by the slightest path-goal duality. His teaching empowers us to be free from the impulse to become free, even from the impulse to liberate others. The deep-seated drive to challenge, to oppose, to change, to improve, to cultivate, to correct, and to clean up dissolves in this alchemical Soto moonlight. Now one can authentically serve all beings as living Buddhas.

Old Buddha, as Dogen Zenji playfully refers in retrospect to his master Ju-ching, is the fiftieth radiant successor of Shakyamuni, the twenty-third Buddha Ancestor in China, and the thirteenth full moon in the Soto lineage. His destined successor, Dogen, father of Japanese Soto Zen, is someone of comparable vastness, an ocean of the fluent expression of nonduality. Consider carefully. Dogen is a destined successor who crosses the planetary ocean to reach his destined master. What wonderful spiritual power! Was Bodhidharma's successor capable of sailing from China to India to find the uncompromising sage?

Only Buddha Ju-ching, called Tendo Nyojo in the wild Japanese tongue, could attract a living diamond as vast as Dogen. Old Buddha is comparable in power to the pivotal figures Nagarjuna, Bodhidharma, Hui-neng, Tung-shan, Tilopa, Naropa, Marpa, Milarepa. Yet after seven centuries of obscurity, Dogen Zenji is now more and more revealed, while his Great Master, Tendo Nyojo, remains concealed. Buddha Dogen resembles a second Shakyamuni. He is the perpetual full moon, even brighter than the sun, who is now circling the planet of global history. His obscure master, Old Buddha, remains an infinite black sun, forgotten by history, unobservable source of Dogen's visible illumination. Ju-ching is the mystery hidden in the heart of his successor Dogen. This concealment is a sign of the inconceivable mastery of the *head cleaning monk*, who secretly inherited the vast responsibility of guarding the radical purity of Zen tradition—its nonduality.

Ju-ching did not publicly acknowledge receiving the transmission of Light. As a living Buddha, he actually continued to clean latrines. Supernatural voices were heard emanating from the Dharma hall, praising the perfect service to all Buddhas and to all sentient beings carried on by this hidden sage. Though remaining fundamentally concealed, he began to be recognized in high centers of governmental authority. His growing reputation as the very embodiment of nondual purity caused the unprecedented elevation of Ju-ching, full moon of Soto, to the abbotship of a prestigious Rinzai monastery. How else would the unknown Japanese pilgrim, Dogen, be able to discover his destined master in the huge expanse of China?

Buddha Dogen chooses to follow the same way of concealment practiced by his ancient Chinese guide, retiring to the mountains of Japan with a small circle of advanced practitioners, thereby infusing power directly into the bloodstream of the Buddha way, rather than engaging in the deceptive task of popular cultural reform. Dogen Zenji's masterwork, *Shobogenzo,* was all but forgotten for centuries until the dawning of the present global era. Now the circular rainbow of the *Shobogenzo,* the Dharma Eye of Nonduality, is visible in the sky over Japan and America. Open your eyes, easterners and westerners! Perceive Dogen Zenji's *Shobogenzo* everywhere!

Buddha Ancestor Ju-ching, empowered by his renunciation of all agendas, all manipulation, is untouchable by the forces of the conventional world. A provincial governor, representative of the emperor, brings ten thousand silver coins to the monastery and requests a Dharma discourse to be delivered at the seat of worldly power. The playful sage requests a Zen word from the high official, an obvious impossibility, and uses his failure to reply profoundly enough as a reason to refuse the invitation. The ten thousand silver coins are carefully packed up and returned.

"I am what is never soiled," Ju-ching proclaims at the opening of Total Awakeness. This very same original purity continues to protect Zen tradition, maintaining its intrinsic freedom from social pressures which always, in every era, attempt to regulate or even steal away with the three precious jewels—Buddha, Dharma, Sangha—the transcendent jewels of refuge from conventionality, from duality, from ideology. Beneath the chaotic surface of Zen history, from Ju-ching's refusal of the ten thousand coins of multiplicity down to the temptations of contemporary secularity, the effortless purity and clarity of this Chinese Buddha and his Japanese successor still remain potent and active.

When the full moon, *what is never soiled,* shines as our heart reality, we can finally engage in the authentic task of cleaning up monastery, family, society, religion—not through programs but through wholeness, not through partial approaches but through completeness. Since there is no more impulse to cleanse, to clear away, even to clarify, nothing impure or obscure can invade Tendo Nyojo's radical Dharma. Nothing can impede his consummate Soto expression from instantly enlightening all beings in the ten directions. Only here, as this non-active, non-cleaning, non-engaged sage, does Dogen find the fragrant cleanness, the uncompromising character, the impeccable nonduality for which he is so deeply longing. It was the fire of this longing, not trade winds, which drove Dogen's small wooden vessel from Japan across the China Sea.

Old Buddha lives, dresses, and eats exactly like his monks. There is not a drop of special privilege or hierarchy. His efforts on behalf of his students are tireless. No other master could demonstrate such patient care, even with the monastery gardener who, under the greening touch of Ju-ching, reaches high levels of realization. The Awakened One praises the deep insight of this uneducated gardener as more advanced than the abbots of most other monasteries. Buddha Ju-ching inspires immense commitment to the Great Way from everyone who spends time with him. Completely unconventional, he opens his monastery to serious non-Buddhist practitioners, making no divisions between human beings. With plain-speaking frankness, untouched by the slightest pride, this cleaner of latrines remarks: "In the last few hundred years, no spiritual guide like me has appeared."

No younger monk in his monastery cleans so intensely and effectively as Old Buddha continues to clean for his whole life. And no one sits so intensively in *zazen.* Sores develop where the sage's body rests on his hard, round cushion. Pain is always with him. Milarepa, the Tibetan master of nonduality, once gave a pith-instruction to a close disciple—direct pointing without words. As the student was leaving the renunciant's cave-retreat, the old *mahasiddha* turned, flipped up his tattered robe, and bent over, revealing his bare bottom layered with dark calluses from incessant sitting. So much for the fantasy that the experience of nonduality is the result of some instant mental decision! Goodbye to the myth that after some discrete moment of enlightenment, nothing more is done!

Zazen, active sitting, completely relaxed and completely intense, is the central and inevitable expression of nonduality in the Soto Way, both before awakening and within the open expanse of awakeness. Where is the border between the two? Such is the direct, existential witness of both Tendo Nyojo and Milarepa.

Zazen is not to enter meditative states of consciousness. It is the meditation beyond meditation, sometimes called *non-meditation* or *mahamudra.* Just sitting, sitting, sitting—shining as naked awareness!

Zazen is the most intense labor of love. It is not sitting down and spacing out. Can a mother sit down and space out? *Zazen* is constantly to bring all beings to birth from the womb of nondual wisdom, feeling the pressure a mother feels during childbirth and the responsibility she feels during child-raising. *Zazen* is tenderly to educate and mature living beings in nonduality and fiercely to protect them with nonduality. *Zazen* is to pour with perspiration, as this new living Buddha does. *Zazen* is to weep internal and external tears of love and aspiration for the full awakening of all conscious beings. We are their mothers. They are our mothers.

This cosmic explosion and implosion, compassion and wisdom, takes place right on the round cushion that often becomes hard as stone. *Zazen* is not to float among moonlit waterlilies nor to wander through green mountain gorges. Old Buddha demonstrates only rigorous, joyful sitting—just sitting, without scriptural study, chanting, bowing, arranging flowers, performing tea. This does not mean that he banishes noble and beautiful activity from the spiritual life. It simply means that active *zazen* is the goalless, pathless way, free from any temptation or tendency to clean, to clear away, to fix, to improve, to beautify, to revolutionize, or to engage in any particular focus. *Zazen* is actually to be what can never be soiled or degenerated in any manner and what can therefore never be cleaned, mended, improved, or elevated in any way.

Ignited by Ju-ching's demonstration of the power of pathless, goalless sitting, Dogen Zenji returns to Japan and composes his famous short treatise on the infinite value of intensely sitting down. *Broad Recommendation for Zazen* offers this unsurpassable diamond sitting to everyone, on every level of society and spiritual development. The radicalness of this universal recommendation, this universal initiation into nonduality, has yet to be appreciated fully by any culture, including those who consider *zazen* an esoteric practice for an elite, who consider awakeness as accessible only to a few practitioners.

After throwing the gates of *zazen* wide open, Dogen Zenji retires into the remote mountains to train intensively with a few ardent monks. This is not a repudiation of his radical proclamation of universal *zazen*. His call reaches us this morning: "Be the Original One twenty-four hours a day, throughout beginningless and endless lifetimes, without indulging any impulse to change or improve. Simply sit down—alert, actionless—each day and night, until you are completely *zazen,* your body and breath spontaneous affirmations of the fullness that the whole cosmos enjoys. No incense burning, chanting, or repenting is necessary!"

This unquenchable fire of *zazen* that consumes both the flames of Hell and the radiance of Paradise was kindled by the Old Buddha in China and carried, blazing, across the sea to Japan in the sacred vessel of Dogen Zenji. It has now been transmitted to America and to planetary civilization. The beautiful traditional form of *zazen* is being demonstrated in the ancient valley of Mexico, at the Sea of Galilee, in the global cities of New York and Los Angeles. Every cell of our body is now enlivened by flames of longing to sit down and be actively complete. May this fire of awakening spread far and wide!

We are not some imperfect being, longing for perfection. *Zazen* is a force infinitely stronger. It is perfection longing to express perfection. There is no easy-going Soto Zen. There can be no compromise with the dangerous illusions of impurity and incompletion. Soto is not gradual. It is more sudden than Rinzai Sudden Enlightenment which, for all its suddenness, focuses great striving on creating a discrete moment of awakening. There is no actual transition from unenlightened to enlightened, though there may appear to be. Soto is the inconceivable suddenness of always being total, real, direct, pure. Soto is free from any need for methods to bring this naked fact into the open.

Nothing needs to be done. Even the attitude *nothing needs to be done* does not need to be cultivated. Just *doing!* Just *zazen!* Whatever action we take to purify or wall off or revolutionize our minds in meditation is a denial of the fact of our basic completeness. Sit on your black cushion as a living Buddha! There is nothing else!

Master Keizan's closing poem this morning presents the case for dynamic sitting, *zazen,* which he describes as a great wind, indestructible as diamond, circulating fluently everywhere and supporting the entire earth. Sitting in *zazen,* we are not supported by the universe. We are supporting the universe! Easily! *Zazen* is our true humanity—transparent, indestructible, circulating everywhere, supporting every atom of spontaneous manifestation, never partial, never soiled.

Waves of *zazen* now flow across the *zendo* from American master to American successor and back again—harmonizing, interlacing, creating fluid patterns. We are sitting together this morning in the palpable presence of Old Buddha. Tendo Nyojo is close family. He feels like our great-grandfather. We are surrounded by his family atmosphere. It has a special fragrance. We can now hear the twenty-third Chinese Buddha Ancestor proclaiming his essence teaching: "*Zazen* is dropping away mind and body!"

The sounds and sights of the *zendo* have certainly dropped away, although in an entirely unexpected manner. They simply no longer need to be cleared away, dropped away, chased away, or organized in any way. What ease! The manifestations we call *body* and *mind* are the subtle set of impulses to clean up, to bring order. They are simply gone. There is no more puttering around, straightening out, arranging, controlling! No more mental broom or busy work! I am what is never disarranged! It is much simpler than we can imagine! The universe is already clean and clear! Now we can go clean *zendo,* sidewalk, neighborhood!

closing poem

> Universe sits as human body,
> gentle breath temporality,
> still hands timelessness,
> part closed eyes transcendent wisdom
> never crystallizing any phenomenon.
> Tongue of power
> against teeth of stability,
> knees of compassion planted firmly,
> living spine nonduality,
> round cushion
> the mountain of transmission.
> Zazen! Zazen! Zazen!

THE TERRIBLE THUNDER OF GREAT COMPASSION

TRANSMISSION FIFTY-ONE
JU-CHING TO DOGEN

koan

During the profound silence of late night sitting, living Buddha speaks quietly yet firmly to the rows of practitioners: "Why are you still inhabiting mind and body? You are sleeping while awake! No incense burning or chanting scripture! No repenting or repeating mantra! No fixating mind and body in concentration! To explore Zen truly, drop away mind and body!" These words of Light powerfully confirm the awakeness of the first Japanese successor, who immediately arises, enters the master's private chambers, and offers incense.

MASTER: Why are you burning incense?

SUCCESSOR: Mind and body are dropped away.

MASTER: Even your dropped-away mind and body are now dropped away.

SUCCESSOR (bowing): This is only a temporary insight.

MASTER: You have now dropped away the very notion of dropping-away.

MASTER'S ATTENDANT: How strange that some non-Chinese monk could reach this unreachable realm!

MASTER: The new living Buddha looks mild and peaceful, yet within him the terrible thunder of Great Compassion is roaring.

comment

That Dogen Zenji could regard Total Awakeness as a temporary insight indicates the supreme enlightenment which drops away any sense of being enlightened. Master Dogen does not even hear the thunder of Great Compassion within him which destines him to become a vast rain of Dharma for the future of the planet.

Born in the year 1200 of this common planetary era, Dogen Zenji's peaceful rain has been falling imperceptibly for nearly eight centuries. He was a child of Prajnaparamita, Mother of the Buddhas. This line of Mother Wisdom was perfectly clear in his formation. He renounced the way of his father and his adopted father in the imperial court, following instead his young mother's dying wish that he pursue Buddha Dharma completely. Beginning at age three, he learned classical Chinese poetry from his grandmother. His maternal aunt was also an important guide for the young boy. Even the two Buddhist monastic uncles who helped him along the path of study, contemplation, and renunciation were maternal uncles. Losing his mother at age seven, this profound boy plumbed the depth of grief and greatly intensified his Buddhist study.

Spontaneously replicating the pattern of Shakyamuni Buddha, Dogen Zenji, from the beginning a child prodigy, left an important future career at the royal court to renounce the conventional world. He was only twelve. His uncle, an abbot wise in the ways of esoteric and metaphysical Buddhism, wept with admiration. The next year, as he persisted firmly in his calling, the boy's head was shaved. At age thirteen, he took the Bodhisattva vow to liberate all suffering beings and became a Buddhist monk. By age seventeen, he had thoroughly studied and assimilated the vast number of volumes that comprise the Buddhist canon.

Dogen's other maternal uncle, also an initiate in the esoteric Buddhist knowledge known as Tantra, now advises his young nephew to prepare to visit distant China and to seek the living seal of Bodhidharma still extant there. So at seventeen, the destined inheritor of Buddhahood abandons study and metaphysical contemplation, entering instead, under the most rigorous monastic regimen, the steep, direct path of Rinzai Zen. During seven years of practice, he swiftly traverses this untraversable way, becoming the successor of his Zen master.

At age twenty-four, deeply mature, Dogen and his Zen master, whose realization the young student has now surpassed, travel together to China on pilgrimage. Every Chinese Zen master the young sage encounters tests and then bows before his radiant awakeness. Several of these old sages, guided by dreams and visions, unveil before Dogen's tender, tear-filled gaze secret Dharma treasures, ancient scrolls fresh as plum blossoms, rare documents of spiritual succession belonging to various lineages of Zen from the vast land of China.

Dogen's rich pilgrimage, guided by invisible Dharma forces, lasts for some three years until he reaches the hidden, unproclaimed sage, the living Buddha who ignites him into flames of sleeplessness and finally brings to an end his display of enlightenment. Immediately after Dogen's very enlightenment drops way, the Awakened One sends him home to Japan to radiate the full moon way, exclaiming: "My finding you is like Shakyamuni Buddha finding Mahakashyapa. You are one of the ancient sages. Remain in the mountains of your distant land and mature, mature, mature! This alone will assure the future authenticity of Living Buddha Zen." Subtle differences among the five principal schools of Zen now become irrelevant to Dogen. His Rinzai training no longer forms him. He is simply the living Buddha, prior to all elaborations of the teaching, no matter how profound they may be.

At age twenty-seven, this magnificent young sage, now virtually invisible, returns to his native land, where he remains secluded in his original Zen monastery and at other quiet places. When he is forty-four, after seventeen years of inconceivable maturing, Dogen finally accepts an old villa in the mountains, leaking rain and covered with brambles, where a few practitioners gather. This eventually becomes the great monastery Eihei-ji. Here, the living Buddha guides dragon-spirits and other visitors from the subtle planes as well as human beings from the planetary plane toward the unveiling of Original Awakeness.

Master Keizan is pouring forth his entire intensity this morning. Our ancient guide is in ecstasy, for he perceives Dogen Zenji as the fifty-first complete Shakyamuni and as the first living Buddha to grace these narrow islands. Previous masters in Japan, venerable as they were, represented various elaborations of Buddhist teaching—the five schools of Zen, as well as Tendai and Shingon—rather than embodying fully, as Dogen did, the root and source of all teaching. Beyond all partial methods and doctrines, Buddha Dogen is the first Soto full moon to rise over this sharp edge of the world. The full moon is always the same moon, without a single degree of fullness missing.

Keizan Zenji now raises the central questions: What are the mind and body that appear and then appear to drop away? Is there any solid, separate body or conventional, individual mind in the first place? What is there that can drop away? Is there both a busy mind and a still mind? Beyond these two, is there a cosmic mind? Beyond the cosmic display, is there some pure radiance which is ultimate mind?

Do not seek answers to these questions, and do not abide in any deep, inward, motionless brightness! Be abodeless! Do not become a Buddha image made of wood or stone! All such elaborations of doctrine—busy mind, still mind, universal mind, ultimate mind, and the partial realizations which they generate—can now simply be dropped away, without any sense of dropping some heavy weight or covering. Drop away the very process of dropping-away, the very notion of dropping-away! No enlightened state! Master Keizan calls this non-state, *bottom falls out of bucket.*

Is successor Dogen now just a useless bucket? Certainly not. He is the diamond body of Buddha. Ever present, never absent. As beloved Roshi Keizan proclaims, transmitting the central principle of Living Buddha Zen: "When everything is utterly emptied out, there is something which cannot be emptied." What? The living Buddhas, appearing throughout past, present, and future. Their sheer brilliance, invisible to dualistic vision, possesses neither inside nor outside, neither stillness nor motion.

The Vedanta of ancient India, teaching nonduality, shows that three states of consciousness—waking, dream, and dreamless sleep—contain all possible experience, all possible elaboration. These three are contrasted with *turiya*—not as another state of consciousness, not as another experience, but as the living principle of all states, the heart of all experience. By Dogen Zenji, all possible elaborations of consciousness, including the various Buddhist schools of philosophy and practice, are called *body-and-mind.* Total

Awakeness, or *turiya,* effortlessly drops away body-and-mind. But not in any nihilistic sense.

Body-and-mind is essentially the functioning of compassion and wisdom, which living Buddhas drop away moment by moment, retaining no sense of the noble activity of the *bodhisattva* warrior, no sense of any special state called enlightenment. This dropping-away does not mean that body-and-mind ceases its marvelous functioning. Such cessation would be absurd, obliterating the precious way of spiritual cultivation, including incense, images, scriptures, bowing, generosity, meditation, and their crown, the transcendent insight which liberates all beings from suffering.

The functioning of body-and-mind is more than the path of spiritual cultivation. It is the inconceivable universe, the priceless, infinite diamond of manifestation. By *dropping away,* the universe becomes transparent to its own central principle—Total Awakeness. The blackboard covered by chalk letters and numbers drops away when we clearly see the mathematical principle that is being illustrated. A naive observer just continues to gaze in awe at the blackboard, as if it alone were the object of conversation. Awake as living principle, we can now offer our being truly to all beings, as Dogen Zenji offered incense in the private chapel of Old Buddha. May we drop away our own dropping-away!

Before Buddha Dogen, the traditional term in Chinese Zen was *mind-and-body.* Dogen reverses the word order after revolutionizing the realization. *Mind* represents wisdom, *body* compassion. Body-and-mind is a realization which places foremost the expanse of relativity and its correlate, compassion.

Another radical visionary of compassion and relativity, accomplishing a similar revolution within the very realm of enlightenment, was Lama Tsongkhapa. He lived in Tibet a century later than Dogen Zenji. These two masters demonstrate that compassion is primary because relationality is already nonduality. Nothing needs to be removed, transcended, transformed, streamlined. The moon is always full. To dedicate every fibre of awareness to awakening all beings into their intrinsic awakeness, their natural fullness, is itself to be completely awake. There is nothing else. Nothing new lies ahead in the distance or just around the corner.

Right before us shines the full moon of body-and-mind. It must be dropped away— playfully, easily. This dropping-away is itself dropped away. Even the slightest sense of dropping-away is now dropped away. Is this realization momentary or timeless? *I do not know! I do not know!*

Since Buddha Ju-ching could perceive the thunder of Great Compassion roaring within the empty space of this non-Chinese monk, the old sage must have also held the secret of compassion's primacy. This is why he proclaimed: "In the last few hundred years, no spiritual guide like me has appeared." Vast wisdom space shines from Zen realization, but the ecstatic primacy of all-embracing compassion is rare, even among Awakened Ones. Shakyamuni Buddha is noted by the Mahayana Sutras as unusual among Buddhas, because he chooses to encompass suffering beings in his Buddha field, even though it remains completely pure and unobstructed in all ten directions.

Tsongkhapa, whose disciple became the first Dalai Lama and eventually the fourteenth Dalai Lama of modern times, and Dogen, whose Soto wave is the largest manifestation of Zen in Japan, provide incontrovertible demonstrations of this primacy of compassion—demonstrations not on the level of doctrine or philosophy but in the turbulent medium of history. They demonstrate enlightenment as the entire expanse of space and time. Total Awakeness as every living being.

closing poem

> Dawn drops away,
> radio news drops away,
> early morning service
> before wooden Buddha
> drops away,
> two thousand five hundred
> years of transmission
> drop away imperceptibly,
> imperceptibly.

SUBTLY PIERCING EVERY ATOM OF JAPAN

TRANSMISSION FIFTY-TWO
DOGEN TO EJO

koan

Already having realized the nature of reality as emptiness, mature practitioner comes to living Buddha for confirmation and discovers an entirely unexpected teaching. For three years, the destined successor drinks in this indescribable full moon way. One morning, during mutual study with his master, a few words from an ancient sage, *single hair pierces many holes,* suddenly open the transmission of Light. Presenting his conscious completeness to Buddha Dogen, the new living Buddha remarks: "What are these *many holes* but the *single hair* itself!" Smiling as he confirms the transmission, the Awakened One replies, "Completely pierced!" Master and successor are now unveiled as one Soto moon, its delicate light subtly piercing every atom of Japan, this intense land floating out on an ocean of moonlight toward the rim of the planetary Buddha mandala, the wide rim called America.

comment

This morning Master Keizan, who has been our close friend now for three years, concludes his *Denkoroku,* his history of the transmission of Light from living Buddha to living Buddha through fifty-two generations. A single full moon rises high in India, crosses the vast expanse of China, and sails out over the sharp edge of Japan. Generations eighty-one and eighty-two are now shining in America. The Shakyamuni moon has become a natural dimension of our modern Western landscape. Planetary history is *completely pierced* by this single hair—not man-made, simpler even than finest thread. Has the process taken two thousand five hundred years? The full moon of Total Awakeness moves through countless universes during a single night.

Dogen's words of Light, *completely pierced,* point to perpetual plenitude. Within every moment. Inside every atom. Upon every life-bearing planet. At the heart of every sacred tradition. As the overarching sky of daily awareness. Perpetual plenitude is the *entirely unexpected teaching* which so surprised successor Ejo and which Dogen Zenji received in China from the Soto lineage of living Buddhas. Master Keizan calls it "an extremely different understanding." It is the rigorous acknowledgment of totality, which can never be any less than total, however it may be experienced throughout the infinite play of relativity. Our ancient Japanese guide comments quite simply about this radical understanding: "Everyone without exception is awake and clear."

This wonderful moon shines panoramically and is not subject to any perspective. Since the moon of Total Awakeness is limitless—as Keizan reports from his direct experience, not from philosophical doctrine—it shines with a brilliance brighter than a universe filled to the brim with suns and moons. This is not white-hot brilliance which repels the gaze, but cool, gem-like brilliance which attracts, heals, and embraces the gaze.

Before being drawn to Buddha Dogen, successor Ejo had already realized emptiness as unincreasable and undecreasable. According to his previous teacher, this realization burned out all karmic seeds and roots of suffering from Ejo's being. Yet it was still an exclusionary realization. Any spiritual experience which generates some basic contrast with former levels of experience cannot be Total Awakeness. The Shakyamuni moon neither revolves around any heavenly body nor even rotates on its own axis, but simply shines as every heart, as every atom. Any spiritual insight which cancels out other dimensions of experience, making the faintest division between real and unreal, between cessation of suffering and suffering, remains exclusionary. How can Total Awakeness exclude? What can it exclude, since it is totality? Contemplative methods are exclusionary. Scriptures and schools of thought are exclusionary. Separate practitioners are exclusionary. As our beloved mentor Keizan remarks with surprising irreverence, methods, scriptures, schools, and meditators are "like a cat waiting for a rat." They are conditioned and conditional experience.

Even *single hair pierces many holes* is exclusionary. After living for three years in the ceaseless radiance of the Soto full moon, Ejo suddenly sees, with peaceful clarity, that the phenomenal *holes* and the absolutely single *hair* piercing them are not two. There is actually no piercing process, no realizing process.

Beginning at age seventeen, Ejo vigorously studied and attained realization in many different Buddhist schools. These were some of the *many holes*. The *single hair,* not composed of strands or schools, extends throughout history as *buddha,* or awakeness, piercing all methods of thought and modes of perception at once.

But this picture is incomplete. For totality, there can be no central axis, or *single hair,* nor peripheral manifestation, or *many holes.* When Dogen Zenji humorously comments, *completely pierced,* he is just playing. As Master Keizan asks: "What *complete piercing* can there be?" What there is, in actual fact, is simply completeness, without any piercing or being pierced. Inspired by Buddha Dogen, we could playfully suggest that only completeness can *completely pierce* completeness.

What remains now is to understand the ardent *zazen,* the powerful sitting with our entire being, the tireless commitment to Living Buddha Zen, which occurs among mature practitioners on this uncompromising way of totality. Why such intensity, expanding in all directions? Because totality is omnidirectional intensity. Totality is *zazen*—infinitely condensed diamond wakefulness.

The *directional* fervor that develops among practitioners along various exclusionary paths allows them to make great sacrifices, to achieve superhuman levels of concentration, and therefore to progress to more and more refined levels of experience. However, the atmosphere around practitioners of the non-exclusionary way of totality generates an *omnidirectional* intensity of an entirely different order. It always produces the unexpected.

Ejo once refused to bend monastery rules covering absences in order to spend more than three days with his dying mother, even after the community of monks met and gave special permission. This event does not occur during some early phase of intensive practice. Ejo is already fully awake. There is no more *single hair*, no more *many holes*. Only sheer intensity, with no subject or object.

In a similar vein, we see Ejo, after being unveiled as a living Buddha, spend twenty years as the personal attendant of Buddha Dogen, while also responsible for the complex ceremonial life of the monastery. After Dogen's *mahasamadhi*, Ejo keeps a portrait of his master always beside him during fifteen years of functioning as the Awakened One for his generation. Before Ejo passes from the conventional world, he makes it known that the crystal of his body will be placed at the foot of Dogen's memorial marker in the position of attendant, without any marker of its own.

Contemplating these events in the life of a fully awakened sage, perhaps we can receive some intuition about the superintensity of totality. In these particular instances, we see that Buddhist discipline and the humility of discipleship are vastly intensified by awakeness, rather than being discarded as mere convention. The sage becomes relaxed and natural but remains inconceivably intense. Ejo's mother once exhorted her son, when he was a young monk: "Do not seek high rank or associate with important leaders. Be a simple recluse, with woven grass rain hat over your back, wandering on foot through open country." Even as the Awakened One, Ejo remains loyal in spirit to his mother's profound instruction.

Master Keizan calls the intensity of the full moon way *deep, strong determination*. It is because we are already infinitely full that we can be infinitely determined to manifest fullness, actualizing Total Awakeness in every cell of our body and thereby unveiling it in all lives as their single radiance. The entire universe is *denkoroku*, the history of transmitting the Light.

Neither our tender affection for all living beings, who are like our mothers, nor our awakening as living Buddhas can distract us from totality. There is no incompleteness and therefore no becoming complete. No *completely pierced*. To excuse himself from monastic vows to extend the visit to his mother, Ejo recognized as subtly exclusionary. To present himself as the next living Buddha, founding his own monastery, Ejo recognized as subtly exclusionary. What mother is there apart from Prajnaparamita, who is Mother Wisdom? What master is there apart from Buddha Dogen, who is Mother Wisdom? What teaching is there other than Dogen's *Shobogenzo,* the spontaneous opening of the treasure house of the eye of nonduality? Eihei-ji Monastery once appeared in a practitioner's dream as a giant Dharma fire, blazing high on a distant northern mountain. This great illumination is Dogen and Ejo, inseparable.

Sitting on the round black cushion this morning, there is vibrant, shimmering intensity. Awakeness. No atom sleeping. Toward the end of the meditation period, some physical discomfort arises. Moving the body to attain a temporary sense of ease would be like Ejo suspending his vows in order to extend his visit. This would be dualistic ease, as Ejo's extension would be dualistic compassion. Buddha nature clearly proclaims: "Sit still where you are! Do not exclude anything from totality!"

The unexpected suddenly manifests. Pain disappears. The previous mode of vibrant, shimmering intensity also disappears. Eyes open normally, neither half-closed nor fully rounded. No sense of concentration remains. No sensation of the body-mind as a drawn bow. Glance moves easily and smoothly around the room. The words of Keizan, our kind Roshi, come forward strongly: *naked, obvious, unmarked.* The high-pitched *zazen* bell sounds, *ching!* There is no meditation period to end.

closing poem

> Cherry blossoms raining,
> mountains dancing,
> rivers dreaming,
> Buddha door opening,
> opening!

LINEAGE CHART OF BUDDHA ANCESTORS FROM SHAKYAMUNI BUDDHA TO THE PRESENT

India

1 Mahakashyapa
2 Ananda
3 Shanavasa
4 Upagupta
5 Dhritaka
6 Michaka
7 Vasumitra
8 Buddhanandi
9 Buddhamitra
10 Parshva
11 Punyashas
12 Ashvaghosa
13 Kapimala
14 Nagarjuna
15 Aryadeva
16 Rahulata
17 Sanghanandi
18 Gayashata
19 Kumarata
20 Jayata
21 Vasubandhu
22 Manorhita
23 Haklenayashas
24 Aryasinha
25 Basiasita
26 Punyamitra
27 Prajnatara
28 Bodhidharma

China

29 T'ai-tsu Hui-k'o
30 Chien-chih Seng-ts'an
31 Ta-i Tao-hsin
32 Ta-man Hung-jen
33 Ta-chien Hui-neng
34 Ch'ing-yüan Hsing-ssu
35 Shih-t'ou Hsi-ch'ien
36 Yao-shan Wei-yen
37 Yün-yen T'an-sheng
38 Tung-shan Liang-chieh
39 Yün-chü Tao-ying
40 T'ung-an Tao-p'i
41 T'ung-an Kuan-chih
42 Liang-shan Yüan-kuan
43 Ta-yang Ching-hsüan
44 T'ou-tzu I-ch'ing
45 Fu-jung Tao-k'ai
46 Tan-hsia Tzu-ch'un
47 Chen-hsieh Ch'ing-liao
48 T'ien-t'ung Tsung-chüeh
49 Chih-chien Hsüeh-tou
50 T'ien-t'ung Ju-ching

Japan

51	Eihei Dogen	69	Hoshi Soon
52	Koun Ejo	70	Goho Kainon
53	Tettsu Gikai	71	Tenkei Denson
54	Keizan Jokin	72	Shozan Monko
55	Gasan Joseki	73	Niken Sekiryo
56	Taigen Soshin	74	Reitan Roryu
57	Baizan Monpon	75	Kakujo Tosai
58	Nyochu Tengin	76	Kakuan Ryogu
59	Kisan Shosan	77	Ryoka Daibai
60	Morin Shihan	78	Ungan Guhaku
61	Shoshi Sotai	79	Baian Hakujun
62	Kenchu Hantetsu	80	Taizan Hakuyu
63	Daiju Soko		(Maezumi Roshi)
64	Kinpo Jusen		
65	Kaiin Sochin		*America*
66	Tetsuei Seiton	81	Baisen Tetsugen
67	Shukoku Choton		(Bernard Glassman)
68	Ketsuzan Tetsuei	82	Jikai (Lex Hixon)

Note: This lineage chart represents the particular line of Maezumi Roshi, simplified in the Soto manner. In his line, the eighty-first generation contains twelve Westerners (four women, eight men) and the eighty-second generation so far contains four Westerners (two women, two men). There are some two dozen Western successors of other Soto masters and, of course, thousands of Japanese Dharma successors. To these numbers for Western Dharma successors we must add perhaps another hundred coming from realized masters in other lines of Zen and other Buddhist lineages.